SCARECROW PRESS INC.

Published in the United States of America
by Scarecrow Press, Inc.
A Member of the Rowman & Littlefield Publishing Group
4720 Boston Way, Lanham, Maryland 20706
www.scarecrowpress.com

12 Hid's Copse Road
Cumnor Hill, Oxford OX2 9JJ, England

British Library Cataloguing in Publication Information Available

Library of Congress Cataloging-in-Publication Data

Hischak, Thomas S.
  Boy loses girl : Broadway's librettists / Thomas S. Hischak
    p. cm.
  Includes bibliographical references (p.) and index.
  ISBN 0-8108-4440-0 (alk. paper)
  1. Librettists—New York (State)—New York. 2. Musicals—New York
  (State)—New York—History and criticism. I. Title

  ML403 .H57 2002
  782.1'4'092273—dc21

                              2002007340

Boy Loses Girl
Broadway's Librettists
Thomas S. Hischak

The Scarecrow Press, Inc.
Lanham, Maryland, and Oxford
2002

For Mark Robinson and Kevin Halpin,
who pay attention to the libretto

CONTENTS

CONTENTS

WRITING LITTLE BOOKS:
AN INTRODUCTION

Whenever Stephen Sondheim is asked the requisite question, "Which comes first? The music or the lyric?" he promptly answers, "The book." Sondheim does not write the librettos for his shows, but he certainly understands the importance of the book in the musical theatre today. And yesterday as well. Before *Oklahoma!* and the integrated musical, even before *Show Boat* and the musical play, the libretto was key to the success of any musical comedy. How easy it is to scoff today as we look back at those early shows. Act 1: boy meets girl. Act 2: boy loses girl. Act 3: boy gets girl. They were already making fun of the formula by the Depression; one of the most successful comedies of the 1935–1936 season was the farce *Boy Meets Girl* by sometime librettists Bella and Sam Spewack. But as ridiculous as the premise seemed, it held many a musical comedy together. How the librettist filled in the formula made all the difference, even when all the plots sounded familiar.

Consider the Gershwin brothers' *Oh, Kay!* (1926) with Gertrude Lawrence, Victor Moore, "Clap Yo' Hands," "Do, Do, Do," and "Someone to Watch Over Me." It was a major hit with 256 performances. Then look at the Gershwins' *Treasure Girl* (1928) with Lawrence again, Clifton Webb, "I've Got a Crush on You," "Feeling I'm Fallin," and "I Don't Think I'll Fall in Love Today." It was a no-go that lasted only sixty-eight performances on the strength of its advance sales. Some may conclude "that's show biz," but Ira Gershwin was closer to the mark when he wrote about *Treasure Girl,* "songwriters to the contrary, [musical] numbers alone do not make a show." While Guy Bolton and P. G. Wodehouse's libretto for *Oh, Kay!* might seem an improbable reason for its success, it worked; Fred Thompson and Vincent Lawrence's book for *Treasure Girl* did not. Boy met, lost, and found girl in both shows, but the formula alone was not enough.

The term "libretto" comes from the Italian, meaning "little book." The scripts for the early Italian operas were often so negligible that one could hardly call them plays. So "libretto" was born, and the subservient writers who provided these second-class books were termed "librettists." The title carried over into operetta and then musical theatre, the billing "libretto by" hanging on into the 1960s. Alan Jay Lerner, who wrote both the book and the lyrics for his shows, despised the term "librettist" and insisted that he was a "playwright." One can see his point; *My Fair Lady* is hardly a "little book" musical. But then the same can be said about the great operas. What is implied in "libretto" is not the size or length or even the integrity of the libretto but the fact that it is secondary to the score. Operas and musicals are all about the score, they keep telling us. But think again. The most popular and beloved operas are the ones with the best stories and most interesting characters. The Broadway musicals that are most often revived are the ones in which the book is revivable. If the score is everything, why worry about the book? Because Sondheim is right; the book comes first—not only in the order of creation but often in the makeup of a successful show.

I am sure anyone could come up with a list of perfectly enjoyable, re-vivable musicals that have ridiculous books. *No, No, Nanette* might appear on most lists. Many would be sure to include *Bye Bye Birdie* or *Li'l Abner* and *Grease.* But let me suggest that, with all their shortcomings, those librettos still work on stage. Boy manages to meet, lose, and get girl in a manner that audiences find palatable. They forgive the contrived or hackneyed nature of the book, chalking it up to nostalgia or satire or even the satisfaction that we are above all that sort of thing today. My guess is that each show on that list would have failed without the libretto it had. That is not to say that the book written for each was the best of all possible librettos, but each one worked. Speaking of the "best of all possible worlds," look at Lillian Hellman's libretto for the original *Candide,* and it is clear how a weak book can sink the most dazzling of scores. When *Candide* and every other flop musical close, blame is usually centered on the book. When a show succeeds, credit is often given to everybody except the librettist. The task of writing "little books" is indeed humbling. (While songs from musicals have been published since the beginning, no Broadway libretto was published until *Of Thee I Sing* in 1931, and then rarely after that.) Everyone seems to know the names and works of the major Broadway composers and lyricists, but how many can recall who wrote the book for *Guys and Dolls* or *Kiss Me, Kate* or even *A Funny Thing Happened on the Way to the Forum*? Fewer, I imagine, than seems right and just in a best of all possible worlds. The librettist must search for new ways for boy and girl to meet so that they can break up for some new reason and then reunite. It seems a thankless task with meager rewards, yet everyone, from composers to producers to stars, knows that it is perhaps the most essential job of all.

A vast majority of Broadway librettos come from previous works: plays, films, novels, short stories, autobiographies, news articles, and so on. In the eyes of some, the art of libretto writing is diminished because the writers are seen as adaptors or rewrite authors. Such reasoning is suspect. One has to look at all the celebrated novelists who have failed and all the classic pieces of literature that have not been successfully musicalized to realize that adaptation is not journeyman's work. The form of the American musical comedy is so unique, so quirky, that it resists simple adaptation. The source material must be reimagined for the musical stage. Editing the original and sticking song and dance into the story is a gross simplification of the librettist's job. To turn *War and Peace* into a play takes a talented editor; to turn it into a musical play takes inspired insight and originality. Why do *Show Boat,* the "Pal Joey" stories, or *The Producers* make such terrific musicals while the singing versions of *David Copperfield,* the *I Remember Mama* stories, and *Some Like It Hot* disappoint? Adaptation is a tricky proposition, and no one knows it better than the people who put together Broadway musicals.

Broadway's librettists have come from various directions. Some, like Oscar Hammerstein and Alan Jay Lerner, were lyricists. Others, such as George S. Kaufman and Maxwell Anderson, were bona fide playwrights. Some came from vaudeville, others from journalism, still others from Hollywood. You will even find directors, press agents, poets, performers, and musicians on the list. Librettists come from all over because there is no one place where one learns to write the book for a musical. It is an art form without a clear path of discovery. College courses in playwriting and musical composition are plentiful, classes in lyric writing few and far between, and those in libretto writing practically nonexistent. Today, as in the days when Hammerstein was starting out, the only preparation for the librettist is hands-on experience. Fledgling librettists used to write original college musicals or summer camp shows; today they are found Off-Off-Broadway or in regional theatres. The all-so-essential task of libretto writing has always been relegated to the school of trial and error. It is a miracle that boy and girl get together at all!

What follows in these pages is a rather selective, frequently critical, and highly personal look at the major Broadway librettists of the past one hundred years. While this study tries to take a chronological path, several of these men and women had long careers that extended over many decades, so sometimes it is necessary to get ahead of oneself. I have limited myself to the American musical theatre and have included only those British librettists who had lengthy careers on Broadway. Only book musicals are considered, although mention is made of those librettists who were also known for writing sketches for musical revues. Both Broadway and Off-Broadway musicals are covered, and the dates used throughout refer to the years of the original New York productions.

I have chosen the facile title of *Boy Loses Girl* for this project because it is the part of the formula that most intrigues me. It is also the part of the plot that causes writers the most difficulty. There are many ways for the two lovers to meet, and possibilities for reconciliation are plentiful. But the trouble or conflict that arises between boy and girl requires both plot and character and offers the most interesting aspect of any libretto. I realize that the simplification of "boy meets girl" is far from accurate; today, it can be "boy meets boy" or "lion loses lioness" or even "bat boy gets girl." But these are just variations on the same old formula. Every "little book" must eventually come around to someone losing someone. Otherwise, there is nothing to sing and dance about.

Finally, a word should be said about the admiration I have for the craft of libretto writing. While few would consider the boy-meets-girl plot to be profound literature, there is something so efficient and ingenious about an expert Broadway libretto that one feels no embarrassment in praising it. The plotting in *Kiss Me, Kate* and the characterizations in *Company,* for example, are glorious moments in American popular culture and need make no apologies to anyone. What the rest of the world has always marveled at (and envied) in American musicals is the unique blending of story, characters, song, and dance. The librettists who somehow make that blending work cannot be overrated.

THE AMERICAN IDEA: GEORGE M. COHAN

The libretto for the American musical theatre, as we know it and enjoy it today, was created by George M. Cohan. This dynamo of a man is most remembered now for his songs (he wrote both music and lyrics) and in his day was acclaimed for his singing and dancing skills. But Cohan was also a shrewd theatrical producer, a proficient director, and, regarding our purposes here, an important playwright-librettist. Of all the hats Cohan wore, librettist probably brought him the least amount of fame. But it was the books for his musicals that propelled them forward into a new art form, and it was the Cohan musicals that jump-started the American kind of musical. Charles Hoyt and others had written about Broadway swells and urban folk, and Edward Harrigan and others had written about ethnic-immigrant types in their late nineteenth-century musical farces but it was Cohan who developed the all-American musical comedy with song, dance, and book racing together to the entertainment finish line. Eschewing the European operetta and the outdated extravaganza shows, the Cohan musicals forged a new kind of fast-paced theatrical entertainment in an efficient little package. We may not revive the Cohan musicals today but their legacy is alive and breathing in *Anything Goes, Guys and Dolls, Hello, Dolly!, The Producers,* and dozens of other shows.

George Michael Cohan was born in Providence, Rhode Island, in 1878. Whether it was on the fourth of July, as he claimed, or July 3, as the unreliable records note, is still a matter for debate; but Cohan believed he was "a real live nephew of my Uncle Sam's," and that belief was the driving force throughout his long career. His parents, Jerry and Nellie Cohan, and his sister Josie were vaudevillians touring the various circuits, so Cohan was on the stage from his youth. By the time he was a teenager, he was writing original songs and even providing sketches for the family act. Thanks to Cohan's wealth of new material and his shrewd management, the Four Cohans became one of the most sought-after acts on the vaude-ville circuit. But Cohan's eye was on Broadway, and he didn't want to go there as part of a revue or extravaganza. He wanted the Cohans to be in a book musical, ideally one written, scored, produced, directed, and starring himself. Before long he would be doing just that.

Crossing over the line from vaudeville to Broadway was seldom done. Some of the major vaudeville stars managed to get featured in a *Follies* show or other kind of revue, but Broadway for the most part looked down on vaudevillians. Theatre was considered "legit," whereas variety was some-thing below that. The twenty-two-year-old Cohan knew this well, so he made a deal with Louis Behman, a producer who booked acts on the Hyde and Behman circuit. Behman could have the Cohans for his theatres for one year if he would produce Cohan's musical on Broadway after the tour. The Four Cohans were so popular that Behman agreed, and in 1901, after the contracted tour, Cohan's *The Governor's Son* opened on Broadway. As expected, he wrote, scored, and starred in the "musical farce" that he based on one of the vaudeville sketches he'd written for the family. While many musicals at the turn of the century suffered from too little plot, *The Gover-nor's Son* was hampered by too much story. There are two main plots, each complicated by and eventually overlapping the other. A married couple (Jerry and Nellie Cohan) suspect each other of inappropriate flirtations, so the husband hires the governor's son (George Cohan) to tempt (and trap) his wife. Running alongside this is the tale of a detective who is hired to lo-cate a philandering brother-in-law. The plot kicker is the fact that the de-tective is the one hiding the slippery relative. Then the mischievous brother-in-law disguises himself as a detective as well and sets off on a merry chase after himself, while it is his wife who is mistakenly wooed by the governor's son. It may have seemed a mishmash of a libretto compared with the slow-moving operetta plots of the time, but at least it was lively, fast paced, and tuneful. *The Governor's Son* managed to run a few weeks in an out-of-the-way theatre, getting only the slightest notice, but Cohan wisely took the show on the road, tinkering with the script and score for two years while it filled playhouses anxious to see the Cohans.

The two years were well spent, because when Cohan's next show, *Run-ning for Office* (1903), opened, its libretto was more streamlined, efficient, and well balanced than *The Governor's Son*. Based on another of the fam-ily's vaudeville sketches, the story centered on the widower John Tiger (Jerry Cohan) and his plans to wed a respectable widow (Nellie Cohan) and run for mayor. John's son Augustus (George Cohan) has fallen for the widow's daughter (Josie Cohan), but neither couple knows about the other couple's plans, so there are a series of complications until the election day victory and a double wedding. *Running for Office* ran only a month on Broadway (followed by another very successful tour), but audiences and critics were starting to notice the multitalented Cohan. Neither show had produced any major Cohan songs yet, but when *Little Johnny Jones* (1904) opened, the future standards "Yankee Doodle Boy" and "Give My Regards to Broadway" helped the musical run two months. Again Cohan took it on a brief tour, polished it, and brought *Little Johnny Jones* back to New York twice in 1905 where it was a major hit with over 200 performances.

While *Little Johnny Jones* might be described more as a musical melodrama than a comedy, it was fast paced and light on its feet. Cohan got the idea for the libretto from reading a newspaper article about the American jockey Tod Sloan, who triumphed at the Royal Derby in England. In the libretto, the all-American jockey Jones (Cohan) arrives in England to ride his horse Yankee Doodle in the Derby but is soon approached by the villainous Anthony Antsey (Jerry Cohan), who offers him a bribe to throw the race. Jones refuses but loses the race fair and square, allowing Anstey to spread a rumor that Jones threw the race for money. The cocky little hero remains in England to clear his name and sends his detective friend to search for evidence to prove his innocence. When he does find proof aboard a ship sailing out of Southampton harbor, the detective signals Jones on the pier by setting off some skyrockets. Jones's jubilation rouses him to sing and dance a celebratory reprise of "Give My Regards to Broadway" in the musical's most famous scene. But Jones's problems continue when Antsey kidnaps the jockey's fiancée, and he and the detective have to rescue her from a Chinatown haunt in San Francisco, settling the score with Antsey for two crimes. The three-act "musical play," as Cohan billed it, was a landmark of sorts. The slangy dialogue, the action-packed plot, the broad yet definite characters, and the tuneful American-sounding score were all refreshingly new to Broadway. The show did not resemble European (or American) operetta in any form, nor did it pile on the spectacle and incidental musical numbers as in the recent extravaganzas. *Little Johnny Jones* was the portent of the future of musical comedy as the libretto became a powerful tool rather than a forgettable but necessary format.

Cohan's next show, *Forty-Five Minutes from Broadway* (1906), was written as a star vehicle for Fay Templeton, a beloved favorite on Broadway. Cohan performed most of his usual tasks (writer, director, songwriter) but did not appear in the show, proving that a Cohan musical did not need its energetic young star to succeed. And succeed it did, trying out in Chicago with a lucrative engagement and running ninety performances on Broadway.

When the wealthy Mr. Castleton of New Rochelle dies intestate, his nephew Tom Bennett (Donald Brian) inherits all the money and is immediately pursued by a power-hungry matron and her high-society daughter. Tom's smart-aleck secretary, Kid Burns (Victor Moore), proclaims, "I'm the real noise around this man's residence" and tries to protect Tom from the social vultures. Kid also meets the late millionaire's faithful servant, Mary (Templeton), with whom he falls in love, and uncovers a will that leaves the whole estate to her. After some wheeler-dealing to save Tom, Kid shows Mary the will and proposes marriage. When she suggests that he is only after the money, Kid vows he'd marry her even if she were poor; so Mary tears up the will, and Kid makes good on his promise.

In many ways *Forty-Five Minutes from Broadway* is Cohan's best libretto, balancing the melodrama with the comedy, the songs with the story. Act 2 of the three-act piece had no songs at all as the plot unfolded rapidly without break. When the songs (the sly title number, "Mary's a Grand Old Name," "So Long, Mary," and two others) appeared, they were pleasant respites from the action. Although Templeton was the star, Moore as Kid Burns was the focal point of the story, and his tough but honest demeanor was much in the same mold as Johnny Jones. (Cohan played Burns in a successful revival of the show in 1912.) All the characters are distinct and well drawn, just as the dialogue throughout is surprisingly adroit. When asked about her former fiancé, Dan Cronin, Mary answers in vaudeville-like statements that are also quite revealing:

ANDY: How long have you been fond of Cronin, Mary?
MARY: It's three years now since he first told me that I loved him.
ANDY: And nobody knew that you were engaged?
MARY: No. I didn't know it myself until he called it off.

The Cohan musical reaches its peak with *Forty-Five Minutes from Broadway*. His many shows after it would return to the ideas and characters of these early musicals, but rarely would they be as accomplished. For example, his next project, *George Washington, Jr.* (1906), was often delightful, but it echoed *Little Johnny Jones* throughout. U.S. Senator Belgrave (Jerry Cohan) is more in love with England and English ways than with his native country and tries to marry off his son George (George Cohan) to the arrogant daughter of a stuffy British lord. But George loves the unpretentious daughter of another American senator, and the father angrily rebukes his son for turning his back on European aristocracy. This ruffles the feathers of the flag-waving George, who breaks with his father:

GEORGE: I disown you as a father. Now what do you think of that!
BELGRAVE: You're a disgrace to the name of Belgrave.
GEORGE: Then take your name! I don't want your name! To hell with
it! I'll take my own name!

So George, taking the same name as the father of his country, marries the American girl, and everyone joins in singing "You're a Grand Old Flag." It was a plot that, with slight variations, would be repeated in a dozen subsequent Cohan shows. *The Honeymooners* (1907) was a revised and retitled version of *Running for Office*, and *The Talk of the Town* (1907) was a sequel of sorts to *Forty-Five Minutes from Broadway* with Kid Burns (again Victor Moore) returning to take the blame for a murder he did not commit. But, like Johnny Jones, his name is eventually cleared, and the plucky American exposes a blackmailer and wins the day. *Fifty Miles from Boston* (1908) sounded like another sequel, and it could have been, the setting of Brookline, Massachusetts, being another rural burg (like the previous show's New Rochelle) that is teased by the hero, Harrigan (Cohan). He loves Sadie (Edna Wallace Hooper), but she loves baseballer Joe Westcott (Laurence Wheat); so Harrigan helps Joe's brother out of a bind (he's stolen money from the post office and lost it gambling) with the understanding that he will try to get his brother Joe to drop Sadie. But Harrigan sees the error of his conniving ways and helps out both Joe and the brother. It was a modest success, but the song "Harrigan" went on to become a standard favorite.

The Yankee Prince (1908) returned to the theme of America versus Europe. The rich Chicago businessman Franklyn Fielding (Jerry Cohan) brings his daughter to Europe to find her a titled husband. But while she is there she meets Percy Springer (George Cohan), an American making the grand tour. Of course she marries him rather than the earl that her father has lined up for her. The same plot was doubled and repeated in *The American Idea* (1908). This time, two Brooklyn millionaires cross the Atlantic to find aristocratic husbands for their daughters. But the girls fall instead for two Brooklyn boys who have disguised themselves as nobility. As stale as these later shows may sound, most of them were popular. Even repeating himself, Cohan made sure the plot moved quickly and nimbly. The librettos had gotten routine, but they were rarely sloppy or tenuous. Cohan may have been limited in his diversity, but he did not lose his touch for fast-paced entertainment.

The title of *The Man Who Owns Broadway* (1909) was not the only autobiographical aspect of Cohan's next musical. Based on his first (and unsuccessful) nonmusical *Popularity* (1906), the story told about the love between a Broadway song-and-dance man, Sydney Lyons (Raymond Hitchcock), and the daughter of a wealthy businessman. Father has a society chap in mind for his daughter, so Sydney seems to be out of the picture until his sweetheart decides to follow her heart and return to the actor. This most contrived of boy-meets-girl stories was given a spark of life by some of Cohan's special touches. One of the first "backstage" musicals, it offered some honest (and sometimes satiric) insight into show business. Cohan managed to spoof some theatre conventions of the day ("My boy," one character notes, "the villains are never handcuffed until 11:00!") and had fun dropping the names of the Shuberts and other theatrical giants of the era. In one scene set backstage, Cohan had all the scenery removed and set the actors in front of the actual back wall of the theatre. In another scene, Sydney is upset that the show cannot go on, so he speaks to the audience in front of the house curtain. Cohan had Hitchcock appear in front of the actual curtain and address the real audience who, prompted by plants in the auditorium, reacted to Sydney's announcement. The librettist may have been running in circles, but he still knew how to tell a story with panache.

The Little Millionaire (1911) was equally familiar but even more popular. Jerry and George Cohan again played father and son in this three-act show that used songs only in the first and last acts. When Henry Spooner's heiress wife dies, her will dictates that her husband must remarry and their son Robert must wed in order to inherit her millions. A couple of stock villains try to stop them, but the younger Spooner eventually wins the heart of Goldie Gray (Lila Rhodes), and dad marries her aunt. The score produced no hits, but Cohan provided plenty of dances, including a lavish, high-stepping double wedding for the finale. The show ran 192 performances, the biggest Cohan hit yet. Just as successful were the producer-songwriter's forays into the revue format, striking gold with *Hello, Broadway!* (1914), *The Cohan Revue of 1916*, and *The Cohan Revue of 1918* (1917). Cohan even ventured into the territory of his old enemy *operetta* when he was asked to doctor the troubled *Cherry Blossoms*, and he turned it into the "Cohanized Opera Comique" *The Royal Vagabond* (1919). The Crown Prince of Bargravia is asked by his mother to put down a revolution, but at the first inn he stops at he is smitten with the innkeeper's daughter who is a member of the uprising. The prince joins the revolutionaries, becomes their leader, then conquers the royal troops by buying them off with his hefty personal allowance. The plot and score were by transplanted Europeans, but Cohan shook up both, writing new lyrics (the opening "tra-la-la" number became a spoof of operetta opening numbers) and adding his brash sense of satire to the libretto:

PRINCE: Doesn't that sound like a horseman approaching?
TUTOR: Not exactly. But it's a good effect.

The Royal Vagabond was also a hit, and it seemed that Cohan was lucky in no matter what genre he tackled. By this time his career as a playwright was also in full swing. He would pen twenty nonmusicals between 1906 and 1940, two of which—*Seven Keys to Baldpate* (1913) and *The Tavern* (1929)—would be regularly revived. But there was a dark side to all this success. Cohan was a popular figure, and his shows promised a satisfying, if old-fashioned, evening of entertainment. But he was not growing, and, more significantly, he did not wish to acknowledge that Broadway was growing. By this time the Princess shows and other hits had featured Jerome Kern and a new breed of composer. Librettists like Guy Bolton and P. G. Wodehouse had introduced a more literate kind of writing to Broadway. In the wings were the Gershwins, Cole Porter, and Rodgers and Hart. The musical theatre was heading for a revolution of sorts, and Cohan tried to resist the tide of change. He certainly resisted it with the famous Actors Equity strike of 1919 when he sided with management and called his fellow actors radical hooligans. When the actors won, Cohan was on the outs with almost everyone, and a new Cohan show would not be seen on Broadway for three years. Ironically, it would be the longest-running hit of his career and his only show to become popular outside the United States.

Little Nellie Kelly (1922) was similar to other Cinderella musicals of the era. (Cohan may have liked to ignore what was going on outside his theatre, but he still knew a good thing when he saw it.) The Irish American lass Nellie (Elizabeth Hines), the daughter of a police officer, is an employee at Devere's department store. She is being wooed by the wealthy playboy Jack Lloyd (Barnett Greenwood), but Nellie is more taken with the cheeky Irish scamp Jerry Conroy (Charles King). Lloyd invites all the working girls at Devere's to a party at his aunt's mansion in order to impress and pursue Nellie. But Jerry crashes the party, and, when the aunt's jewelry is stolen, he is fingered as the obvious suspect. Jerry is eventually cleared, and Nellie goes to him, preferring his wisecracking ways over the civility of the upper classes. "Nellie Kelly, I Love You" was the hit song from the show, but it was the whole package that thrilled audiences: Cohan's lively dialogue and sharp direction, the agreeable performances, and sparkling choreography by Julian Mitchell. *Little Nellie Kelly* ran a very profitable 276 performances, followed by a popular tour and subsequent hit versions in London and Australia.

A year later Cohan returned with another Irish heroine in *The Rise of Rosie O'Reilly* (1923). Virginia O'Brien played the title lass, a poor but plucky gal who sells flowers under the Brooklyn Bridge. She is wooed by the high-society swell Bob Morgan (Jack McGowan), but he makes little headway until he is disinherited by his father and has to take a job in a florist shop. Once he has sunk to her level, Rosie can fall in love with him. She even loves him after Bob's father has a change of heart and restores his money. Another Cinderella gets her prince. Less than a runaway hit on Broadway, the musical did very well on the road. A new Cohan libretto wouldn't be seen on Broadway for four years, though the plot of *The Merry Malones* (1927) could hardly be called new. This time the Irish heroine is Molly Malone (Polly Walker), and she won't give the wealthy Joe Wescott (Alan Edwards) the time of day because of all his money. So Joe tries to get his father to disinherit him, hoping it will do the trick. But the old man is on to him and arranges a happy ending for the couple. What was most remembered about *The Merry Malones* was a chorus number called "The Bronx Express" that was set in a realistically recreated subway car. What history notes about the show is that it ran a lucrative 208 performances and marked for Cohan, who played Molly's father, his last stage appearance in one of his own musicals.

Polly Walker played the title heroine again in *Billie* (1928), the last Cohan musical to play Broadway. Based on his 1912 play *Broadway Jones,* the plot featured another rich playboy falling for a common gal. Jackson "Broadway" Jones (Joseph Wagstaff) has left his Connecticut burg and spent all his money living the high life in New York. When he finds himself thousands of dollars in debt, he decides to marry a widow who is lacking in good looks but overflowing with cash. But before the wedding can take place, word comes that Jackson's uncle has died and left him the family chewing-gum factory back home. Jackson's plan is to sell off the factory to an anxious buyer and return to Broadway with the profits. But the dedicated factory secretary Billie (who, she sings, has a masculine name because her parents were expecting a boy) explains to him that the buyer only wants to close the plant and put all the locals out of work. Jackson falls not only for her plea to keep the factory open but also for Billie and decides to settle down with her in Connecticut and run the family business. The old-fashioned show looked like a museum piece in the midst of the Jazz Age, but audiences found enough to enjoy to keep it running for 112 performances. The title song was charming, and some of the libretto still had the recognizable Cohan punch:

BILLIE: What is Broadway?
JONES: Broadway?

BILLIE: A street?
JONES: Sure, it's the greatest street in the world.
BILLIE: Some people say it's terrible.
JONES: Philadelphia people.

These lines originally came from the 1912 play version and didn't seem out of place in a Cohan show sixteen years later. That's how little the Cohan musicals had changed. After *Billie,* Cohan concentrated on writing nonmusicals and even returned to performing, but in other men's works. His success in Eugene O'Neill's comedy *Ah, Wilderness!* (1933) and the Rodgers and Hart musical *I'd Rather Be Right* (1937) endeared him to a public that soon forgot that he had written all those old musicals. Cohan's legacy was a trunkful of song favorites; his work as a librettist was ignored or forgotten. He died in 1942, the same year the film bio *Yankee Doodle Dandy* was released. Decades later his story was told in the Broadway musical *George M!* (1968). Would Cohan have liked it? The flag waving and the songs, yes. But he wouldn't have liked the sloppy, meandering libretto. It wasn't a Cohan show.

One might suspect that the Cohan librettos are inferior because the shows are not revived today. But how many American musicals (or comedies and dramas) from the first two decades of the twentieth century are revived today? Remarkably few. Groundbreaking works often come across to later generations as more a curiosity than a satisfying theatre experience. Who produces the Princess musicals today? Or the early concept musicals like *Lady in the Dark* (1941) or *Love Life* (1948)? They seem destined to be admired but not seen. The Cohan librettos broke new ground, and everyone knew it at the time. *Little Johnny Jones* was so refreshingly different that even the critics who did not like it had to take notice. The audiences, on the other hand, quickly embraced the new style of musical storytelling. They may not have been able to explain exactly how it was different, but they knew they enjoyed it. Cohan's librettos are popular literature, not unlike the melodramas that dominated the American theatre during the nineteenth century. Most of the same elements were there: swiftly moving well-plotted stories, moral and upright heroes, innocent but eager heroines, strong poetic justice, down-to-earth prose dialogue, and American values that overrode foreign trivialities. The only area in which Cohan departed from *The Old Homestead* (1887) and the many other melodramas of its nature was in his approach to the city. In most melodramas, life on the farm was noble and pure while urban centers were decadent and destructive. Cohan made fun of the country rubes and glorified the white lights of Broadway. He made New York City an all-American place, and across the country many viewed Broadway through his celebratory songs.

Just as those old melodramas are no longer produced, the Cohan librettos have a difficult time of it on the modern stage. But *Little Johnny Jones* and *Forty-Five Minutes from Broadway,* which have the sharpest and most entertaining librettos, could be enjoyed today. A Goodspeed Opera House production of the former was a hit in 1981, but a Broadway revival the next year was clobbered by the critics. Broadway believes that it is so sophisticated these days, but we forget that it was Cohan who started the musical theatre on the road to better stories, believable characters, and efficient staging. For many years the director-playwright George Abbott was praised for his "Abbott Touch" in writing and directing fast-paced musical comedies. But what of the Cohan touch? How did the great innovator come to be old hat so quickly? His lack of adaptability is some of the reason. Cohan came up with a bright and new variation on the boy-meets-girl formula, but he never let it develop. He resisted change and stuck to what succeeded. Audiences, who often resist change as well, stuck with him for nearly thirty years. But the revolution that Cohan had started soon engulfed him. He created an American kind of musical, then stood still while others took his American idea and ran with it. How telling it must have been when Cohan's last show, the predictable *Billie,* opened a little less than a year after the startlingly bold *Show Boat* (1927). Without the early Cohan librettos, Oscar Hammerstein would not have been able to write a script like *Show Boat.* They seem worlds apart, but in truth the Hammerstein–Kern classic is just a more ambitious and refined version of Cohan's American idea.

Cohan's legacy for well-structured librettos is still evident today, even though Broadway has taken a more lackadaisical view toward musical storytelling as it explores conceptual and other plotless forms of musicals. It seems we've slowed the musical down these past twenty years or so, and the Cohan touch or the Abbott touch is gone. But consider how few musical *comedies* Broadway has produced of late. As the shows have gotten darker, the pace has slackened. Many of Cohan's works were melodramas, yet they moved like farces. Can you imagine how he would have plotted and directed *Les Miserables?* Perhaps we are still doing the Cohan melodramas but in slow motion and with more ponderous scores. Yet the Cohan approach to libretto writing can still be found in such varied works as *42nd Street, Little Shop of Horrors, City of Angels, Falsettos, The Lion King,* and *The Producers.* These are plot-driven shows that tell their stories well. They may use dance or puppetry or even mock opera instead of rapid Cohan dialogue to do the job, but each has a strong libretto on which everything else rests. So old and yet so new, the Cohan musical is still with us.

CHAPTER TWO
OH, BOY! OH, LADY!
GUY BOLTON AND P. G. WODEHOUSE

Ⅰf the Broadway musical grew up quickly and sometimes awkwardly with Cohan, it started to mature with the Princess musicals and other shows written by Guy Bolton, often collaborating with lyricist P. G. Wodehouse on the libretto. The Cohan musicals can be described as brash and adolescent; the Bolton shows illustrate the breezy, pseudosophisticated demeanor of a college lad. The difference is one of tone and content rather than true maturity. But the Bolton librettos are so cheeky and self-satisfying that one easily falls prey to their charm. Like the Cohan musicals, the Bolton–Wodehouse shows are rarely revived today. The former are perhaps too mechanical, the latter possibly too trivial and lightweight. Yet these contrived, often ridiculous, musicals represent a major step for the American theatre. They are literate without being ponderous, escapist without being embarrassing. Just like their often-gushing titles, the Bolton shows exude confidence and a celebratory feeling. The Broadway musical can be great fun, they seem to say, and no apologies are necessary.

Guy Reginald Bolton was an American but brought to Broadway a European background. He was born in 1884 in Hertfordshire, England, to American parents and was educated in Paris and New York. Bolton studied to become an architect and began a promising career (he designed the Soldiers and Sailors Monument still seen on Manhattan's Riverside Drive) before turning to the theatre full time when his first play was produced in London in 1912. For the next forty years, he would write over fifty scripts for musicals and nonmusicals for both Broadway and the West End. *Ninety in the Shade* (1915) was his first libretto for Broadway. It was a small-scale, romantic musical about a ladies' man (Richard Carle) in the Philippines whose romancing of a "Hot Tamale" (Jean Newcomb) is temporarily upset by the arrival of his fiancée Polly (Marie Cahill). Despite a pleasant score by a young Jerome Kern, the show failed to run; but this first teaming of the two men was the beginning of one of Broadway's most illustrious collaborations.

Their next effort, *Nobody Home* (1915), was the first of the famed Princess shows. This series of intimate musicals in the 299-seat Princess Theatre lasted only four years, but in many ways it changed the face of the Broadway musical. It also was the inspiration for Richard Rodgers, Lorenz Hart, Cole Porter, the Gershwins, and a whole generation of young songwriters. Literary agent Elisabeth Marbury and theatre owner F. Ray Comstock initiated the idea of presenting contemporary shows by new composers in a theatre that, by the nature of its size, limited the number in the cast and in the orchestra. Wodehouse later would jokingly refer to the project as "midget musical comedy," but there was nothing small about the aspirations of the project. While not all of the seven Princess shows were hits, each was an event, starting with *Nobody Home*. Schulyer Greene provided the rather pedestrian lyrics, but Kern's music and Bolton's book were highly promising. An Americanized version of a British musical called *Mr. Popple of Ippleton*, Bolton's script sets the story in the Blitz (read Ritz) Hotel and in the Manhattan apartment of showgirl Violet (Alice Dovey), who is going on tour and wishes to sublet the place. Although she is in love with "society dancer" Vernon Popple (George Anderson), the boy's overbearing aunt (Maude Odell) disapproves of the match, and Vernon's wandering eye has landed on music hall star Tony Miller (Adele Rowland). When Vernon's staid brother Freddy (Lawrence Goldsmith) comes to town and considers renting Violet's apartment, they fall in love and wed, though not until Vernon, his aunt, and everyone else converges on the apartment as prospective tenants. *Nobody Home* was sharper and tighter than most musical comedies of the day but not anything approaching a landmark. All the same, it managed a run of 135 performances (moving to a larger theatre later on) and toured successfully.

Marbury and Comstock were impressed enough to engage Bolton, Kern, and Greene for their next Princess show, *Very Good Eddie* (1915), which *did* turn out to be a landmark. The libretto was again based on a previous work, Philip Bartholomae's comedy *Over Night* (1911), but Bartholomae's adaptation failed out of town, so Bolton was added to the team. The result was a delicious bedroom farce set along the Hudson River, one that thrilled audiences and critics with its lighthearted plot, likable characters, and superb score. Two newlywed couples, Eddie (Ernest Truex) and Georgina Kettle (Helen Raymond), and Percy (John Willard) and Elsie Darling (Alice Dovey), board a Hudson River Day Line boat for a trip upriver. But when Eddie and Elsie miss the ship at a short stop at Poughkeepsie, the two are forced to pretend to be honeymooners and check into the Rip Van Winkle Inn. Also on board is the dashing Dick Rivers (Oscar Shaw), who pursues a different girl named Elsie (Ann Orr), convincing her singing teacher Madame Matroppo (Ada Lewis) that he needs to interview her for a magazine. The meek Eddie and the diminutive Elsie Darling get separate rooms at the inn, but a mouse frightens her into Eddie's room, leading to all kinds of misunderstandings that are further complicated by some characters mistaking one Elsie for the other. By morning, the confusions are untangled, and mousy Eddie learns to stand up to his domineering wife. While the events were improbable, they were at least possible, and each character had a thread of believability that was engaging. Also, Bolton's dialogue was more droll and understated than the usual musical comedy jokes:

> MRS. KETTLE: So this is the Hudson, is it? When do we get out of sight of land?
> MR. KETTLE: This is a river.

The songs were somewhat tied into the story, so that the farcical tone of the libretto was not broken for musical numbers. The only aspect of the show that was rather routine was Greene's lyrics. When Bolton asked the newly arrived Englishman P. G. Wodehouse what he thought of *Very Good Eddie*, the Brit expressed enthusiasm for everything but the lyrics. Having written lyrics back in London, Wodehouse offered his services, and the illustrious trio of Bolton, Wodehouse, and Kern was born.

Pelham Grenville Wodehouse enjoyed one of the longest and most varied careers of any twentieth-century writer. He was born in Guilford, England, in 1881 and educated at London's Dulwich College for a career in the financial world. But he loved to write and turned to journalism and later fiction. His first of many comic novels, featuring such character favorites as Psmith, Mr. Mulliner, and the wise servant Jeeves, came out in 1902, by which time he was contributing lyrics and sketches to West End musicals. (He even collaborated with the young Jerome Kern on *The Beauty of Bath* in 1906.) By the age of twenty-four, Wodehouse had twenty novels published and felt he wanted to settle in New York, a place he had visited twice before. He emigrated to America in 1915 and stayed for sixty years, becoming a naturalized citizen and eventually completing ninety-six novels; hundreds of short stories; six nonmusical plays; dozens of articles, essays, and screenplays; and some two dozen Broadway musicals. Oddly, Wodehouse's libretto- and lyric-writing career was confined mostly to one decade, 1917–1928, but he made a considerable impact on Broadway, particularly in bringing a slangy-poetic style to lyric writing.

Although he was hired to write lyrics only for *Have a Heart* (1917), the first Bolton–Wodehouse–Kern musical, Wodehouse ended up contributing so much to the libretto that he was credited as co-author with Bolton. (They would share similar writing duties for eight future musicals as well.) *Have a Heart* was intended as a Princess show, but it opened at the larger Liberty Theatre instead. Less than a hit at seventy-eight performances, the musical nonetheless had the flavor and skill of a Princess success. Another honeymoon is the basis of the plot, but this time it is a second honeymoon. Store owner Rutherford Schoonmaker (Thurston Hall) and his wife Peggy (Eileen Van Biene) have had a bumpy marriage of late and have filed for divorce. But on the eve of the finalization, "Rudy" convinces Peggy to "elope" with him and hide away at a seaside resort. It looks like the couple will have a second chance until the arrival of Dolly Barbizon (Louise Dresser), a former employee of Rudy's who has become a silent movie star. Her flirtations with Rudy nearly send the Schoonmakers back to the divorce courts, until the complications are explained away by Henry (Billy B. Van), a wily elevator boy from Rudy's store who arrives to save the day. Not only were the lyrics an improvement over *Very Good Eddie*, but the Wodehouse–Bolton libretto was even more literate and playful. (The expert Kern score included the later standards "And I Am All Alone" and "You Said Something.") Critical reaction to the show was favorable, but, maybe because it wasn't at the Princess Theatre, audiences did not associate it with the popular *Very Good Eddie* and failed to make it a hit.

Their next musical, *Oh, Boy!* (1917), *was* at the Princess and it *was* a hit. The libretto used one of the most familiar situations of French comedy: a girl mistakenly found in the rooms of a married man. But there was nothing old hat about the Bolton–Wodehouse story that was carefully plotted and filled with delicious dialogue. George Budd (Tom Powers) brings his new wife Lou Ellen (Marie Carroll) to his Manhattan apartment, where a telegram from his Quaker aunt awaits him, threatening a visit. The stern old dragon holds George's purse strings, and, having married without her permission, he fears she will cut him off. He sends his bride to her mother's house for the wedding night just as Jackie (Anna Wheaton), a sexy gal running away from a policeman, climbs in through the window. It seems Jackie, fleeing from a masher, punched a cop in the eye. So when the officer pounds on the door, George shows him the marriage license and tells him that there must be some mistake: Jackie is his wife, and she has been with him all evening. Soon the aunt (Edna May Oliver), Lou Ellen and her mother, and George's playboy friend Jim (Hal Forde), accompanied by some showgirls arrive at the apartment, and Jackie is forced to play both wife and aunt, depending on who's in the room. The dialogue sparkles, especially when the streetwise Jackie tries to talk like a Quaker: "I will even give thy good wife mine if thee will only beat it." The libretto, an original concoction by Bolton and Wodehouse, was complemented by Kern's finest score yet ("Till the Clouds Roll By" was the immediate hit), and *Oh, Boy!* ran a lucrative 463 performances before a popular tour and later productions in London and Australia.

The most durable of the Princess shows was *Leave It to Jane* (1917), which did not play at the Princess Theatre (that house was still packing them in with *Oh, Boy!*) but retained the same creative team and boasted the same kind of small-scale production with large-scale entertainment value. One of the earliest of many musicals set on a college campus, *Leave It to Jane* was based on George Ade's comedy hit *The College Widow* (1904) and did not stray far from the original. Jane Witherspoon (Edith Hallor), the daughter of the president of Atwater College, is known for her resourcefulness, so when word reaches campus that Billy Bingham (Robert Pitkin), the finest athlete in the area, is going to play football for Atwater's arch rival, the students turn to Jane. She convinces Billy to enroll at Atwater and to play football under an assumed name. He agrees, but later, feeling as though he has been taken advantage of, Billy is disenchanted with everything until he learns that Jane loves him for himself, not his gridiron abilities. Much of the comedy came from such delightfully wacky characters as the man-hungry Flora (Georgia O'Ramey), a football-crazy pair played by Oscar Shaw and Ann Orr, and Billy's tyrant of a father (Will C. Crimans) who is whisked away by the Atwater students whenever he comes close to seeing his son. The Kern–Wodehouse songs, which included "Cleopatterer," "The Siren's Song," and the title number, had the same youthful buoyancy as the script, and *Leave It to Jane* settled in for 167 performances in the larger Longacre Theatre. It remains the most revived of the Princess musicals, a 1959 Off-Broadway production running two years.

Oh, Lady! Lady! (1918) echoed *Oh, Boy!* in more than explanation points, and it was nearly as popular, but the libretto seems less accomplished and Kern's score less known. The Bolton–Wodehouse plot revolved around a theft at a mansion, something they and others would use in future librettos, such as *Oh, Kay!* (1926) and *Animal Crackers* (1928). Heiress Mollie (Vivienne Segal) is engaged to Willoughby Farringdon (Carl Randall), but Mollie's mother is not taken with "Bill" and is more than happy to suspect him when the family jewels are stolen. The real culprit is Fanny Weld (Florence Shirley), a girl who claims to be a boyhood friend of Bill's but is really the ambitious girlfriend of Spike (Edward Ables), Bill's valet. Spike steals the jewels back, replaces them, and saves the romance of Mollie and Bill. It is more an efficient script than an inspired one, everything fitting together nicely but nothing very special coming out of it. The same could be said for the Kern–Wodehouse songs, the best one of the lot, the torchy "Bill," being dropped while the show was out of town and not heard on Broadway for another decade. *Oh, Lady! Lady!* was the last Princess musical by Bolton, Wodehouse, and Kern (other writers contributed to the series that ended in 1919), but they would work together on three more shows before going off in different directions.

Several lyricists (including Wodehouse) contributed to the score for Kern's *Sally* (1920), but Bolton wrote the libretto alone this time. One of the best of the Cinderella-like vehicles that were so beloved in the 1920s, *Sally* featured Florenz Ziegfeld's dancing star Marilyn Miller as an orphan who dreams of becoming, not surprisingly, a *Ziegfeld Follies* dancing star. While working as a dishwasher in a Greenwich Village restaurant, Sally meets the Long Island heir Blair Farquar (Irving Fisher), who has come to book a private party. Although they are strongly attracted to each other, the likelihood of their getting together is thin. But luck shines on Sally when Blair's father is desperate for a replacement to perform at a bash at his Long Island mansion (an exotic foreign dancer has backed out), and a theatrical agent hires Sally to go disguised in her place. Sally is reunited with Blair (who doesn't recognize her at first), but they quarrel and part ways until the agent gets Sally booked into the *Follies*, where she becomes a star and gets her man back. A clever supporting character in the plot is Sally's co-worker "Connie," the ex-Duke Constantine of Czechogovinia (Leon Errol), who is reduced to working as a waiter but still enjoys the social high life of royalty. Helped by the sterling Kern score ("Look for the Silver Lining," "Wild Rose," "Whip-Poor-Will," and other gems) and Miller's wide appeal, *Sally* was, at 570 performances, the most popular musical of the decade.

While Bolton and Wodehouse each worked with other writers and composers in between these shows, they reunited with Kern one last time for *Sitting Pretty* (1924), an intimate musical that recalled the glory days of the Princess shows before World War I. Horace (Dwight Frye) is a small-time burglar who breaks into wealthy homes with only a modicum of success. When he tries to pilfer from the Pennington mansion, he only ends up falling for May Tolliver (Gertrude Bryan), who works there. May and her sister Dixie (Queenie Smith) take it on themselves to reform Horace, which they do, and May ends up with an honest Horace while Dixie gets Harold (Rudolf Cameron), the Pennington heir. Despite an expert book and superior songs (none of which became a standard), *Sitting Pretty* failed to run any longer than ninety-five performances. After that, the members of the famous triumvirate went separate ways, only occasionally crossing paths. Bolton latched on to a new composer, the young George Gershwin, with *Lady, Be Good!* (1924). Ira Gershwin supplied the lyrics, and Bolton collaborated with Fred Thompson on the libretto. Like Wodehouse, Thompson was a transplanted Englishman whom Bolton had worked with on some West End shows. Newly arrived in New York, he and Bolton would co-write a handful of Broadway musicals together, none more important than *Lady, Be Good!*.

Generally considered to be the first musical to effectively use jazz in its score, *Lady, Be Good!* was also the first major hit for the Gershwins and made Fred and Adele Astaire bona fide Broadway stars. The Bolton–Thompson libretto is more far fetched than necessary and lacks the cohesiveness of Bolton's earlier work, but it provided ample opportunity for the many talents involved. When Dick Trevor (Fred Astaire) turns down the romantic urgings of wealthy Josephine Vanderwater (Jayne Auburn), she sees to it that he and his sister Susie (Adele Astaire) are evicted from the Vanderwater-owned apartment building, and they take up housekeeping on the street. But the down-and-out couple is helped by the crafty lawyer Watty Watkins (Walter Catlett), who desperately needs someone to masquerade as a Mexican wife to collect an inheritance. Susie agrees to the deception, only to learn that Jack Robinson (Alan Edwards), the man she loves, is supposedly the real Mexican lady's husband. But that marriage turns out to be illegal, Susie gets her man, and Dick ends up with the girl he preferred over Josephine. Barely worked into the plot was comedian-singer Cliff Edwards, who sang "Fascinating Rhythm" and other numbers from the scintillating Gershwin score.

Bolton and Thompson also provided the script for the Gershwins' *Tip-Toes* (1925), another variation on the Cinderella musical. A vaudeville trio, consisting of the amiable Tip-Toes (Queenie Smith), her brother Al (Andrew Tombes), and their uncle Hen (Harry Watson Jr.), find themselves stranded and out of work in Florida, so they make arrangements for Tip-Toes to pass herself off as a society gal and snag a vacationing millionaire. But when she goes after the glue magnate Steve Burton (Allen Kearns), she actually falls in love with him and reveals the con game. Even though he risks social disgrace, Steve remains true to Tip-Toes for a happy ending. In a season filled with musical hits, *Tip-Toes* held its own at 192 performances. Even more successful was *The Ramblers* (1926), a vehicle for comics Bobby Clark and Paul McCullough that Bolton co-wrote with songwriters Harry

Ruby and Bert Kalmar. The farcical and illogical libretto concerned Professor Cunningham (Clark), a phony spiritualist medium, and his stooge Sparrow (McCullough), who travel the countryside and get mixed up with a film crew making a movie on location. The book was a series of chases, and the score was mostly forgettable, but the two stars triumphed.

Another star vehicle, but much better written, was *Oh, Kay!* (1926), which featured Gertrude Lawrence in one of her most beloved roles. The Gershwins wrote the wonderful score and Bolton reteamed with Wodehouse on the libretto. It may have echoed earlier shows (another Long Island mansion, down-and-out aristocracy, lovable crooks), but the tale, now set in the Prohibition era, played like a breath of fresh air. Since he lost his titled lands through taxes, the Duke of Durham (Gerald Oliver Smith) has turned to rum-running with the help of his sister Kay (Lawrence) and their bootlegging cohort Shorty McKee (Victor Moore). They are using the Long Island home of the often absent (and often engaged) Jimmy Winter (Oscar Shaw) for their delivery depot. But when Jimmy returns home unexpectedly, the trio takes on false identities (including Kay as a housemaid and Shorty as a revenue officer), and the plot complicates efficiently. After getting out of a seemingly endless series of betrothals, Jimmy ends up with Lady Kay. It was one of Bolton and Wodehouse's most delectable librettos. But it was followed by one of their sorriest efforts, a stuffy romance called *The Nightingale* (1927), which used real people in a fictional and dull manner. Songbird Jenny Lind (Eleanor Painter) falls in love with Captain Rex Gurnee (Glen Dale) of West Point, but she eventually puts an end to their affair because she fears her stage career will hurt his promising military career. P. T. Barnum, Robert E. Lee, and Cornelius Vanderbilt were among the personages to fill out the cast of characters, without much effect. Armand Vecsey's score was somewhat to blame, but one cannot credit the libretto with helping matters. *The Nightingale* struggled on for twelve weeks.

Bolton was represented again on Broadway a month later, and this time he and co-author Fred Thompson had a hit. *Rio Rita* (1927) was an atypical Bolton show in that it was very large and lavish (Ziegfeld produced it, using it to open his new theatre named after himself), and it was an operetta. Captain Jim Stewart (J. Harold Murray) and his Texas Rangers are on the hunt across the Lone Star State for a mysterious bandit labeled the Kinkajou. Jim is also trying to capture the heart of the beautiful Rio Rita Furguson (Ethelind Terry) and is making progress until the evil General Esteban (Vincent Serrano), who lusts after Rita, convinces her that Jim is only wooing her because he wants to capture Kinkajou, whom he believes is her brother. But Jim eventually reveals Esteban to be the bandit, and the captain is reunited with Rita. The comedy came from the team of Bert Wheeler and Robert Woolsey, who were worked into the plot as bumbling lawyers, and Ada May as the saucy cabaret singer Dolly. It was all very old fashioned but surprisingly enjoyable, helped by the pseudo-operatic score by tunesmiths Harry Tierney (music) and Joseph McCarthy (lyrics), who had as little experience with operetta as Bolton and Thompson. Both the new theatre and the new show were a hit.

Closer to home for Bolton was *The Five O'Clock Girl* (1927), a "fairy tale in modern dress" that Bolton and Thompson wrote for Harry Ruby and Bert Kalmar's score. The girl of the title is Patricia Brown (Mary Eaton), who works at the Snow Flake Cleaner's Shop in Manhattan and, leaving work every day promptly at five, phones the same number and speaks with her mysterious admirer. He turns out to be the swell Gerald Brooks (Oscar Shaw), so Patricia "borrows" fancy clothes from the shop when she finally gets to meet him and tries to pass herself off as a society miss. Her deception is soon unmasked, but the two are brought together by the machinations of Patricia's co-worker Susie Snow (Pert Kelton) and Gerald's valet, Hudgins (Louis John Bartels), who end up in each other's arms. If the plot seemed tired, the songs and the dialogue were not. (When Susie asks Hudgins why they can't live with his parents after they wed, he replies, "Because they're still living with their folks.") *The Five O'Clock Girl* was another success for Bolton, who continued to be one of the most sought after librettists in the business.

It is no wonder that Ziegfeld wanted him for his extravaganza *Rosalie* (1928), another vehicle for Marilyn Miller that tried (and nearly succeeded) to match the success of *Sally*. To cover his bets, Ziegfeld hired both Sigmund Romberg and George Gershwin to write the music, Wodehouse and Ira Gershwin for the lyrics, and Bolton and Anthony McGuire for the book. Oddly, none of them was up to par. The Gershwins did provide "How Long Has This Been Going On?" (left over from a previous show), and the librettists had some fun mocking operetta plots, but *Rosalie* ended up being about Miller's dancing and Joseph Urban's lavish sets. Princess Rosalie of Romanza (Miller) falls for the Lindbergh-like flyer Lieutenant Richard Fay (Oliver McLennan), an American and a West Point officer who flies across the Atlantic to be with her. But the princess cannot marry a commoner as long as her father (Frank Morgan) is king, so the old boy abdicates and joins other ex-royalty in a song and dance, and the ex-princess gets her flyer. With a stage full of Ruritanian townfolk, waltzing ballroom couples, marching hussars, and Miller dancing her way through the story, audiences (and most critics) had no complaints, and *Rosalie* ran a very profitable 335 performances.

Bolton finally got to work with songwriters Richard Rodgers (music) and Lorenz Hart (lyrics) with *Simple Simon* (1930), another Ziegfeld vehicle, this time for comic Ed Wynn. The "perfect fool" scripted much of the libretto himself, coming up with sketches that allowed him to show off his favorite bits. Bolton was probably responsible for giving the show some sort of shape and keeping it from turning into a revue. Coney Island newspaper vendor Simon (Wynn) refuses to look at the bad news of the day. He reads only fairy tales and dreams of himself as the hero in a series of fantasy adventures involving Snow White, Cinderella, a giant frog, and so on. It was pretty lame stuff, but Wynn was a master at what he did, and his fans were not disappointed. Two of the best Rodgers and Hart songs, "He Was Too Good for Me" and "Dancing on the Ceiling," were cut before opening, but Ruth Etting did get to sing "Ten Cents a Dance," which launched her career. The Depression was already having its effect on Broadway, and Ziegfeld had to take *Simple Simon* on the road in order to make any money.

Bolton's next project, the Gershwins' *Girl Crazy* (1930), had no such problems, becoming the hit of the 1930–1931 season. The show is remembered mostly for its treasure chest of Gershwin standards and for introducing Ethel Merman to Broadway, but the libretto by Bolton and John McGowan is first class. (Sloppily revised years later as *Crazy for You*, it was still a crowd pleaser.) New Yorker Danny Churchill (Allen Kearns) is so besotted with wine, women, and nightclubs that his father sends him out to Custerville, Arizona, where all three are in short supply. Danny goes to Custerville by taxi, and the Jewish cabbie Gieber Goldfarb (Willie Howard) likes the look of the place and stays, eventually becoming the sheriff and talking to the local Indians in Yiddish. As for Danny, he turns a dude ranch into a swinging gambling casino, and soon Custerville is looking like a miniature Manhattan. He also falls for the town's postmistress Polly (Ginger Rogers), and before you know it the saloon keeper's daughter Kate (Merman) leads the town in discovering "I Got Rhythm." *Girl Crazy* was Bolton's last major hit and an apt testament to his remarkable storytelling talents.

It is ironic that the last Bolton–Wodehouse libretto never made it to Broadway. Working with Cole Porter for the first time, they fashioned a shipboard musical comedy they called *Bon Voyage*, in which the passengers on a chic oceanliner find themselves shipwrecked on an island in the third act. The story was fashioned around its stars (Ethel Merman, William Gaxton, and Victor Moore) and contained such familiar Bolton touches as a comic gangster and characters taking on various disguises to win their sweethearts. With the script, songs, and scenery finished, Wodehouse took off for London and Bolton for Paris. Then disaster struck: the real ocean liner *Castle Morro* caught fire off the coast of New Jersey and sank, killing 125 passengers. Producer Vinton Freedley knew his shipwreck musical as written was doomed, so he hired the show's director, Howard Lindsay, and a publicist, Russel Crouse, to fashion a new script using the Porter score, the shipboard sets, and the already-signed cast. The result was *Anything Goes* (1934), the quintessential 1930s musical and the most revived show from that decade. How much of the Bolton–Wodehouse libretto survives in the new script is difficult to say. But Lindsay and Crouse were the ones to pull off the last-minute hat trick, and it initiated one of the most fruitful collaborations of the American theatre (see chapter 6).

Bon Voyage was Wodehouse's last libretto. He left the musical theatre to concentrate on novels and nonmusical plays. Broadway lost one of its finest lyricists and librettists in one fell swoop. Bolton continued writing librettos for another twenty years, but rarely did he produce anything beyond the mediocre. *Walk with Music* (1940), which he wrote with Parke Levy and Alan Lipscott, had a premise that Hollywood would copy more than once. Three farm girls from New Hampshire set off for Florida to make their fortune; one of them, Pamela (Kitty Carlisle), will pose as an heiress, the other two as her maid and chaperone. The plan goes awry when Pamela falls for a penniless lad, but all is well when one of her sisters *does* land a millionaire. The score by Hoagy Carmichael (music), Johnny Mercer (lyrics), and others had some bright moments, but the rest of the show disappointed and failed to run. A few months later, *Hold On to Your Hats* (1940) opened with a libretto by Bolton, Matt Brooks, and Eddie Davis. The show marked Al Jolson's return to Broadway after decades in Hollywood, but the libretto was more than just a star vehicle. A cowboy radio star, "The Lone Rider" (Jolson), finds himself and his Russian-accented sidekick Concho (Bert Gordon) mixed up in some real-life adventure when they pursue a villain. It was lighthearted fun with a tuneful score by Burton Lane (music) and E. Y. Harburg (lyrics), but the musical had to close when Jolson became dissatisfied with New York and returned to California.

There was no star to blame when *Jackpot* (1944) flopped. The libretto by Bolton, Sidney Sheldon, and Ben Roberts was a comic lark but seemed too inconsequential in those post-*Oklahoma!* days. In order to sell government bonds, Sally Madison (Nanette Fabray) puts herself up as first prize at a bond rally. Three marines pick the lucky number, so complications ensue until two of them find other true loves. Not much better but certainly more popular was *Follow the Girls* (1944), which Bolton wrote with Eddie Davis and his old partner Fred Thompson. It was a slapdash affair that often resembled a burlesque or variety show more than a book musical, but, with its ribald jokes and long line of chorines, *Follow the Girls* entertained servicemen on leave and many others for two years. The story, such as it was, centered on burlesque queen Bubbles La Marr (Gertrude Niesen), who takes over a Long Island servicemen's canteen to aid her country. Her beau, the rotund Goofy Gale (Jackie Gleason), has been rejected by the army and has no other way to break into the place to court Bubbles than to dress up as one of the buxom chorus girls. Much of the show consisted of specialty acts, and its stars were encouraged to ad lib and work in their own bits. *Follow the Girls* was the kind of musical that Bolton had fought against in the Princess days; now he was writing them himself. His last Broadway musical, *Ankles Aweigh* (1955), written with Davis again, seemed like a peacetime version of *Follow the Girls*. Hollywood starlet Wynne (Jane Kean) weds a navy pilot (Mark Dawson), but their wedding night keeps getting postponed as the studio moves her from one film location to another and the military keeps transferring him to inconvenient bases. The score by Sammy Fain (music) and Dan Shapiro (lyrics) was bright and tuneful, but *Ankles Aweigh* seemed even more antique in the heyday of more logical book musicals.

By the time he died in London in 1979, Guy Bolton was pretty much forgotten by those working on Broadway and the West End, two venues he dominated a half century earlier. Just as most librettists are doomed to obscurity, Bolton seemed to disappear while the giants he worked with (Kern, Porter, Rodgers and Hart, the Gershwins) grew in stature as the years passed. But to those putting on musicals in the 1910s, 1920s, and 1930s, Bolton was one of those giants. The billing of "Bolton–Wodehouse–Kern" during the Princess musicals' day was not accidental. The book writer was important enough to be noticed because anyone could see that it was the librettos for those shows that seemed so different. The subtle but revolutionary changes Wodehouse made in lyric writing and that Kern made in composing theatre scores strike us as obvious today, but Bolton's contribution, so clear then and so misunderstood now, was just as vital. Only a handful of his shows are revived today, but when they are, this vitality shines. New York revivals of *Very Good Eddie, Leave It to Jane, Oh, Kay!, The Five O'Clock Girl,* and others do not take the town by storm as they did in their era, but each one impressed on theatregoers that the man who brought the Broadway libretto out of adolescence could not easily be dismissed.

CHAPTER THREE

HIGH JINKS AND PIPE DREAMS: OTTO HARBACH AND OSCAR HAMMERSTEIN II

Oscar Hammerstein led the American musical into maturity; Otto Harbach taught Hammerstein how to do it. Together they not only transformed the Broadway libretto but also created the modern musical play. Interestingly, neither man was a composer. If musicals are about music then the revolution should have been led by a musical artist. But despite the advances made by Kern, Gershwin, Rodgers, and others, the Broadway musical grew to maturity only when the librettos did. Sophisticated and complex music arrived before scriptwriting was taken as seriously. It was the nonmusical Harbach and Hammerstein who brought the libretto up to the level of the music, and, once there, the possibilities were awe inspiring.

Both men were also accomplished lyricists, so their libretto careers have rarely gotten the attention they deserved. If theatregoers are at all aware of Harbach, they know him as the lyricist of "Smoke Gets in Your Eyes" and other pre–World War II songs. And as well known as Hammerstein is, few realize that he wrote the books for almost every one of his Broadway shows. It took Hammerstein to bring to fruition the ideas that Harbach initiated. They were teacher-pupil at first, then partners, then finally pipe-dreaming father and wish-fulfilling son. (It seems like a strange and unique theatre relationship until one sees a similar pattern years later with Hammerstein and Stephen Sondheim.) While few would consider Harbach and Hammerstein as equals when it came to craftsmanship and talent, they should be viewed as a team when looking at the development of the Broadway libretto.

Harbach was born Otto Abels Hauerbach in Salt Lake City in 1873, the son of Danish descendants whose name was originally Christiansen. (The family took the name of their employer's farm, a common practice in the early 1800s.) Hauerbach worked his way through college and planned to have a career in academia. He was hired as an English and public speaking instructor at Whitman College in the state of Washington, but after a few years he left to go to New York, hoping to earn a graduate degree from Columbia University. To pay tuition, Hauerbach worked in insurance and then in journalism, but it wasn't enough, and he had to leave Columbia before finishing his studies. While making ends meet writing for small Manhattan newspapers, he discovered the theatre and thought that the writing in musicals was greatly lacking. So he started penning his own librettos and lyrics and, teaming up with composer Karl Hoschna, completed some musicals that were turned down by several producers. But when Hoschna was asked to score a musical called *Three Twins* (1908), he suggested Hauerbach as the lyricist, and the ex-teacher had his first of many hits. Charles Dickson wrote the libretto about a disinherited heir who disguises himself as a brother to a pair of twins (thus the odd title), and it was efficient and playable. But much of the show's popularity rested on the score, which included the immediate standard "Cuddle Up a Little Closer, Lovey Mine."

Dickson, Hoschna, and Hauerbach were reunited for a backstage musical called *Bright Eyes* (1910), but it did not succeed, and Hauerbach felt the reason was the script. Convinced that he could come up with better libretto writing, he wrote book and lyrics for *Madame Sherry* (1910), and it was such a hit that Hauerbach was able to quit his newspaper job and devote all his time to the musical theatre. The libretto was based loosely on a German musical, but Hauerbach made significant changes (and improvements) in the book, and he and Hoschna provided a whole new score. Manhattan dandy Edward Sherry (Jack Gardner) has been put in charge of running the Sherry School of Aesthetic Dancing by his eccentric Uncle Theophilus (Ralph Herz), a millionaire who is a fan of archaeology. ("For the last twenty-five years he has been digging around the ruins of Greece for the lost arms of the Venus de Milo," says Edward. "Seems to have been the only arms he ever really cared for.") Edward has written his uncle that he has a wife and two children to make him think that his nephew has settled down. In reality he is sweet on the instructor, Lulu (Frances Demarest), who teaches her young pupils in an Isadora Duncan–like style of dancing. When Theophilus's niece Yvonne (Lina Arbarbanell) arrives from a convent school to taste the high life of New York, Edward falls for her, and Lulu's affections move toward the South American gent Leonard Gomez (John Reinhard). But before the two couples can find happiness, the uncle shows up, and Edward has to employ his housekeeper and two young pupils to pretend to be his wife and children. As the housekeeper is already married, the ruse becomes difficult when her real husband comes on the scene. But all is untangled on Theophilus's yacht, the uncle is told the truth, and the correct couples are paired off. The Hoschna–Hauerbach score was superior, but it was the way the libretto utilized the songs that made *Madame Sherry* so special. For example, the rhythmic "Every Little Movement (Has a Meaning All Its Own)" was used first as a dance exercise for the pupils, then as a sensual wooing song for Leonard, and later as a sincere love duet for Edward and Yvonne. Some songs took their title directly from a line in the libretto and then developed the idea that normally would be handled with dialogue. Although it could not be mistaken as an integrated musical in the modern sense, *Madame Sherry* is Hauerbach's first attempt to merge book and score.

Hoschna and Hauerbach would collaborate on nine musicals, but none was as accomplished as *Madame Sherry*. The most interesting of them included *Doctor DeLuxe* (1911), about a suitor who is mistaken as a physician and continues the charade to win the girl he loves, and *The Girl of My Dreams* (1911), in which a Quaker girl tries to reform her wayward sweetheart. While neither had a long run, there was no question about the team's proficiency. But the collaboration was cut short by Hoschna's untimely death in 1912 at the age of thirty-four. Since Hauerbach had not worked with any other composer, the loss of his partner devastated him. Yet luck came his way in the form of Rudolf Friml, a Czech composer who had emigrated to America in 1906. Friml's career as a classical violinist and composer was floundering, so he turned to operetta with little success until he was hired to write the score for *The Firefly* (1912), a much-ballyhooed vehicle for soprano Emma Trentini. Operetta king Victor Herbert had refused to work with the temperamental star, so the task fell to Friml with Hauerbach writing the libretto and lyrics. *The Firefly* was a hit in its day and remains one of very few revivable operettas from the 1910s. Hauerbach's original book served its star well but was also a well-balanced tale with interesting character types. The street singer Nina (Trentini) wishes to escape the wrath of her drunken guardian, so she disguises herself as a cabin boy and gets a job on a private yacht heading for Bermuda. On board she is smitten with Jack Travers (Craig Campbell), who is engaged to the society girl Geraldine Van Dare (Audrey Maple). Nina excites the music professor Franz (Henry Vogel), who has heard her sing and thinks he's discovered a brilliant boy tenor. Her disguise creates all kinds of confusions and jealousies (especially with Geraldine and her predatory mother) before everything is cleared up and Nina wins Jack with the help of the comic supporting characters. Again Hauerbach was able to fit the songs into the plot with ease, even if he had to make his main character a singer by profession. His dialogue was uneven but still more adept than the usual operetta libretto. (When Nina is offered the job of Jack's valet and is told she will have to dress him, she replies, "I'm not that kind of boy.") Of course it was the Friml–Hauerbach score that triumphed, but one cannot dismiss the efficient libretto that allows *The Firefly* to still work on stage.

Hauerbach would work with Friml on eight more musicals over the next fourteen years, beginning with *High Jinks* (1913), the biggest hit of its season. Hauerbach collaborated with Leo Ditrichstein on adapting a French comedy into a "musical jollity" that was very different in tone from *The Firefly*. A Parisian neurologist, Dr. Gaston Thorne (Robert Pitkin), gets hold of a magic potion that he dispenses to his patients as a perfume. A little spray near the ear brings on the most giddy reactions, thereby setting off a series of complications involving a married couple, an explorer, an American lumber mogul, a runaway wife, and Thorne's own inamorata. It is a patchwork libretto filled with unmotivated songs and vaudeville bits, but the score is infectious, and the song "Something Seems a Tingle-Ingling" is used throughout as a way to tie the shenanigans together. After two major hits in a row, Hauerbach was now in great demand and worked on shows with various composers, sometimes contributing to five or more musicals each season. For *The Crinoline Girl* (1914), he collaborated with Tin Pan Alley songwriter Percy Wenrich on a vehicle for the cross-dressing star Julian Eltinge. Tom Hale (Eltinge) can marry the heiress he loves only if he can prove himself to her father by earning $10,000. So Tom discovers the identity of the female jewel thief called "the crinoline girl," disguises himself as a woman to infiltrate her world and nab her accomplices, and gets a $25,000 reward. Well plotted but musically disappointing, the show was a failure. So was *Suzi* (1914), Hauerbach's English version of a Hungarian operetta.

Reunited with Friml, Hauerbach wrote the European-flavored operetta *Katinka* (1915), which ran a very profitable 220 performances. The libretto is filled with so many familiar clichés that at times it seems like a spoof of an operetta, but Hauerbach saved the comedy for a bumbling American character who stumbles onto the exotic setting. Although she loves the Russian attaché Ivan Dimitri (Samuel Ash), the pretty Katinka (May Naudain) marries Ivan's boss, Boris Strogoff (Lorrie Grimaldi), the Russian ambassador in Vienna. But on her wedding night she steals away and finds refuge in the home of the American Thaddeus Hopper (Franklin Ardell). He hopes to hide her from Boris by sending Katinka to a harem, but Thaddeus's suspicious mother is accidentally sent there instead. After much comic confusion, Boris's first wife shows up, his marriage to Katinka is found illegal, and she can wed Ivan. In many ways the high jinks in *Katinka* were even more far fetched than *High Jinks*, but Friml's soaring melodies and Hauerbach's expert handling of the material made the operetta very satisfying on several levels. When Friml and Hauerbach returned with *You're in Love* (1917), the result was more traditional but less fun. Edward Clark co-wrote the book with Hauerbach, a competent affair about a honeymooning couple who are constantly at odds with an obnoxious aunt.

With America's antagonism toward Germany growing in the late 1910s, Hauerbach decided to Anglicize his name to Harbach to avoid any prejudicial feelings. His first musical under his new name was another Friml work, *Kitty Darlin'* (1917), but it failed to run. But Harbach was back on top with *Going Up!* (1917), a lighter-than-air musical based on James Montgomery's comedy *The Aviator* (1910). Robert Street (Frank Craven) has written a best-selling book about flying, but in truth he has never even been in an airplane. That changes when he has to win a flying race in order to get the girl he loves. (He manages to stay in the air the longest because he doesn't know how to land the plane.) Harbach collaborated on the merry libretto with Montgomery and Louis Hirsch (also the show's composer), and it was so pleasingly effective that the show can still be revived on occasion. The same certainly cannot be said for *Tumble Inn* (1919) and *The Little Whopper* (1919), both with Friml. The latter musical, which managed to run six months, is worth pointing out because it was the first Friml–Harbach show with a contemporary American setting rather than the usual European costume pieces. Friml would never be able to capture an American up-to-date flavor in his music, but Harbach had done very well with such pieces and hoped to move more in that direction. He would pursue it with various composers and with a young writer who would become his pupil, his most constant collaborator, and the man to bring Harbach's ideas to light.

Oscar Greeley Clendenning Hammerstein II was born in New York in 1895 to a famous theatrical family: his grandfather, Oscar Hammerstein I, was a colorful producer, theatre builder, and opera impresario; his father, William Hammerstein, was a favored theatre manager; and his uncle, Arthur Hammerstein, was a successful theatre producer who had presented a handful of Friml–Harbach hits. Educated at Columbia University for a law career, Hammerstein started writing lyrics and librettos for the college shows and after graduation worked as an assistant manager for some of his uncle's productions. His first writing effort, the nonmusical *The Light* (1919), closed out of town, but his first musical, *Always You* (1920), showed promise. Hammerstein's plot dealt with a former doughboy who is torn between his engagement to his American sweetheart and his love for the French girl he fell for while "over there." Hammerstein also wrote the lyrics to Herbert Stothart's music, and in both efforts he received modest praise from the press. Arthur Hammerstein was impressed enough to add his nephew to the creative team of *Tickle Me* (1920), Hammerstein writing the book and lyrics with Harbach and Frank Mandel while Stothart provided the music. Although the show was a success (thanks to its star, Frank Tinney), the musical was not very accomplished. Tinney played a screenwriter who goes on location in Tibet when they film his script, only to find swirling dancing peasants, comic misunderstandings, and true love. Better plotted (but not as popular) was *Jimmie* (1920) with the same authors. The title character is the long-lost daughter (Frances White) of a millionaire; unbeknownst to her, she stands to inherit a fortune. But the conniving Vincenzo Carlotti (Paul Porcasi) knows about it, and he tries to substitute his own daughter in her place. Eventually the truth comes out; Jimmie is reunited with her father and even becomes a cabaret star in the bargain. The libretto and score were splendid, but *Jimmie* did not catch on. Some blame *Mary* (1920), the popular musical that opened soon after. Harbach provided the libretto (with Mandel) and the lyrics for that show, and "Love Nest" became the most popular song of the year. But *Mary* has a weak plot, about a speculator who hopes to make a fortune selling "portable homes" in Kansas, and many of the musical numbers are awkward interruptions usually ignoring the story.

Harbach would contribute to a handful of other shows before reuniting with Hammerstein on *Wildflower* (1923), an interesting collaboration with the young composer Vincent Youmans. The plot had a ridiculous premise: according to a will, French farm girl Nina Benedetto (Edith Day) will inherit a large sum of money if she can go a whole year without losing her temper; if not, the fortune goes to her nasty cousin. The writing did not do much to improve this contrived story, but the score (with Stothard and Youmans each writing half the numbers) was delightful. ("Bambalina" was the hit song.) Although *Wildflower* was the biggest success of the season, Harbach and Hammerstein would not come up with a worthwhile libretto together until the next year. In the meantime, Harbach contributed to the forgettable *Jack and Jill* (1923) and *Kid Boots* (1923). Hammerstein worked on *Daffy Dill* (1922) and *Queen of Hearts* (1922), short-lived vehicles for, respectively, Frank Tinney and Nora Bayes, and collaborated with Youmans again on *Mary Jane McKane* (1923), a mediocre show that ran because of its star Mary Hay. Both Harbach and Hammerstein had ambitious ideas about the American musical theatre, but it was hard to see it in such substandard librettos. It was their next collaboration, the phenomenally successful *Rose-Marie* (1924), that indicated the direction Broadway would travel.

As familiar as the score of *Rose-Marie* is, the show is seldom revived, and the plot is not as well known. (The later film versions departed radically from the original libretto.) It is a very melodramatic plot, hinging on a murder, no less, but a substantial story with vivid characters, even though they easily fall into stereotype when viewed today. Rose-Marie la Flamme (Mary Ellis), the daughter of a French trapper, works as a singer at a small hotel in the Canadian Rockies. She is in love with the miner Jim Kenyon (Dennis King), even though she is persistently pursued by the devious city slicker Edward Hawley (Frank Greene). When there is a disagreement over land rights with the Indian Black Eagle (Arthur Ludwig), Jim brings his maps to Black Eagle's cabin to show him that Jim has not been infringing on his land. The drunken Black Eagle is gone, but his mistress, the half-breed Wanda (Pearl Regay), confronts Jim. Wanda is in love with Hawley (who is hidden in the cabin), and, after Jim departs, Black Eagle arrives to find her in Hawley's embrace. In the fight that ensues, Wanda stabs Black Eagle to death, and Hawley goes off to put the blame on Jim. Because of the known land dispute, everyone believes that Jim is the murderer, even Rose-Marie, who finally agrees to marry Hawley. But Hard-Boiled Herman (William Kent), a wily trader who is Jim's friend, gets the truth out of Wanda, who stops Rose-Marie's wedding to Hawley. Rose-Marie and Jim are reunited in his forest hideout as the Mounties arrest the real murderer.

While this story may not be much of an improvement over a late nineteenth-century melodrama, it was fairly unique for a musical, especially in operetta, where the issues at hand are usually more trivial. The dialogue is sometimes stilted, especially with the characters who speak with dialects that are French ("I am take sleigh ride with Jeem") or Native American ("I no promise nothing"). At the same time it is vigorous writing that is not afraid to mine all the passion out of the situations. Hammerstein and Harbach were proud of how the songs were incorporated into the plot (they even refused to list the musical numbers in the playbill program, seeing them as part of the whole), but, frankly, *Rose-Marie* was no more an integrated musical than a handful of others at the time. What it was instead was a bold attempt to bring integrity to the Broadway libretto. The superb score (music by Friml with some help by Stothart) was immediately embraced, and that certainly helped make *Rose-Marie* the hit of the decade. (In addition to the long Broadway run and four road companies, the musical was a hit in London, Paris, Berlin, Stockholm, Moscow, and Sydney.) But, integrated or not, it was the libretto that gave the show its bite. And even if it is too hopelessly dated now to be easily revived, *Rose-Marie* is a minor landmark and one that would lead to major landmarks.

Although Hammerstein was the collaborator who most shared his ideas, the ever-busy Harbach found himself working with others in between the

Hammerstein projects. The most notable of these 1920s musicals without Hammerstein was that quintessential of all Roaring Twenties shows, *No, No, Nanette* (1925). Harbach co-authored the libretto with Frank Mandel and shared lyric responsibilities with Irving Caesar for Youman's music. In many ways *No, No, Nanette* is the antithesis of *Rose-Marie:* frivolous, naive, and deliciously inconsequential. Based on an earlier Mandel comedy called *My Lady Friends,* the libretto concerned Bible publisher Jimmy Smith (Charles Winninger) and his ward, the flippant flapper Nanette (Louise Groody). Both are upsetting the status quo, Jimmy by giving money to three different financially strapped ladies (which doesn't go down well with his wife) and Nanette by flying in the face of convention and setting off for Atlantic City on her own (causing grief for her beau). A third plot, about Jimmy's philandering lawyer Billy Early (Wellington Cross) and his shaky marriage to Lucille (Josephine Whittell), managed to make connubial discord charming. Even the Smiths' comic maid Pauline (Georgia O'Ramey) was woven into the silly story with ease. While Harbach's libretto seemed to make no efforts toward his and Hammerstein's goal of an integrated musical theatre, *No, No, Nanette* is modern in its own wacky way. It is also the most revived of all 1920s musicals (especially since the blockbuster 1971 Broadway revival) because it wears its light-headedness so well.

Harbach and Hammerstein reteamed for *Sunny* (1925), the first of many collaborations with composer Jerome Kern for each man. When producer Charles Dillingham hired the team, he insisted that various specialty acts be worked into the plot, such as Cliff "Ukelele Ike" Edwards, whose contract specified that he do his strumming bit at around ten o'clock each evening. So Harbach and Hammerstein set their tale in an American circus touring Great Britain and let the loose ends be part of the Big Top show. Sunny Peters (Marilyn Miller) is a bareback rider in the circus who tumbles off her horse and into love for the visiting American Tom Warren (Paul Frawley). When Tom heads for the States, Sunny stows away aboard the oceanliner because she can't afford a ticket. Soon she is caught, so she agrees to marry Tom's best friend, Jim Denning (Jack Donahue), to avoid being thrown into the brig. The plan is to get divorced as soon as they arrive in New York, but during the trip Sunny's affections turn away from Tom and toward Jim, and a happily married couple disembarks in New York. Circus acts aside, it was a pretty tight libretto. But Miller was the box office draw, and the splendid Kern score was what made the musical special.

When Harbach and Hammerstein worked with composer George Gershwin for the first (and only) time, it was under unusual circumstances. *Song of the Flame* (1925) was an operetta and not the comic brand to be found later in Gershwin's *Of Thee I Sing* (1931); instead, it was in the traditional European mode. (Operetta veteran Stothart also contributed to the score.) The Russian aristocrat Aniuta (Tess Kosta) has a second identity: she is the revolutionary spitfire whom the peasants call "the flame" because of the bright red dress she wears into the fray. Prince Volodyn (Guy Robertson) is in love with the upper-class Aniuta, but after the revolution, when they meet again in Paris, he discovers that she is the flaming revolutionary and falls in love with her new persona as well. The lavish production helped the costume piece run, but the musical was an oddity for Gershwin and a throwback for the librettist-lyricists. More modern, but equally uninspired, were two shows Harbach did without Hammerstein. *Kitty's Kisses* (1926) was a complicated bedroom farce that he co-wrote with Philip Bartholomae, and *Cross Cross* (1926) was a vehicle for the veteran performer Fred Stone and his daughter Dorothy. The second featured music by Kern with Anne Caldwell collaborating with Harbach on the book and lyrics. Reunited with Hammerstein and Friml, Harbach aimed for another *Rose-Marie* but came up with only *The Wild Rose* (1926), a musical flop in which only the scenery got good notices.

When Harbach and Hammerstein were teamed with Sigmund Romberg, Broadway's other great operetta composer, the result was *The Desert Song* (1926), one of the most beloved of musical romances. With its exotic setting (the North African desert) and colorful leading character (a dashing and mysterious revolutionary), the operetta was strictly in the European style. Yet the libretto, by Harbach, Hammerstein, and Mandel, creates it own reality, and Romberg's music is lush and otherworldly. The story was inspired by recent history (the uprising of the Riffs in Morocco led by the Arab guerrilla Abd-el-Krim) as well as the public fascination with the exotic Sahara as evidenced in the popular Rudolph Valentino film *The Sheik* (1922). The musical acknowledged Hollywood also with the song "It" about alluring cinema star Clara Bow. But *The Desert Song* is traditional operetta with its harmonizing lovers, deceptive villains, and comic foils. The French governor's son Pierre Birabeau (Robert Halliday) pretends to be a bumbling coward, but he has a second identity: the mysterious Red Shadow who leads the Riffs in raiding colonial outposts. The beautiful French mademoiselle Margot Bonvalet (Vivienne Segal) won't give Pierre the time of day (she is engaged to a French captain), but when the Red Shadow steals into her bedroom and convinces her to go off into the desert with him, she agrees. When the two lovers are surrounded in their Sahara paradise by the governor and his soldiers, the disguised Pierre yields his sword rather than fight his own father and escapes without his identity being revealed. The Riffs declare the Red Shadow a traitor, and Pierre comes back to the outpost with the Shadow's scarlet garments, declaring he has slain the outlaw. Margot weeps for her beloved kidnapper until Pierre reveals the truth and the couple are united without disguises. In many ways the libretto was a male version of the earlier *Song of the Flame*, both revolutionaries sporting the same red attire. But *The Desert Song* is much more tightly constructed, even with the interpolation of two comic Americans: a wayward journalist trying to cover the uprising and his amorous secretary. The musical is revived without difficulty because the romantic libretto supports Romberg's flowing music so well.

Harbach, working with Youmans and Kern, found little success with, respectively, *Oh, Please!* (1926) and *Lucky* (1927); and when he reteamed with Hammerstein for *Golden Dawn* (1927), the result was a profitable but poorly written show. But the combination of Kern and Hammerstein (in his first solo effort at book and lyrics) a month later produced *Show Boat* (1927), and Broadway saw its first mature and fully realized musical play.

So much has been written about the score, the production, and even the plot of *Show Boat* that I would just like to make some observations about the nature of the libretto. Consider first the unlikeliness of the project. Even Edna Ferber thought it was a bad idea to turn her sprawling novel into a stage musical. Aside from the novel's epic scope (dozens of characters, the elapse of many years, the various locations), there were the many themes that were not usual musical fare: gambling addiction, alcoholism, miscegenation, and racial inequality. Ferber was right; her book could not be an ordinary Broadway musical. But it could be a musical play. Everything Hammerstein had (rather wrongly) boasted about concerning *Rose-Marie* actually came true in *Show Boat*. The songs *did* grow from the plot and the characters, and the book *did* reach a level of drama expected only on the nonmusical stage. That said, it must also be pointed out that Hammerstein's libretto is not very tight or economic. The nature of the epic form practically defies such neat and careful construction. Instead, *Show Boat* flows, sometimes unsteadily, from episode to episode. Both Kern and Hammerstein were never totally satisfied with the sometimes-disjointed second act, and most of the revisions of the script over the years for revivals and film versions have concentrated on the many scattered events in that act. (For the celebrated Broadway revival in 1994, a masterful dance sequence was used to show the passage of time and to bring unity to the act.) But I do not think that *Show Boat* is diminished by its sprawling nature and untidy plotting. It is as vast in its ambitions as it is in its subject matter, and part of the musical's glory is its out-of-control vitality.

When one examines Ferber's original novel, Hammerstein's craftsmanship is more evident. He eliminates characters and scenes productively and combines elements to turn a prose work into a powerful stage piece. The mulatto Julie La Verne is a much more vivid character, and Magnolia Hawks's maturity is more clearly worked out in the libretto. Many of the principal characters are dead by the end of Ferber's story, but Hammerstein wisely keeps some of them alive for the final scenes, not for a happy ending but for a more focused, dramatic finale. Even the racial aspects of the novel are handled more subtly and effectively in Hammerstein's version. (Joe and Queenie are very minor characters in the novel.) Ferber is very good at the details that make the novel form so engrossing. The description of the oil-cloth floor in the pilot house or Parthy's severe hairstyle are typical of her eye for detail. But Hammerstein has a better dramatic sense. In the musical's most powerful nonmusic scene, in which Steve cuts Julie's finger and drinks a few drops of her mulatto blood to prove that he has "Negro blood in me," the dialogue comes directly from Ferber. But Hammerstein sets the scene during a rehearsal on the showboat, making a commentary on the melodramatics on the stage mirroring those happening in real life. Some of the novel seems dated today, and not everyone would rank it as a masterpiece of American literature, but *Show Boat* the musical *is* a theatre masterpiece. Its many revivals testify to its timeliness. It is a musical that can be rethought and re-realized by every generation. A song may be moved or added, a scene cut or revised, or a new directorial concept introduced, yet it is still *Show Boat*. It not only survives meddling but sometimes grows richer because of it. Sadly, no musical that Harbach ever worked on would come close to achieving what Kern and Hammerstein did with *Show Boat*. He worked with his no-longer pupil on three later musicals, but the teacher did not seem to have the talent to create what he had taught and so firmly believed.

Harbach and Hammerstein's *Good Boy* (1928) was a contemporary piece that looked at show business with a rather cynical frame of mind. It was atypical of both men, but the libretto (written with Henry Myers), about an Arkansas hoofer who tries to make it on Broadway, was sharp and knowing. Quite the opposite was *The New Moon* (1928), generally considered the last of the great American operettas. Hammerstein collaborated on the book with Frank Mandel and Lawrence Schwab and provided the lyrics for Romberg's celebrated music. Although it was set in New Orleans and on board the ship of the title, it was very European in flavor. Robert Misson (Robert Halliday), a French aristocrat turned revolutionary, falls for the well-bred Marianne Beaunoir (Evelyn Herbert), even though his "stouthearted" comrades warn him about trusting a woman. When an evil policeman, the

Vicomte Ribaud (Max Figman), arrives from France to arrest Robert, he also is smitten with Marianne. Ribaud manages to apprehend Robert, lying to him that Marianne betrayed his whereabouts, and they board the *New Moon* for Europe. Marianne joins them (to be near Ribaud, she tells them) and cannot understand why Robert is so cold to her. Robert organizes a mutiny on board, Ribaud is overturned, and they land on an island where news of the French Revolution reaches them. With the end of royalty and the aristocracy in France, Marianne (who is merely a citizen now) and Robert are reunited, and he will serve as governor on the utopia-like island. The whole libretto is robust and not a little ridiculous, but somehow it holds together well and can be effectively revived.

With the crash of 1929, old-time operetta (like *The New Moon*) passed out of the mainstream of Broadway. Only by giving it a modern look or disguising some of its more obvious characteristics could operetta survive in the 1930s. This would cause trouble for both Harbach and Hammerstein, who strongly felt that operetta, not joke-filled musical comedy, was the road to the true musical play. Except for a 1938 musical that closed out of town, the two men would not work together again. Each pursued the integrated musical with various composers and with variable results. Harbach teamed up with Romberg again for the very foreign *Nina Rosa* (1930), a romance set in the Andes Mountains, and with Kern for the "modern" operetta *The Cat and the Fiddle* (1931). While the former was as dizzy and light-headed as might be expected at such a high altitude, the other was a small gem of a musical. Although *The Cat and the Fiddle* was set in Brussels, it was not a costume piece. The contemporary setting led to a very contemporary approach to the operetta form. There was no chorus or lavish spectacle, and the tale was told simply and in a straightforward manner that did not need villains or disguises to keep the plot moving. The young American composer Shirley Sheridan (Bettina Hall), who is in Brussels to study and, it is hoped, to be discovered, writes light jazz; the young Romanian composer Victor Florescu (Georges Metaxa) writes opera. Despite their musical differences, they are drawn to each other romantically. But when a producer wants to interpolate some of Shirley's songs into a production of Victor's opera, the love affair is strained until the two are finally reconciled, the two kinds of music blending as harmoniously as the two lovers. Practically a chamber opera, the show used such quaint devices as a street singer to keep the tale flowing musically and intimately. It is a lovely show that demonstrated that Harbach was not so out of date after all.

Also very contemporary, but not as well written, was *Roberta* (1933), the last Broadway success for both Harbach and Kern. The score is a lasting testament to the composer's genius, but Harbach's libretto is not an apt tribute to his talents. Based on a novel titled *Gowns by Roberta,* the script contrived to have an American football player, John Kent (Ray Middleton), inherit a Paris dress shop from his aunt (Fay Templeton). Once in Europe, he is smitten by the shop assistant, the foreign-accented Stephanie (Tamara), even though Sophie (Helen Grey), his obnoxious girl friend from the States, comes on the scene and almost gets John to marry her. Harbach shamelessly has the shop girl reveal that she is really a Russian princess as his deus ex machina, a device that only barely worked two decades earlier. The comedy came from Bob Hope as John's wisecracking sidekick Huckleberry Haines, and there was a requisite fashion show to beef up the sagging story. *Roberta* had a profitable run because of one song (it was known about town as the "Smoke Gets in Your Eyes" show) and lots of Paris gowns.

For the man who used to contribute to four or five shows each season, Harbach was represented less and less often on Broadway in the 1930s. His last New York project was the Romberg operetta *Forbidden Melody* (1936), a costume piece set in Romania, but it might as well have been on the moon, it was so out of touch with the times. The short-lived show was a sad swan song for Harbach, a name fewer and fewer theatregoers recognized. Although he lived until 1963, he was mostly forgotten except by Hammerstein and others who knew that Harbach was one of the cornerstones of the modern American musical. His shows were remembered mostly for the scores, too few people realizing that it was Harbach who had written the lyrics for those as well. It was left to his pupil to carry on the work. The trouble was, Hammerstein's career seemed to be nose-diving as musical after musical of his failed at the box office. Some were quite expert, and he often provided lyrics for superior scores, but Hammerstein was quickly turning into one of Broadway's youngest has-beens.

Rainbow (1928), for example, was very accomplished with an ambitious libretto by Hammerstein and Lawrence Stallings and a blues-jazz score by Vincent Youmans that is now considered ahead of its time. Like *Show Boat,* the story had a wide sweep and dealt with a gambler trying to better himself by marrying the right girl. The tale is set during the Gold Rush of 1849, and the hero hopes to take on a new identity after he accidentally kills a man in a brawl. Despite some potent scenes and noteworthy songs, *Rainbow* collected only a few compliments from the press and quickly closed. *Sweet Adeline* (1929) was the most popular Hammerstein show of the period, though the stock market crash a month after it opened kept it from enjoying a long run. Set during the Spanish-American War, it tells about

Addie Schmidt (Helen Morgan), a saloon singer in Hoboken, New Jersey, who dreams of making it to Broadway. It was a familiar story, but Hammerstein's libretto had some realistic touches, such as Addie's turning to drink when the man she loves runs off with her sister. The Kern score produced a handful of standards long associated with Morgan (most notably "Why Was I Born?") and a lesser-known gem called "A Girl Is on Your Mind," which was another in a series of dramatic song-scenes that Hammerstein was experimenting with.

A string of Hammerstein failures followed. *Ballyhoo* (1930) was a vehicle for W. C. Fields that flopped despite the star's presence. *The Gang's All Here* (1931) was a scattershot farce about rival bootleggers that pleased few. *Free for All* (1931), a musical comedy about a New York playboy trying to run a copper mine out West, quickly closed. Hammerstein returned to the operetta form with the Romberg musical *East Wind* (1931), an exotic romance about two French lovers in Saigon. Despite a beautiful and generally acclaimed production, Depression audiences didn't buy it. Hammerstein's luck improved somewhat with *Music in the Air* (1932), an operetta with Kern that, like *The Cat and the Fiddle*, was rather modern (though still European). Dr. Walther Lessing (Al Shean), an aged music teacher in Bavaria, writes a song called "I've Told Ev'ry Little Star" with his pupil Karl Reder (Walter Slezak). They leave their small mountain village with Karl's sweetheart Sieglinde (Katherine Carrington) to travel to Munich to get the song published. Once in the big city, the young lovers are nearly torn apart by a womanizing composer and an egomaniacal opera diva, and their sweet song is to be commercialized by money-hungry businessmen. So the three gladly return home, pleased to give up fame and fortune and settle for happiness and a simple life. The melodious score produced a few hits ("There's a Hill beyond a Hill" and "The Song Is You"), and the libretto mostly avoided the tired clichés of past operettas. If Kern and Hammerstein were still convinced that operetta was the ideal format for more realistic musicals, *Music in the Air* seemed to bear them out somewhat. It managed to run 342 performances during the darkest days of the Depression.

When Kern and Hammerstein reunited for *Very Warm for May* (1939), they stumbled badly, even though the show did produce one of the most beloved of all Broadway songs, "All the Things You Are." The libretto was a sloppy affair about various romances among performers at a summer stock theatre. The musical's short run is especially sad in retrospect: it was Kern's last new show with Hammerstein and, in fact, his last for Broadway. After the failure of *Very Warm for May*, Kern went to Hollywood and later died before being represented again on the Great

White Way. Hammerstein's last collaboration with Romberg, *Sunny River* (1941), did not fare any better. A contrived romance set along the banks of the Mississippi River, the libretto was roundly blamed, though the score was just as unmemorable.

Hammerstein was pretty much written off by most of the Broadway community, so it was somewhat surprising that Richard Rodgers turned to him when his partnership with Lorenz Hart was faltering. Perhaps Rodgers was looking for a very different kind of artist (and personality) from Hart. If so, he could not have chosen better. The erratic, brilliant Hart, who had to be badgered into writing and then dashed off lyrics quickly before disappearing from sight, would lead one to the very different Hammerstein, a methodical, slow writer whose concentration and dedication were prodigious. Hart wrote only a few librettos during his career, whereas Hammerstein had very few credits in which he wrote only lyrics. Hart usually wrote the lyric after Rodgers completed the music (mostly because Rodgers couldn't wait around idle any longer), but Hammerstein almost always would provide Rodgers with a script and a lyric before a note was written. As far as contrast goes, it was an ideal collaboration. But to insiders the teaming of Rodgers and Hammerstein seemed to spell disaster. Not only had Hammerstein's recent shows been flops, but the blame had usually been placed on his librettos and even his lyrics. Also, Rodgers was still considered modern and jazzy, while Hammerstein was labeled old fashioned and past his prime. Add to that the unlikely prospects surrounding the cowboy musical they were to present as their first collaboration, and it's no wonder the advance word on *Oklahoma!* was so negative.

Most of the distinctions attributed to *Oklahoma!* (1943) are not exaggerations. The songs and dances growing out of the character's psyches; the return to homespun, folk comedy rather than sarcastic penthouse humor; the whole new look and feel to the piece; the arrival of the mature integrated musical—these have been more than adequately discussed elsewhere. But looking at Hammerstein's libretto by itself offers a few noteworthy insights. The source material, *Green Grow the Lilacs* (1931), was far from a hit play, so few theatregoers in 1943 compared it to its musical version. Lynn Riggs's folk comedy actually has less plot than *Oklahoma!* Ado Annie is a very minor role, and Hammerstein created Will Parker and the comic subplot for the musical. The romance between Laurey and Curly is central to both play and musical, with the villain, Jud (Jeeter in Riggs's version), forming the third side of the triangle. Yet all three characters seem to have more flesh and blood in *Oklahoma!* Jud is sometimes a comic villain (as seen in the duet "Pore Jud Is Daid"), yet with his dark solo "Lonely

Room" and his far-from-comic lust for Laurey and hatred for Curly, he is much more interesting than Jeeter:

> JUD: Don't want nuthin' from no peddler. Want real things! Whut am I doin' set up here—like that feller says—a-crawlin' and a-festerin'? Whut am I doin' in this lousy smokehouse?

Laurey's growing maturity is also more fully realized in the musical. Hammerstein remains faithful to Riggs's play throughout (the famous opening with Aunt Eller churning butter while a singing Curly is heard approaching is taken directly from the original) but wisely elaborates here and cuts there. In the play, Curly is arrested for the murder of Jeeter, is sent to jail, escapes, and then is tried and freed. Hammerstein tightens the whole sequence and brings things to a cleaner and more effective finale. One of the other changes was a matter of practicality: Jeeter tries to set fire to a haystack during the knife fight with Curly. Hammerstein cut the fire for the musical, but, interestingly, it was put back in the 1955 film version. A masterpiece of adaptation, *Oklahoma!* shows Hammerstein's playwriting skills finally matching his remarkable lyric-writing talents.

The success and history of *Oklahoma!* and most of the subsequent Rodgers and Hammerstein shows have been well chronicled. But again I would like to look briefly at the Hammerstein librettos, starting with his only subsequent musical without Rodgers. *Carmen Jones* (1943) must have seemed as foolhardy a venture as *Oklahoma!* Previous attempts to modernize classic operas had always failed. Even the light-hearted *The Mikado* had resisted Broadway tampering. But Hammerstein's take on the Prosper Merimée story of the sultry, tragic Carmen worked well, retaining an opera milieu (and Bizet's music) while using the slang and informality of a Broadway musical. Merimée's cigarette factory worker becomes Carmen Jones, an African American southerner who labors in a parachute factory during World War II. Dashing military officers and bullring matadors become American GIs and boxing ring champs. The same tragic events unfolded in the musical, but they seemed less remote to American theatre audiences, and, while making no effort to eclipse the original, the new version proved to be very satisfying. *Carmen Jones* also proved to be a hit, running 502 performances, and the flop-burdened Hammerstein was back in the forefront of Broadway creators.

The transition of Ferenc Molnár's *Liliom* (1909) to *Carousel* (1945) is also quite proficient. Broadway had seen the Molnár tragedy in 1921 in a successful Theatre Guild production, but again few theatregoers twenty-five years later were drawing comparisons with the musical. Hammerstein made more radical alterations than in *Oklahoma!*, changing the setting from turn-of-the-century Budapest to a New England mill town in 1873, re-naming all the characters, and bringing an American temperament to the dark fantasy. Once again he expanded on the comic subplot, added humor to the piece without weakening the integrity of the tragicomedy, and fleshed out some of the secondary characters. (Only the oily villain Jigger Craigin still comes across as a stock type in the musical.) The libretto ends much like the play, but with some of the edges softened and wistful hope-fulness pervading the air. It is a typical Hammerstein ending rather than a truly tragic one, yet Molnár, who had written operetta plots in Hungary, ap-proved of *Carousel*'s finale. The central role of Billy Bigelow (John Raitt) was the most complex and multifaceted character yet seen in a Broadway musical. Molnár and Rodgers are somewhat responsible, but Hammer-stein's book and lyrics deserve most of the credit:

> BILLY: You're a funny kid. Don't remember ever meetin' a girl like you.
> ... You—are you tryin' to get me to marry you?
> JULIE: No.
> BILLY: Then what's puttin' it into my head? ... You're different all right.
> Don't know what it is. You look up at me with that little kid face like—
> like you trusted me. .... I wonder what it'd be like.
> JULIE: What?
> BILLY: Nothin'. I know what it'd be like. It'd be awful.

The integration of song and libretto reaches some sort of high point in *Carousel*. The so-called bench scene, in which "If I Loved You" and dialogue intertwine so beautifully, is the most potent example. Very rarely would ei-ther Rodgers and Hammerstein or anyone else be able to surpass the inge-nuity and inspiration of that musical scene.

Hammerstein's ideas about self-respect and honest values in life were expressed in a full-blown manner in *Allegro* (1947), an original musical that contained some of his best and worst writing. The loose, episodic tale, told with the help of a Greek chorus-like ensemble of commentators, followed the life of Joseph Taylor (John Battles) from birth to midlife crisis. Raised in a small community by loving parents, Joe pursues the medical profession, but unlike his father, who remains a local G.P., he is prodded by ambition and a greedy wife to reach higher. Eventually he is a slick Chicago physician who has lost touch with anything that was once important to him. When he discovers his wife's infidelity, Joe declines a lucrative new city position and returns home to his roots and more steadfast ideals. Despite its happy ending, *Allegro* is sometimes bitter, angry, and even sarcastic (a rare trait in Hammerstein's works). Like *Carousel,* boy gets girl early in the musical, but it does not bring lasting happiness. Life is so much more complicated than the old formula ever suggested. Hammerstein wanted to show this, but without a strong, structured story to build on, parts of *Allegro* are preachy and sanctimonious. More disappointing, the characters are not all that interesting. Joe's worldly-wise nurse, Emily (Lisa Kirk), who secretly loves him despite the fact that she realizes "The Gentleman Is a Dope," is the only character in the libretto who seems to sparkle with life. In trying to say so much, Hammerstein forgot the importance of plot and character.

He certainly had plenty of plot to deal with in *South Pacific* (1949). James A. Michener's anthology *Tales of the South Pacific* had many stories to tell, and Hammerstein, for the first time since *Show Boat,* was faced with the challenge of whittling something on a epic scale down to the musical stage. Because Hammerstein had never been in the military, he relied on director Joshua Logan, who had served in World War II, to help him make the world of GIs in the wartime Pacific believable. (Logan's contribution was significant enough that he was eventually credited as co-author.) The primary story about the French planter Emile de Becque (Ezio Pinza) and the American nurse Nellie Forbush (Mary Martin) came from Michener's story "Our Heroine," while the tragic subplot concerning the conniving native Bloody Mary (Juanita Hall), her daughter Liat (Betta St. John), and the American Lieutenant Joe Cable (William Tabbert), who loves her, originated in a tale called "Fo' Dollar." Hammerstein and Logan tie the two stories together plotwise (the characters easily overlap into each other's tale) but thematically as well. Cable's New England hypocrisy keeps him from wedding Liat just as Nellie's southern prejudices make her shun the idea of marrying Emile, who has two Polynesian children. Both plots are resolved in a manner that is somewhat contrived (Cable dies on a mission, and Nellie's doubts are softened by Emile's brush with death), but there was really no other way for the libretto to end and still be palatable musical theatre fare. Besides, Hammerstein's point about being "Carefully Taught" to continue prejudice is made, and the outcome of the characters is more important theatrically than thematically. Unlike *Allegro, South Pacific* manages to say a lot and still be highly satisfying and entertaining. Hammerstein excelled as both a writer and a showman.

The King and I (1951) was the first Rodgers and Hammerstein musical to break away from their series of shows dealing with America and Americans. It was also unusual in that it was a star vehicle, written for Gertrude

Lawrence at her request. [Yet it hardly seems like a star vehicle today when it is the role of the King that is often highlighted.] Hammerstein's source was Margaret Landon's historical (but romanticized) novel *Anna and the King of Siam*, which had been filmed in 1946. There are similarities between the screenplay and the musical, yet the tone of *The King and I* seems warmer than in its sources. For example, the novel's King is a cool and detached character who rarely lets down his regal mask. But in the musical, we see the tortured man behind the mask. Without developing any form of overt romance between the King (Yul Brynner) and the English governess Anna (Lawrence), the libretto explores both the humanity and the stubbornness in each character. The tragic subplot this time is important thematically, but it occupies little stage time (most of their scenes being in song), and neither the concubine Tuptim (Doretta Morrow) nor her lover Lun Tha (Larry Douglas) are fleshed out very well. But there is so much in *The King and I* that is potent, enjoyable, and even bold that its continued popularity is easy to understand.

When Hammerstein attempted another original libretto, the result was much more conventional than *Allegro*. *Me and Juliet* (1953) is a backstager in the old sense of the term. Rodgers and Hammerstein took pains to avoid the familiar clichés found in such show biz musicals. No understudy took over for the star, a failing show didn't become a blockbuster, and there were no temperamental divas or eccentric financial backers to lend the story some panache. Instead *Me and Juliet* told about the day-to-day routine of performing a musical that was off and running. There were two love stories: a triangle consisting of chorine Jeanie (Isabel Bigley); the assistant stage manager Larry (Bill Hayes), whom she loves; and the jealous electrician Bob (Mark Dawson), who craves her. The comic subplot concerned a dancer, Betty (Joan McCracken), who is smitten with the stage manager, Mac (Ray Walston), but he has a policy of not dating members of the company. Both plots were rather dull with little excitement in either the romance or the comedy. The closest thing to action is when Bob drops a lighting instrument from the flies in an attempt to kill Larry, but he misses. The libretto did likewise. Nothing much happened, and the two happy endings were long in coming and lackluster on arrival. There is much to recommend in the score, and *Me and Juliet* managed a barely profitable run, but it remains the least interesting of the partners' works.

Less successful but far more intriguing was *Pipe Dream* (1955), Rodgers and Hammerstein's least-known musical. John Steinbeck's novella *Sweet Thursday* concerned a group of misfits and castoffs in Monterey, California, yet it had a genial optimism that must have appealed to

41

Hammerstein. Marine biologist Doc (Bill Johnson) is so poor he can't even afford a microscope to examine his seaside specimens. The wandering, small-time thief Suzy (Judy Tyler) gets picked up by the police but is released and taken in by Fauna (Helen Traubel), the madame of the local flophouse. Doc and Suzy drift into an affair (with Fauna acting as matchmaker), while Doc's layabout friends stage a phony raffle to raise money for a microscope for their pal. They succeed, but Suzy and Doc break up over a disagreement, her telling the others she never wants to see him again unless he needs her. So one of Doc's cronies breaks the biologist's arm with a baseball bat while he is sleeping. Suzy returns to nurse him, and life continues in this ragtag world of lovable losers. It is an odd musical in many ways, and it's not difficult to see why it failed. But Steinbeck's book and Hammerstein's libretto both have a quirky kind of charm. Perhaps another Broadway artist might have found a way to make the piece work (Frank Loesser was originally interested in the property), but Rodgers and Hammerstein's *Pipe Dream* remains an unrevivable curiosity.

The team's most commercial musical comedy was *Flower Drum Song* (1958), an unpretentious show about Chinese Americans living in San Francisco. It was based on C. Y. Lee's novel of the same name, and Joseph Fields co-authored the adaptation with Hammerstein. Nightclub owner Sammy Fong (Larry Blyden) loves the fully Americanized dancer-singer Linda Low (Pat Suzuki), but he is betrothed to the newly arrived immigrant Mei Li (Miyoshi Umeki). The more traditional Chinese American youth Wang Ta (Ed Kenney) also loves Linda, but Sammy destroys any hope for that relationship when he arranges for Wang Ta's father (Keye Luke) and aunt (Juanita Hall) to see Linda's striptease act. Luckily for all concerned parties, Wang Ta is drawn to the gentle Mei Li, and it looks like Sammy will get Linda. But the Chinatown community insists that Sammy go through with the arranged marriage with Mei Li. A wedding is held, but when the bride lifts her veil after the vows, it turns out to be Linda. It is a well-balanced romantic comedy except for the awkward presence of Helen Charo (Arabella Chong), a friend of Mei Li who has an unrequited passion for Wang Tu. The librettists use her to continue the complications, but, having created a sincere and selfless character, it is very unsatisfactory when she is dumped by both Wang Tu and the writers. (In Lee's book she commits suicide.) *Flower Drum Song* has many of Hammerstein's favorite themes, particularly regarding the generation gap and the breaking of old traditions, but everything is on such a playful level that the musical seems to be about nothing in particular—a sort of comic version of *The King and I*. (In 2001, Henry David Hwang rewote the libretto, and the new version managed to bring up some intriguing ideas about East-West relationships.) More than any other Rodgers and Hammerstein musical, this one has jokes:

> WANG SR.: This is the first time Ta has ever stayed away all night. What could he be doing?
> AUNT: If this was a quiz program I could win a trip to Europe.

Perhaps the comedy veteran Fields was responsible for the lighter touch. One thing is known: Hammerstein was very ill, and it is questionable just how much of the libretto he actually wrote. His cancer had spread far enough that Hammerstein turned over the libretto for their next production, *The Sound of Music* (1959), to Howard Lindsay and Russel Crouse. Hammerstein managed to complete the lyrics for the musical but died nine months after it opened.

The legacy of Harbach and Hammerstein cannot be overestimated. Even if none of their shows were produced any longer, their contribution to the development of the American musical would be extensive. In addition to their often superb craftsmanship and bold ambitions, the two men must be credited with turning Broadway musical writing into a serious art form. Harbach was perhaps the first librettist to believe that the book for a musical should be as carefully planned and meticulously written as any other kind of literary effort. He approached the musical in the same manner that he viewed literature when he taught English in college. Harbach then instilled this kind of dedication in his pupil, who had the talent to make such lofty ideas take flight. The Harbach–Hammerstein librettos are not great literature, but the fact that they tried to be makes them important. When Hammerstein later wrote theatre masterpieces on his own, it was because of all those early efforts by the two men.

Before Harbach, there were mainly hack writers turning out the books for musicals. Hack writing would continue (sometimes very successfully), but Broadway had learned that the libretto could do better than just boy-meets-girl plots. Hammerstein and Harbach took musicals seriously. Sometimes this led to pretentious and overearnest works. Other times it shone and opened up possibilities for the musical theatre. This kind of dedication can be illustrated in a story that Harbach's son often told. When he was in his eighties, wheelchair ridden and mostly blind, Harbach complained one morning of sleeping badly during the night. When the son asked what the reason might be, Harbach said he couldn't sleep because he suddenly realized what was wrong with his lyric for "Smoke Gets in Your Eyes" (a song he had written nearly thirty years before). This striving for perfection characterizes the work of Harbach and Hammerstein. They both dreamed big, made big demands on themselves, and delivered big. Their dedication is the American musical maturing.

CHAPTER FOUR
STRIKE UP THE BAND: GEORGE S. KAUFMAN AND FELLOW WITS

George S. Kaufman, who coined the warning "Satire is what closes on Saturday night," saw many of his plays and musicals pack houses on many a Saturday night. Yet the celebrated playwright was right: Broadway has never been a stronghold of satire. That is, unless the work just happened to be co-written by Kaufman. Not only is he America's best theatre satirist, he is just about our *only* author of successful stage satires. He comes out of a school of humor that flourished in the 1920s, the Algonquin wits, which included such comic talents as Robert Benchley and Dorothy Parker. But Kaufman is the only one of the group to bring his satirical humor to the stage. With few exceptions, all of his forty-five librettos and nonmusicals were written with someone else. Dubbed the Great Collaborator, he liked to be part of a team. But whether he was writing with Edna Ferber, Moss Hart, Morrie Ryskind, Marc Connelly, or any other of his numerous partners, the unmistakable Kaufman mark is evident. He was the master of the wisecrack, the barbed put-down, the dry riposte, the exaggerated observation, and the ridiculous understatement. He also wrote some of the funniest librettos ever presented on Broadway.

George Simon Kaufman was born in Pittsburgh, Pennsylvania, in 1889. An elder brother had died in childhood, so Kaufman was raised in a pampered and protective environment with little physical activity allowed. But he was a voracious reader from his youth, and he decided to become a writer of some sort. He went into journalism, getting his first job in Washington, D.C.; then he landed a position with New York's *Evening Mail.* By 1915, he had progressed to the *Tribune* and then later the *New York Times,* writing theatre reviews for both papers. Once his playwriting career took off, he gave up the critic post but still contributed articles and comic pieces to newspapers and magazines. Kaufman's first play was *Among Those Present* (1918), written with Larry Evans and Walter Percival, but he gained recognition as a playwright with the hit comedy *Dulcy* (1922), which he co-authored with Marc Connelly. The two would collaborate on six other plays, most memorably *Merton of the Movies* (1922) and *Beggar on Horseback* (1924). With Edna Ferber he would pen such hits as *The Royal Family* (1927) and *Stage Door* (1936). But Kaufman's most famous collaborator was Moss Hart, the two of them providing such beloved classics as *Once in a Lifetime* (1930), *You Can't Take It with You* (1936), and *The Man Who Came to Dinner* (1939). Kaufman also wrote sketches for several musical revues and enjoyed a prestigious career as a director as well.

His first musical to make it to Broadway was *Helen of Troy, New York* (1923) with Connelly as his co-author and Harry Ruby and Bert Kalmar (in their first musical) providing the score. Critics found more favor with the book than the songs, but the show managed a profitable run. Helen McGuffey (Helen Ford) is a stenographer for a shirt collar factory in the upstate town of the title. When her son starts dating the boss's daughter, Helen gets the sack, so she invents a softer, more comfortable men's collar and sells it to a rival company. The libretto was a satire on big business, but the Kaufman barbs were more silly than pointed in this early effort. He and Connelly took on Tennessee hillbillies in their next libretto, *Be Yourself* (1924). Based on the team's 1917 unproduced comedy *Miss Moonshine*, it told of a feud between the McLeans and the Brennans, their rivalry taking on the spirit of a college football game with cheering from the sidelines and letter sweaters to indicate the two "teams." Again it was a modest success.

Kaufman's first musical hit was the Marx Brothers farce *The Cocoanuts* (1925) with a score by Irving Berlin. Although Kaufman was the only credited author, he received help from Morrie Ryskind, and the brothers themselves provided many of the lines, the whole show changing nightly during its 377-performance run. The libretto spoofs the real estate boom in Florida with speculator and hotel owner Henry W. Schlemmer (Groucho) selling off lots of swampland as bits of paradise. What plot there was concerned some stolen jewels belonging to the wealthy Mrs. Potter (Margaret Dumont) and how the blame is wrongly put on the young man who wants to marry her daughter. Chico and Harpo were Schlemmer's cronies who, when they were not busy stealing silverware or chasing girls, unwittingly reveal the real thieves. The show has more of the Marx Brother surreal humor ("The next number on the program will be a piccolo solo which we will omit.") than the wisecracking Kaufman wit, and even he admitted there was not much of his material left once the brothers took over the stage. But *The Cocoanuts* was a success, and Kaufman gladly worked again with the zany comics on *Animal Crackers* (1928), this time giving program credit to Ryskind.

Morrie Ryskind was a native New Yorker, born in 1895 and writing sketches for vaudeville and musical revues at a young age. His work was seen in such Broadway variety shows as *The 49ers* (1922), *The Garrick Gaieties* (1925), and *Merry Go Round* (1927). His first libretto, *Pardon Me,* written with Ralph Murphy, closed out of town in 1927. But Ryskind was firmly on Broadway with *Animal Crackers.* Instead of jewels, this time it was a painting that was stolen. The African explorer Captain Spaulding (Groucho) is a guest of Mrs. Rittenhouse (Dumont) at her Long Island mansion when the heist occurs, so he and his spies, Chico and Harpo, again help catch the culprit. There was a lot of door-slamming farce, fake copies of the painting being circulated about the house, and the expected Marx mayhem. Again it is difficult to determine the work of the librettists from that of the brothers. For example, when Groucho is asked if he has seen a habeas corpus, he replies, "No, but I've seen Habeas Irish Rose"; it's a delicious pun (kidding the current hit *Abie's Irish Rose*) that could have been written by a Marx, a Kaufman, or a Ryskind. The score this time was by Kalmar and Ruby, and, like Berlin's songs for *The Cocoanuts,* it received little attention despite some pleasant numbers. *Animal Crackers* ran a profitable six months, toured the country, then took the Marx Brothers to Hollywood. (Kaufman and Ryskind contributed to the screenplays of a handful of the brothers' films.)

The true Kaufman wit was first evidenced in the musical *Strike Up the Band* (1930), a merry Gershwin show that had a difficult birth. In 1927, Kaufman wrote a libretto that satirized everything from international politics to the ingredients of cheese. When the U.S. government puts a high tariff on Swiss cheese, the dairy mogul Horace J. Fletcher pushes America into a war with Switzerland, offering to pay for the war if they will name it after him. The war goes so well, both sides getting an economic boost from the hostilities, that when a tariff is put on caviar, the United States decides to go to war with Russia next. It was a biting and merciless libretto but too abrasive for the slaphappy Roaring Twenties; *Strike Up the Band* closed in Philadelphia. The producers did not give up on the show (and the sparkling Gershwin brothers' score), and it was given to Morrie Ryskind to soften up the touchier points. As a way of removing the tale further from reality, Ryskind turned the whole plot into a dream that Fletcher (Dudley Clements) has one night. In the new version, America goes to war with Switzerland over Swiss chocolate, and the role of a silly politician, brilliantly played by comic Bobby Clark, was expanded. But most of what was potent in *Strike Up the Band* was in the original Kaufman script, including greedy Swiss hotel owners who charge the American troops inflated prices to stay at their inns and a secret code that uses yodeling to relate military information. Rarely produced today (probably because the next Kaufman and Ryskind satire is so much more revivable), *Strike Up the Band* managed to please audiences for 191 performances during those early years of the Depression.

That next musical was *Of Thee I Sing* (1931), an American classic on many fronts. Again the Gershwins provided the score, and once again the subject was politics and international relations. The plot is as outlandish as the chocolate war in *Strike Up the Band*. Yet it seems to be only slightly more exaggerated than politics as usual, so the satire was more direct and the effect more exhilarating. In order to boost the sagging presidential campaign for John P. Wintergreen (William Gaxton), his party leaders decide to build their political platform on love. They come up with a national beauty contest held in Atlantic City, the winner getting to marry Wintergreen, who will then win the race to the White House with love as his campaign slogan. The sexy Diana Devereaux (Grace Brinkley) from the South wins the contest, but by this time Wintergreen has fallen in love with office secretary Mary Turner (Lois Moran) because she bakes terrific corn muffins. Wintergreen wins the election but no sooner takes office when Diana sues for breach of promise. The French government declares the jilting of Diana an international insult because she is, after all, distantly (and illegitimately) related to Napoleon. Wintergreen is impeached by the Senate, under the supervision of his mousy vice president, Alexander Throttlebottom (Victor Moore), but not convicted because Mary announces that she is pregnant and the government has never convicted an expectant president. Mary has twins, and France is placated when Diana gets to marry the vice president. It is a wacky story but not all that improbable. Kaufman and Ryskind do not target any individuals but rather the political system in toto. Here is Wintergreen's advice to Throttlebottom when it looks like his conviction will put the vice president in the White House:

> WINTERGREEN: Of course the first four years are easy. You don't do anything except try to get reelected.
> THROTTLEBOTTOM: That's pretty hard these days.
> WINTERGREEN: And the next four years you wonder why the hell you wanted to get reelected. Then you go fishing.
> THROTTLEBOTTOM: Well, couldn't I save a lot of time and go fishing right now?
> WINTERGREEN: No, you got to wait until an important matter comes up and then you go fishing.

Some of the comedy does take into account the real world of 1931. With Europe already arming itself for another world war, there is something stinging about Wintergreen's order: "Tell the Secretary of the Navy to scrap two battleships. . . . Scrap two and build four. Disarmament." *Of Thee I Sing* is arguably the best political satire of the American theatre. Not only did it not close on Saturday night, but it ran 411 performances and won the Pulitzer Prize for drama, the first time the distinguished award was given to a musical. Just as noteworthy, it was the first Broadway libretto to be published. The idea of sitting down and *reading* a musical was as absurd as it was unknown. (Even *Show Boat* had not been published after it was acclaimed in 1927.) But when a libretto was as literary as *Of Thee I Sing,* it was time to rethink the significance of the Broadway musical comedy.

Kaufman, Ryskind, the Gershwins, Gaxton, Moore, and Moran all returned to the world of John P. Wintergreen with the sequel *Let 'Em Eat Cake* (1933), but this time they could not find an audience for any more than ninety performances. The reasons for its failure are not clear. Some blame the more serious situation in Europe that made a comedy about international politics too uncomfortable. Others suggest that the script and score were inferior. There is also the belief that Broadway was tired of the Wintergreens and their follies. Perhaps all three reasons can be credited, though the Gershwin score, in retrospect, has been declared to be as distinguished as that of the first show. As for the libretto, it is just as sharp and funny as *Of Thee I Sing,* but maybe too sharp and too eerily funny. When Wintergreen and Throttlebottom fail to get reelected to a second term, they turn to Mary, whose talent for corn muffins is matched by her sewing of blue dresses. But their venture into the garment business also fails, so Wintergreen decides to start a revolution patterned after the Fascist movements in Europe. "Italy—black shirts! Germany—brown shirts! America—blue shirts!" he proclaims as his party of Blue Shirts storms the country and keeps Mary's garment shops busy. A farcical baseball game between the Supreme Court and the League of Nations over who will pay the war debt turns ugly when umpire Throttlebottom makes a controversial call and is scheduled to be guillotined. Counterrevolutionaries throw out the Blue Shirts, but Mary unites the women of America, thereby making Throttlebottom president and turning blue into the color of choice in fashion houses. Ira Gershwin may have pointed out the show's problem when years later he said that the satire was too scattered in its targets. He may have been right, but *Let 'Em Eat Cake* remains one of Broadway most unusual and ambitious attempts at political satire.

While Kaufman was struggling with his two Wintergreen musicals, his playwriting partner Hart was breaking into the musical genre. Moss Hart was born in 1904 in New York City to a poor working-class family. He was educated at public schools before breaking into the theatre as an actor. Hart's summer jobs at Jewish adult camps gave him his first writing experience, and he turned to playwriting, finding little success until he teamed up with veteran Kaufman on *Once in a Lifetime* (1930). His first musical effort was *Jonica* (1930), a short-lived piece co-authored with Dorothy Heyward about a convent schoolgirl and her misadventures when she goes to the big city to attend a wedding. But Hart found modest success with his next musical, *Face the Music* (1932), which marked Irving Berlin's return to Broadway after nearly five years. Hart's libretto skewered New York politics as Kaufman and Ryskind had done to national and international policies. The city, in the depths of the Depression, finds its former millionaires dining at the Automat (a low-cost eatery) with the commoners. Also getting a cheap meal there is Broadway producer Hal Reisman (Andrew Tombes), who cannot raise a cent for his next show until the wealthy Mrs. Martin Van Buren Meshbesher (Mary Boland) offers to back his musical extravaganza. It seems her husband is a corrupt police sergeant, and, with a muckraking commission looking into city spending, the cops need a place to hide all their illegal funds. The musical Reisman puts on, a *Follies* spoof called *Rhinestones of 1932*, is in trouble, but the cops suggest that some good old-fashioned smut be added, and the show becomes a hit. Hart's satire was more specific than Kaufman's (the libretto dropped many current names, and the plot paralleled much of what was going on in Mayor Jimmy Walker's administration), even though Hart's barbs were never as piercing as his partner's. But *Face the Music* delighted critics and managed to run 165 performances during a very difficult season.

Hart contributed comic sketches to two of the decade's finest musical revues, *As Thousands Cheer* (1933) and *Sing Out the News* (1938), as well as writing the American version of *The Great Waltz* (1934), a European operetta that told the story of Johann Strauss and his son, using the composers' famous melodies for songs. Hart provided a routine operetta libretto, something very atypical of his work, but the spectacular costume musical was a big hit all the same. His next original book musical, *Jubilee* (1935), was with Cole Porter, and it proved to be quite masterful, even though its box office appeal was disappointing. Taking his cue from the Silver Jubilee that King George V of Great Britain was celebrating, Hart created a fictional English family who, threatened with an uprising led by a wicked nephew, disguise themselves as commoners and travel to America. King Henry (Melville

Cooper) and his queen (Mary Boland) become Mr. and Mrs. Smith and, released from the constraints of royal life, get to pursue their own whims. He spends his days playing parlor games while she hobnobs with movie stars and flirts with Charles Rausmiller (Mark Plant), a Johnny Weissmiller–like athlete who plays the ape-man Mowgli on the silver screen. The royal couple's grown children also have a taste of adventure: the princess (June Knight) has a fling with a dashing writer, and the prince (Charles Walter) dances the night away in a nightclub to Porter's "Begin the Beguine." Just as the revolution back in England fails, the royals' true identity is discovered, and they head back home. Except for making fun of American celebrities, there is little satire in *Jubilee*. Instead, it is a breezy and sophisticated romp, Hart's book and Porter's songs blending in a carefree manner.

Although Kaufman had directed Hart's *Face the Music*, the two did not collaborate on a libretto until *I'd Rather Be Right* (1937), a gentle spoof on FDR with a score by Rodgers and Hart and with the aging showman George M. Cohan playing the current president. It was an ugly preparation period (Cohan hated the songwriters, the librettists, and Roosevelt and let everyone know it), but the result was a genial musical comedy with lots of harmless ribbing in the script. Two young lovers in Central Park lament that they cannot afford to marry because his low wage cannot be lifted until FDR can balance the budget. When the boy falls asleep in the park, he dreams that the president has heard of their woe, and Roosevelt sets out to try and bring fiscal security to the nation. All his attempts fail, from asking the women of America to give up cosmetics and donate the money to the country to issuing one-hundred-dollar postage stamps to taxing the government. Finally, FDR encourages the youngsters to go ahead and marry because better times lie ahead. It was a feeble and totally unengrossing plotline, but it allowed for plenty of scenes and characters (almost all based on real people in government) in which Kaufman and Hart got to display their topical humor. Alf Landon, Roosevelt's opponent in the last election, came on as a White House butler. When the Wagner Act was called for, an acrobatic vaudeville act appeared. The Federal Theatre Project and other New Deal organizations were lampooned. The dialogue was vintage Kaufman and Hart: when FDR urges that national encumbrances be disposed of, an aide suggests, "Do we need Baltimore?" Or such a facile exchange as this:

FARLEY: This fellow is Chairman of the Fourth Assembly District in Seattle. He wants to be Collector of the Port of New York.
ROOSEVELT: But we've got a Collector of the Port of New York.
FARLEY: Not in Seattle.

The script often resembles a revue with its parade of sketch-like scenes, and the Rodgers and Hart score is not one of their most memorable. But audiences wanted to see Cohan on stage again, so *I'd Rather Be Right* had a profitable run.

Morrie Ryskind took a break from Hollywood assignments to write the libretto for Irving Berlin's *Louisiana Purchase* (1940), yet another political satire. This time the idea came from the corrupt dealings of the Southern giant Huey Long and his family dynasty. The Louisiana Purchase Company is being investigated, so the squeaky-clean Senator Oliver P. Loganberry (Victor Moore) travels from Washington to New Orleans to look into the matter. Jim Taylor (William Gaxton), the lawyer for the company, tries to put the senator in a compromising position with two sultry Southern belles (Vera Zorina and Irene Bordoni), but the fumbling politician escapes scandal and even ends up marrying one of the gals. The satire was far from incisive, but Ryskind's libretto was a competently built vehicle for its stars, and the show was the biggest hit of its season.

Topical shows like *Louisiana Purchase, Of Thee I Sing,* and *Face the Music* were rarely attempted once American entered World War II. Making fun of the government drew few laughs, and audiences wanted escapism or new subjects for musical comedy. Moss Hart certainly came upon a new subject with *Lady in the Dark* (1941), one of the most innovative of all American musicals. Having undergone psychoanalysis for years, Hart was intrigued by the relatively young science and its dramatic possibilities. He started writing a seriocomic play about psychiatry but then realized that the heroine's dreams could best be illustrated in a musical. With Ira Gershwin writing the lyrics and Kurt Weill the music, *Lady in the Dark* unfolded in a unique way. Except for a childhood nursery rhyme that ran through the evening as a leitmotif, all the songs were confined to the dream sequences. The book scenes were written in a realistic, joke-free manner with very real characters and naturalistic dialogue. The result is an intelligent play that bursts into a musical when entering the world of the subconscious. The plot is rather simple and straightforward: fashion magazine editor Liza Elliott (Gertrude Lawrence) has risen to the top of the business world, yet still feels inadequate because of bits of memory of her unhappy childhood. At the present she is being forced to make several decisions, from choosing the cover of the next magazine issue to whom she ought to marry. The men in her life present an interesting picture of Liza's dilemma: her married lover Kendall Nesbitt (Bert Lytell), the gay fashion photographer Randall Paxton (Danny Kaye), the dashing but vapid movie star Randy Curtis (Victor Mature), and her quarreling advertising manager Charley Johnson (Mac-donald Carey). These men appear in different guises in her dreams as Liza confronts all her inadequacies with musical and surreal production numbers. Finally, she realizes that Charley is the only man in her life who could possibly understand her, so when he is able to complete the childhood ditty "My Ship" that has been haunting her, Liza decides to marry him. While Hart's view of psychiatry was often simpleminded (Liza has hang-ups about her beauty because her father once told her as a child that she'd never be as pretty as her mother), his approach to character and dialogue was not. Liza is a modern woman and nobody's fool; at the same time she realizes that she is wanting. The scenes with her adversary Charley best show both sides of Liza Elliott:

> LIZA: This is Boss Lady speaking. You see, it occurred to me, Johnson, that in all the years you've been here, in all these charming talks we've had together, you've always had all the answers. And now that you're leaving, I thought I'd like at least one little talk in which I had the answers.
> CHARLEY: Yes.
> LIZA: Is that the end of a sentence?
> CHARLEY: Uh-huh.
> LIZA: Oh, come on, Johnson. Put 'em up. It's the kid's last fight.

Despite its unconventional manner, *Lady in the Dark* was popular with audiences and ran 467 performances. Some of its success can be attributed to the star power of Lawrence and newcomer Kaye, but credit must also be given to Hart's libretto that experimented with the musical theatre format and came up with a satisfyingly new experience. The infrequent number of revivals the musical has enjoyed in America cannot be justified. (A London production in 1997 was a critical and popular hit.) *Lady in the Dark* was Hart's last libretto and far from typical of his work, yet it is, in many ways, his finest stage effort.

Kaufman would write three more musicals before his death in 1961, but they do not measure up to his previous work. *Hollywood Pinafore* (1945) was a clever take on the Gilbert and Sullivan classic, now set in California. Instead of admirals, captains, and sailors, the cast featured movie moguls, screenwriters, and talent agents. The original's bum boatwoman Little Buttercup became a gossip columnist, Louhedda Hopsons (Shirley Booth), who sang how she could "butter up" to the best of them. Kaufman rewrote Gilbert's libretto and lyrics, and the Sullivan music was retained. It was an enjoyable burlesque, but still not as much fun as the original Victorian operetta. *Hollywood Pinafore* was modestly popular, but Kaufman's next effort,

Park Avenue (1946), failed to please critics or audiences. The creative team was top notch: music by Arthur Schwartz, lyrics by Ira Gershwin, and a libretto by Kaufman and ace screenwriter Nunnally Johnson. But none of them was in top form. The heavy-going plot revolved around the high-society matron Mrs. Sybil Bennett (Leonora Corbett), whose charity work during the war gave her life purpose. But now in peacetime all she seems to do is get married too many times, which causes problems when her daughter hopes to wed her Southern beau. *Park Avenue* struggled on for nine weeks. Sadly, it was Ira Gershwin's last Broadway musical. Kaufman's final libretto was *Silk Stockings* (1955), which he co-wrote with his wife Leueen McGrath. But the show was floundering on the road, and Abe Burrows was brought in to rewrite the script. So little of Kaufman's work remained that he asked that his name be removed as librettist.

Kaufman and his fellow wits were seasoned professionals who often turned to politics and social issues of the day for their satirical jaunts. But they brought more than a sly sense of humor to the musical stage. In the case of Kaufman and Hart, they were much-in-demand directors as well. Kaufman staged such classics as *The Front Page* (1928) and *Guys and Dolls* (1950), while Hart directed some of his own works as well as those by others, such as *My Fair Lady* (1956) and *Camelot* (1960). In other words, they were consummate theatre men, not just joke writers. Kaufman and company brought a literary gift to the art of libretto writing. They always stayed within the confines of musical comedy and had no desire to move into the more serious territory where Harbach and Hammerstein ventured. But light comedy and topical satire were challenging fields in themselves, and often Kaufman and his collaborators were able to reach the dizzying heights of a W. S. Gilbert. Broadway needed its serious poets with lyrical subtlety, but just as often it required writers who could just strike up the band.

CHAPTER FIVE
BLOSSOM TIME: DOROTHY DONNELLY AND OTHER EARLY LIBRETTISTS

It would be easy (but inaccurate) to dismiss all the librettists before George M. Cohan as journeymen or hack writers. The men and women who wrote the nineteenth-century musicals and operettas were pioneers in many ways, writing "little books" for shows that were often constructed piecemeal, songs and stars added indiscriminately, and the plots often buried in the spectacle. If legend is correct, the very first musical, *The Black Crook* in 1866, came about because the book was so weak that its producer hoped to spice it up by adding songs and a French ballet troupe who had lost their theatre to a fire. It was not an auspicious start for the art of libretto writing, and it would take decades before the books were considered a major component of those newfangled song-and-dance shows. The only American musicals from before 1900 that are revived today are a small handful of operettas, and those are noted primarily for their scores. But there were several librettists from those difficult, floundering decades who managed to write commendable books for the new genre of musical theatre. It is worth looking at some of these men and women from the last decades of the nineteenth century up through the 1920s.

One of the earliest of these pioneering librettists was J. Cheever Goodwin (1850–1912), a Harvard-educated journalist who turned to writing librettos and lyrics in the 1870s. Between 1873 and 1903, he was represented on the New York and London stage by some two dozen musicals, many of them adapted from European works. Yet Goodwin's most accomplished works were his original creations, including his first success, *Evangeline* (1873). Subtitled "The Belle of Arcadia," the musical "extravaganza" was based on Longfellow's 1847 epic poem, but was more a burlesque of the original than an adaptation of it. When the title heroine and her sweetheart Gabriel are driven from their village by the British, they set off on an odyssey that takes them not only to some of Longfellow's locales but to the

Wild West and the jungles of Africa as well. Among the most memorable of the non-Longfellow characters they encountered were a whale who is sweet on Evangeline, a lone and mute fisherman who keeps popping up wherever the lovers travel, and (the audience's favorite) a dancing cow whose syncopated footwork was the talk of the town. Edward E. Rice wrote the music for the varied and (unique for its day) original score. Goodwin relied on familiar opéra-bouffe techniques, such as Gabriel written as a trouser role to be played by a woman and the bombastic comic villainess performed by a man. But his colloquial lyrics and his fanciful storytelling kept *Evangeline* in the style of the new musical comedy genre. Its initial New York run was short, but it gained popularity on the road and became one of the most often revived musicals of the next two decades.

Goodwin's other memorable musical was *Wang* (1891), a comic opera of sorts that was set in Siam but with an American vaudeville mentality. The libretto is actually quite compact with few unconnected characters or disjointed musical numbers. The comic favorite De Wolf Hopper played Wang, the Regent of Siam and, since the death of his brother the king, an impoverished royal figure trying to find out what the late monarch did with the royal treasury. The wealthiest personage in the kingdom is La Veuve Frimousse, the widow of the former French consul, who has enough daughters to make up the show's chorus. Wang woos the widow while the young Prince Mataya (another trouser role) tries to win one of the widow's daughters, Gillette. Both are eventually successful, but not until a lot of comical and musical shenanigans have filled the stage. The score (music by Woolson Morse) was bright and very non-Asian with "Ask the Man in the Moon" becoming one of the biggest hit songs of its era. But it is Goodwin's smart-alecky dialogue and amusing characters that point the way to later musical comedy. Wang is a delightful comic villain who endears the audience by confiding in them in his very sarcastic manner:

> WANG: Between ourselves, what I want to be alone for, is to think. I never can think in a crowd, and I have got enough to think about to kill a cat. When my brother, the late king, died six years ago, he left the royal coffer a howling vacuum. What in the name of Daniel Dancer he did with all the shekels he raked in during his reign, staggered me. He didn't take them with him, I'll swear, for I had a post mortem made that developed nothing except a quarrel among the surgeons.

Wang was a popular staple on Broadway and the road for a dozen years (Hopper was said to have played the Regent over 500 times) and proved to be Goodwin's most durable work. But he was also a successful adapter of European operettas and burlesques into Broadway musicals, and the writing in his shows was much more polished than the norm. As Gerald Bordman has noted, Goodwin was the "first professional librettist to leave his mark on the American Musical Theatre."

Coming on the scene a little later and finding even greater success was Charles Hoyt (1860–1900), who had several hit plays and musicals in the 1880s and 1890s. Hoyt was one of America's masters of farce, and both his musical works and his plays abound in fast-paced plots, larger-than-life characters, and dazzling theatrical effects. He was born in Concord, New Hampshire, and studied for the law before turning to journalism. Hoyt embarked on his first play when a producer friend needed to fill an empty week in a Boston theatre. Soon he was doctoring others' works and writing his own, finding his first major success with the musical *A Bunch of Keys* (1883). Hoyt worked quickly and furiously for the next sixteen years, penning some eighteen musicals before burning himself out; he ended up in an insane asylum and died at the age of forty.

Hoyt's two most notable musicals were *A Parlour Match* (1884) and *A Trip to Chinatown* (1890), both fine examples of musical farces that would lay the groundwork for later and more sophisticated musical comedies. The former show concerned two con men, McCorker and Old Hoss, who invade the wealthy home of Captain William Kidd and convince the old man that McCorker is a gifted medium who can communicate with the dead. With the help of the captain's daughter, mischievously named Innocent, they hold a séance in which a series of spirits sing and dance and encourage the old captain to fund whatever schemes that McCorker and Hoss come up with. In one memorable farce scene, McCorker rummages through a dresser in the Kidd household and hides in a drawer when a relative enters the room. But the relative is so drunk that when he discovers McCorker, he assumes he is simply experiencing delirium tremens, and the thief gets away. The songs were cobbled from various sources and changed during the many different versions of *A Parlor Match* that were produced with success over the next fifteen years.

But Hoyt's fame rests on *A Trip to Chinatown,* described by some as the American theatre's first true musical comedy. It was also the most successful musical yet seen (657 performances), a record it would hold for thirty years. Hoyt wrote the libretto and most of the lyrics, and Percy Gaunt composed the score directly for the show, an unusual practice at the time except for operettas. The plot is a well-constructed farce that allows for easy song opportunities and, later, interpolations. (In fact, the musical's most famous number, "After the Ball," by Charles K. Harris, was added to the touring version in 1892.) Subtitled *An Idyl of San Francisco,* it is a merry adventure about a foursome of young people who wish to attend a riotous masquerade ball but lie and tell Uncle Ben, the guardian of two of them, that they are going to take a tour of Chinatown. The youths have sought the services of the lively widow Mrs. Guyer to act as their chaperone, but when Ben accidentally gets her letter of acceptance, he assumes she is propositioning him and decides to meet her at the restaurant mentioned in her note. The young partygoers are dining at the same restaurant before going to the ball, so when Ben shows up, there is plenty of hide-and-seek. Ben gets intoxicated waiting for the widow to show up, and when he goes to pay his bill (and gets stuck with the youngsters' bill as well), he realizes that he has left his wallet at home. Once everything is sorted out, Ben finds he cannot scold his nephew and niece and their friends because they are in an equal position to scold him. The similarities between this plot and the one for *Hello, Dolly!* (1964) are uncanny, and much of *A Trip to Chinatown* has the free-wheeling sense of joy of the later musical. And with such song hits as "Reuben and Cynthia" and "The Bowery," the show was as strong musically as it was storywise.

Hoyt's comic touches throughout the libretto are vaudeville-like in their sensibility. There is a much put-upon servant named Slavin Payne, a saucy maid called Flirt, a droll waiter named Noah Heap, and the audience's favorite, Welland Strong, a perpetual hypochondriac who keeps a careful record in his notebook of all the things that are killing him:

> TONY: And what do the doctors say?
> STRONG: No two agree.
> TONY: And who shall decide when doctors disagree?
> STRONG: Usually the coroner. . . . Do you know, the only man who really understood my case was a horse doctor! He said if I stayed in Boston I'd die in sixty days. Out here I'd live two years if I obeyed certain rules. Here's the book of rules and it tells how much I shorten my life each time I break one. That glass of wine shortened it nineteen hours.

A Trip to Chinatown, in its various versions, would remain a popular favorite across America for twenty years. It is Hoyt's finest contribution to the developing musical theatre.

Edward Harrigan (1844–1911) is often compared to Hoyt. His musical farces had the same kind of rambunctious flavor, but Harrigan specialized in ethnic humor, and his musicals concentrated on working-class folk.

Born in New York and trained as a comic in touring acts across the country, Harrigan entered Broadway through the back door. The vaudeville sketches he wrote and starred in with his partner Tony Hart became so popular in neighborhood variety houses that they were expanded and by the 1880s were turned into full-length librettos playing in Broadway theatres. Always broad and outrageous burlesques, the Harrigan and Hart shows were known for their robust and even crude humor. Ethnic types from Irish immigrants to displaced Negroes filled Harrigan's scripts, the most acclaimed being the *Mulligan Guard* series. These musical farces (with David Braham usually composing the music for Harrigan's lyrics) centered on paramilitary groups of Jews, Germans, blacks, Italians, and Irishmen who battled each other in harmless confusion. Harrigan usually played the boisterous Dan Mulligan, and Hart often appeared in drag as his wife, sister, or maid. *The Mulligan Guard's Ball* (1979) and *Cordelia's Aspirations* (1883) are considered two of the finest of the series. The first conveys the chaos that results when two rival groups, the Irish Mulligan Guard and the Negro Skidmore Guard, book the same dance hall for a party on the same night. Cordelia of the second work is Dan's wife, who, fueled by the talk of visiting relatives, has pretensions of grandeur and forces the Mulligans to move uptown. But the plan soon finds them penniless, and Cordelia tries to commit suicide by drinking roach poison. Luckily, it was really the maid Rebecca's hidden cache of booze, and Cordelia recovers and returns back to the happy slums where they started.

Harrigan's shows depended on a lot of physical comedy, but he knew how to tell a verbal joke as well:

> DAN: Cordelia's dying. She drank the roach poison from the bottle.
> REBECCA: She drank out of dis bottle?
> DAN: Cordelia's dead!
> REBECCA: Drunk.

Harrigan wrote nearly forty librettos before he retired in 1896. George M. Cohan was so impressed by (and indebted to) him that he wrote the song "Harrigan" for a 1908 musical and invited the old comic on opening night to be his guest. Long gone and forgotten, the Harrigan and Hart shows were the film and television for a whole generation of lower-class New Yorkers and for plenty of swells as well.

The most prolific librettist (as well as lyricist) of the American theatre was Harry B. Smith (1861–1936), a tireless dynamo who penned over 120 Broadway shows between 1887 and 1932. Add to that the many musicals he wrote that were produced only outside of New York, and Smith's libretto output is twice that number. He was born in Buffalo but grew up in Chicago, where he later worked as a journalist, serving at different times as a music and drama critic. Smith turned to writing for the stage when he met composer Reginald De Koven, and the two men were convinced that such a thing as an American operetta could find success. Their initial effort, *The Begum* (1887), was typical of Smith's later work: contrived, facile, unpretentious, and filled with mistaken identity and farcical names. The tale is set in a mythical Asian land where the Begum of Oude has had many husbands, killing off each one when she got bored with him. She would name her spouse a General, declare war on someone, and send him off to die in battle. But when her latest spouse, Howja-Dhu, returns to the palace victorious, the Begum has to settle down and stay married to him. Other characters had such silly names as Jhustt-Naut, Klahm-Chowdee, and Myhnt-Jhuleep.

The Begum was not a hit, but Smith would collaborate on sixteen more musicals with De Koven, the best being *Robin Hood* (1891), the most popular operetta of the century. Smith's libretto remains faithful to the old English legend but adds contemporary humor. The Sheriff of Nottingham is a comic villain and the operetta's central figure. Several characters, from Maid Marion to Will Scarlet to Robin himself, disguise themselves at different points of the story. The archery contest, the wedding interrupted by Robin and his men, and the thrilling climax, with King Richard arriving in the nick of time and pardoning the "bandits," were all theatrical showpieces. The score (lyrics by Smith) was also a treat with the drinking song "Brown October Ale" and the wedding ballad "Oh, Promise Me" both becoming famous. *Robin Hood* was regularly revived over the next thirty years.

Smith wrote fourteen operettas with Victor Herbert, including the composer's first major success, *The Fortune Teller* (1898). Set in Budapest, it told of an heiress who tries to substitute a gypsy girl, who looks remarkably like her, in her place when she must wed a count she does not love. Another piece filled with disguises and mistaken identity, the libretto managed to be both comic and romantic at the same time, and with such exotic numbers as "The Gypsy Love Song" it entertained audiences over the first three decades of the new century.

Smith was not limited to operettas and also wrote musical comedies, fairy tale shows, adaptations of European works, and even revue sketches for the *Ziegfeld Follies*. He penned *The Girl from Utah* (1914), Jerome Kern's first notable Broadway musical, as well as *Watch Your Step* (1914), Irving Berlin's first book musical. The former was a revised English musical about an American girl who escapes from her Mormon husband and flees to London, where she is saved by a song-and-dance man. *Watch Your Step* had a slight story about two possible heirs who, according to a millionaire's will, must prove that they have never been in love in order to inherit a fortune. Neither show boasted a strong story—Smith's self-deprecating program credit in the latter musical ran "Book (if any) by Harry B. Smith"—but each served as a workable framework for two of Broadway's most important scores. Often dismissed as a journeyman hack, Smith wrote quickly and often. (It was not unusual for him to have five shows in one Broadway season.) But if he was more prolific than profound, he was also an expert play builder and created librettos that served their scores and stars well.

Henry Blossom (1866–1919) was perhaps a better writer and provided Victor Herbert with even stronger librettos. Blossom was born in St. Louis and worked in insurance until he turned to writing novels. When he adapted one of his books for the stage, he became more interested in the theatre and devoted most of his Broadway career (the first two decades of the twentieth century) to writing librettos. Two of the Herbert–Blossom collaborations deserve special attention. *Mlle. Modiste* (1905) was an early and effective version of the Cinderella tale told in modern terms. Parisian salesgirl Fifi longs to become a stage star and loves the dashing Captain Etienne. Both dreams are stalled by her lower-class station. But with the help of a sassy American, Hiram Bent, Fifi gets voice lessons, eventually becomes the singing sensation Mme. Bellini, and overrides Etienne's family's objections to their marriage. It was a simple and unembellished libretto that worked such song hits as "I Want What I Want When I Want It" and "Kiss Me Again" into the story without too much contrivance. Blossom's dialogue (he also wrote the lyrics) was both lyrical and slangy so that the effect was a very modern operetta:

HIRAM: See here. There's a sign in your window "One Speaks English Here." I guess I'm the one.
FIFI: I "guess" you're not. You don't speak English. You speak American. Englishmen don't guess, they know.

On a more farcical tone, *The Red Mill* (1906) gave Herbert his most comic libretto to score, and the show ended up being closer to musical comedy than comic operetta. Two clownish Americans abroad, Con Kidder and Kid Conner, find themselves out of money in a small Dutch village. But this doesn't keep the two buffoons from getting involved in a local love triangle: the burgomaster wants his daughter to wed the governor, but she is in love with a sea captain. When the suspicious father locks his daughter up in a windmill, Con and Kid help her escape and also find the funds to return home to America. Blossom's libretto was a vehicle for the two beloved stage comics David Montgomery and Fred Stone, but it was more than just a series of bits. Such song favorites as "The Isle of Our Dreams" and "The Streets of New York" were far from integrated into the plot, but at least their placement there made sense. Blossom wrote the librettos and lyrics for eighteen musicals, but his half dozen with Herbert were cherished for their vitality and charm.

While women composers on Broadway would be rare for too many years, there were several distaff librettists and lyricists in the early decades of the twentieth century. Three women writers during this period deserve attention. Anne Caldwell (1867–1936) had few runaway hits, but she was much respected in the business and was a favorite of some prominent songwriters. She was born in Boston and attempted careers as a singer and then a composer before teaming up to write songs with her husband James O'Dea. Their work was interpolated into some Broadway shows, and by 1907 Caldwell had her own libretto and lyrics heard on the musical stage. Although she wrote with Victor Herbert, Jerome Kern, Vincent Youmans, and others, her most notable show was *Chin-Chin* (1914) with music by Ivan Caryll, another Montgomery–Stone vehicle that was the biggest hit of its season. Caldwell and R. H. Burnside co-authored the libretto that was a modern take on the Aladdin tale, emphasizing comedy over adventure and letting its two genies carry the show. The impoverished Aladdin hopes to marry the daughter of an American business tycoon, Cornelius Bond. Aladdin believes he can win the family's approval after he finds the magic lamp. But the evil Abanazar plots to steal the lamp from Aladdin, break up the romance, and sell the magical item to Bond. Montgomery and Stone played the two slaves of the lamp, Chin Hop Lo and Chin Hop Hi, as well as several other characters in disguise, from a Polish ventriloquist to a Paris gendarme. The story traveled all over the globe as the fast-paced extravaganza refused to take itself at all seriously:

CHING: Now you can go.
ABANAZAR: Why?
CHING: Because you are the villain and we can't finish the story with you here!
ABANAZAR: And you can't start without me, so I will be here tomorrow night at eight-thirty. Matinee at two-fifteen.

Caldwell was represented on Broadway by two dozen musicals between 1907 and 1928, a handful of them written specifically for Stone. As a lyricist, she had her fair share of hit songs, but her libretto talents were considerable as well.

Similarly gifted was Rida Johnson Young (1866–1926), who wrote the libretto and lyrics for two operetta classics, *Naughty Marietta* (1910) and *Maytime* (1917). She was born Rida Johnson to a prosperous Baltimore family and moved in high society as she enjoyed a notable acting career, often performing with her husband James Young. But she left the stage to work in music publishing and then turned to writing, her first play appearing on Broadway in 1906. Her first libretto was *Just One of the Boys* (1910), but her new career was secured when she wrote *Barry of Bally-more* (1910) with her hit song "Mother Machree" (music by Ernest R. Ball and Chauncey Olcott). Young collaborated with Victor Herbert on *Naughty Marietta*, which many consider his finest operetta. Both the plot and the score are now considered the stuff of parody, but the impact of "Ah! Sweet Mystery of Life," "I'm Falling in Love with Someone," "Tramp, Tramp, Tramp," "Italian Street Song," and others cannot not be underestimated. The Broadway stage had not heard such full-throated operatics before, and the musical's plot was reused for many a subsequent show. In eighteenth-century New Orleans, the American Captain Dick and his men are searching for the elusive pirate Bras Priqué, who is tormenting the colonies. Marietta, a French countess, flees a forced engagement in France and disguises herself as a street singer. She and Dick fall in love, but Marietta is pursued by the arrogant Etienne Grandet, the son of the governor. Etienne discovers her true identity, but before he can expose her, his own secret is revealed: he is Bras Priqué. Young incorporated the score into the story well, especially concerning "Ah! Sweet Mystery of Life." Marietta sings fragments of the song and vows that she will marry the man who can complete this melody that came to her in a dream. Of course, Dick is the man, and the final, full duet version of the ballad brings both the score and the story to a climax.

Young teamed up with Sigmund Romberg for *Maytime,* and the result was one of that operetta composer's finest works. The libretto is loosely based on a German tale, but because of growing animosity in America against all things Teutonic, she Americanized the story, and the producers never credited its European origins. It is an ambitious tale, covering sixty years of New York City life. The heiress Ottillie Van Zandt loves Richard Wayne, an eager young man trying to recover from his family's financial descent. But Ottillie's family insists that she marry her upper-class cousin, so she and Richard are forced to part one day in May, burying his love poem to her in the garden and vowing to remember each other forever. Over the years,

Richard's fortunes rise, and when they meet fifteen years later, they find that their love has not died. Twenty-five years later, Ottillie's husband dies and leaves her destitute. When her house and possessions are auctioned to pay off debts, Richard buys them and gives them back to Ottillie. Thirty years later, with both Richard and Ottillie dead, the two lovers' grandchildren meet and fall in love in May. Finding the love poem in the garden, the couple discover their families' past history, and the romance comes full circle. Young's dialogue might seem a bit stiff by today's standards ("Begone! Out of my sight!," Ottillie's father declares when he finds Richard embracing his daughter), but she knew how to create a dramatic situation and how to get the most out of it. Again a song ("Will You Remember?") is repeated effectively, and the whole musical holds together beautifully. Young's output was limited since she did not begin writing until she was forty years old, but she managed to complete some eighteen librettos and many lyrics as well.

Although she had fewer credits and worked primarily with only one composer, Dorothy Donnelly (1880–1928) was perhaps the best of the three women librettists of the era. She was born in New York to a show business family (her father was the manager of the Grand Opera House) and enjoyed a successful acting career in nonmusicals, tackling major roles in plays by Yeats, Shaw, and Ibsen. Donnelly began writing librettos when she was in her thirties and found her first success when she provided the book and lyrics for *Blossom Time* (1921), a musical bio about Franz Schubert in which Sigmund Romberg adapted the famous composer's compositions into songs. The libretto was more a romance than an accurate biography, and it ended on a tragic note. The young composer Schubert is in love with the Viennese lady Mitzi Kranz, but she is being wooed by Baron Franz Schober. Because the names are so similar, Mitzi mistakes a written declaration of love from Schubert as coming from Schober and marries him, leaving the composer to die heartbroken. The operetta was the most successful show of its season and remained a familiar favorite for twenty years. It also prompted many other biographical musicals, but few were as well constructed as Donnelly's libretto.

Donnelly's other major success was *The Student Prince* (1924), in which she wrote the book and lyrics for Romberg's original music. Another romance with an unhappy ending, the libretto concerned a German prince, Karl-Franz, who goes to study at Heidelberg University and falls in love with the tavern barmaid Kathie. After a few passionate and soaring duets, the love affair is broken off when the king dies, and Karl-Franz must return to the capital and take his father's place. For political reasons, he must also marry Princess Margaret, so the farewell between Kathie and the prince is a final goodbye. In rehearsals, the producing Shubert brothers fought Donnelly and Romberg, insisting that the conclusion be changed to a happy ending and that the large male chorus of students be replaced by a line of chorines. But the authors and their lawyers won out, and *The Student Prince* became one of the Shuberts' greatest hits. In addition to her expert lyrics for such Romberg favorites as "Golden Days," "The Drinking Song," and "Deep in My Heart, Dear," Donnelly's tone throughout the libretto is romantic but far from gushing. The prince's wily tutor, Dr. Engel, and his snobby valet, Lutz, provided the humor, and the lively chorus of carousing students kept the piece from becoming too somber. The love scenes, like the duets, were rhapsodic but much more immediate than one usually found in operettas set in foreign locales. *The Student Prince* is still revived and still offers many pleasures.

Once her writing career took off, Donnelly gave up acting and managed to write eight musicals before her untimely death at the age of forty-eight. All but one were profitable, and, more important, all showed a remarkable talent for storytelling. The Depression pretty much killed off old-time American operetta, but Donnelly, had she lived into the adventurous 1930s, would probably have contributed noteworthy librettos in the new style of musical as well.

CHAPTER SIX

HOORAY FOR ANYTHING RED, HOT, AND BLUE! HOWARD LINDSAY AND RUSSEL CROUSE

The playwriting team of Howard Lindsay and Russel Crouse was one of the most successful of the nonmusical theatre, penning such plays as the prize-winning *State of the Union* (1945) and the longest-running champ *Life with Father* (1948). They also wrote the librettos for ten Broadway musical comedies over a period of thirty years. Rarely inspired but often proficient craftsmen, Lindsay and Crouse represented the high professionalism of the American theatre at a time when show business was busy and there were plenty of pros to provide quality scripts for the high demand for entertainment. There is no central theme or particular style running through their plays and musicals because they were usually at-hire artists, tackling each job efficiently as it came along. Like the title of one of their librettos, anything goes in a Lindsay–Crouse script.

Russel McKinley Crouse was born in 1893 in the small city of Findlay, Ohio, and educated in Toledo, where as a teenager he had aspirations to becoming a journalist. He pursued this occupation first in Cincinnati and then in New York City, where he became enamored of the theatre. In 1928, Crouse made his first attempt to have an acting career, but when he got a job as publicist for the Theatre Guild, he gave up newspaper work and started writing for the stage. His first Broadway credit was as one of the three librettists for *The Gang's All Here* (1931), a musical farce about gangsters that he wrote with Oscar Hammerstein and Morrie Ryskind. The show quickly shuttered, and Crouse's next effort, the musical farce *Hold Your Horses* (1933), about corrupt New York politics, did little better. But Crouse's luck changed when he met theatre veteran Lindsay. Born Herman Nelke in Waterford, New York, in 1889, Howard Lindsay was educated at Harvard, then went to New York to have an acting career. He appeared on Broadway and on tour up through the 1920s, gradually moving into directing. Lindsay staged such popular plays as the Kaufman–Connolly comedy

Dulcy (1921) and the Cole Porter musical *The Gay Divorce* (1932), acting only infrequently from then on (although he did later play the title role in his *Life with Father*). Lindsay's writing career began with the nonmusical *Tommy* (1927), and his first libretto experience came with *She Loves Me Not* (1933), a play with songs.

The story behind the debut of the team of Lindsay and Crouse resembles a backstage tale in which the star is incapacitated and the understudy goes on at the last minute to high acclaim. In this case, the stars were Guy Bolton and P. G. Wodehouse, who wrote a frolicsome libretto about an ocean liner that is shipwrecked on an island. Cole Porter provided the score, and the director (Lindsay), stars (Ethel Merman, William Gaxton, and Victor Moore), scenery, and costumes were set. Then tragedy struck: the liner *Morro Castle* caught fire and sank off the coast of New Jersey with the loss of 135 lives. The libretto needed to be rewritten using the same songs, cast, scenery, and costumes, avoiding any reference to a sea disaster. Bolton and Wodehouse were out of the country, so Lindsay and Crouse were given the unenviable task and came up with *Anything Goes* (1934), the most popular musical comedy of the decade (as well as the most revived). The script uses many of the typical devices of the day (lovers separated by class, a comic gangster, a stowaway on an ocean liner, a silly-ass Englishman, a bombastic dowager-mother, characters in disguise, and so on), but Lindsay and Crouse put them together in a package that is much more fun than the norm. The new librettists made Merman the nightclub singer and former evangelist Reno Sweeney, a far-fetched idea but one that fit her and their new story comfortably. Billy Crocker (Gaxton) loves the wealthy Hope Harcourt (Bettina Hall), but she is to sail to England with her mother and her fiancé Sir Evelyn Oakleigh (Leslie Barrie). So Billy stows away, takes on various disguises, and tries to win back her affections during the voyage. Besides Reno and her chorus girls, also on board is the Reverend Moon (Moore), "public enemy number 13" on the FBI list and always hoping to make his way to the number one position. Reno has always been romantically inclined toward Billy, but love turns to friendship as she falls for the silly Evelyn and Billy wins Hope back again. It is a fairly tight libretto considering its slapdash birth and the many shenanigans going on in the plots. Porter's songs are sandwiched in on the slightest pretense, but that was true for most of his (and others') shows at the time. What is noteworthy about the script is the way the dialogue echoes Porter's lyrics so well. No other Porter musical (with the possible exception of *Kiss Me, Kate*) has a libretto in which the same kind of humor runs through both the book and the songs:

BISHOP: China! I've served in China for years.
MOON: [disguised as a missionary] Well, I wasn't exactly in China, you see, I was more in . . . in . . .
BISHOP: Oh, I see. You were in Indo China.
MOON: That's it! I was in Indoor China and you were in Outdoor China!

Anything Goes has gone through book revisions for various revivals over the years, but in each case the changes made are minor, usually repositioning (or adding) a song or trimming a scene here and there. It began as and remains one of Broadway's most delightful musical comedies.

Lindsay, Crouse, Porter, and Merman reteamed for *Red, Hot and Blue!* (1936), which was only a modest success but still a superior piece of musical clowning. The libretto has one of the craziest of premises: when Peaches La Fleur (Polly Walters) was a little girl, she accidentally sat on a hot waffle iron and has its marks branded on her posterior. Bob Hale (Bob Hope), the boy who loved her then, has grown up but has never forgotten his long-lost Peaches, her memory keeping him from committing to any other woman. "Nails" O'Reilly Dusquesne (Merman), a former manicurist and now a very wealthy widow, likes Bob, so she decides to help him find Peaches by throwing a huge contest for charity: whoever finds Peaches is the winner. Nails gets the convict Policy Pinky (Jimmy Durante) released from Larks Nest Prison to aid in the search, but he misses jail life, especially since he was made captain of the polo team. Although Peaches is found, Bob realizes that it is Nails whom he loves. But his agreement with Peaches is null and void when the Supreme Court declares that any contest that benefits the American people is illegal. There were some similarities to the political satire *Of Thee I Sing* (1931), but the humor in *Red, Hot and Blue!* was not nearly as pointed as in that classic. Still, there is much to recommend in the farcical piece. Lindsay and Crouse's libretto provided its three stars with terrific comic material and told a ridiculous fable with glee:

PINKY: Don't cry. Please don't cry. Don't be lugubrious.
NAILS: What's lugubrious mean?
PINKY: Go ahead and cry.

The duo collaborated with the activist librettist-lyricist E. Y. Harburg on their next musical, *Hooray for What!* (1937), which was intended to be even more political, but the show's star, the lisping Ed Wynn, saw that much of the punch was removed from the script, and it ended up being another zany Wynn vehicle. Enough of the satire survived to give one an idea of how pointed the original must have been. Horticulturalist Dr. Chuckles (Wynn) invents a gas that kills apple worms, but when he discovers that it kills humans as well, unfriendly nations try to steal the formula from him. In Geneva, where Chuckles addresses the delegates of the League of Nations ("The trouble with the world ith that Italy'th in Ethiopia, Japan ith in China, and Germany ith in Authtria. Nobody thtayth home."), a female spy catches a sight of the formula with her hand mirror. But she copies down the instructions backwards, and so the gas that the enemy makes turns out to be a laughing gas that causes nothing but brotherly love. With Europe building up its armaments and another world war about to explore, *Hooray for What!* was pretty potent comedy. This time Lindsay and Crouse were actually close to the kind of high-flying satire of *Of Thee I Sing*. Chuckles's admonition to the delegates— "Don't you fellowth know that if you mith two more paymentth, America will own the latht war outright?"—was worthy of Kaufman. Harburg and Harold Arlen wrote the score, filled with ribbing numbers, and audiences accepted the uncomfortable comedy without too much problem, probably because in the hands of Wynn no one could take anything on stage too seriously.

Busy writing and producing nonmusicals throughout the 1940s, Lindsay and Crouse did not write another libretto until *Call Me Madam* (1950), again with Ethel Merman and again a political comedy. But the times were less volatile, and the satire in this musical is more charming than biting. Shamelessly based on the Washington hostess Perle Mesta, whom President Truman had appointed ambassador to Luxembourg, Lindsay and Crouse set their libretto in "two mythical countries . . . one is called Lichtenburg, the other is the United States of America." The widowed Mrs. Sally Adams (Merman), a high-society mover because of the millions she's made in Texas oil fields, has been named ambassador to the little European country, where she throws her money around and falls in love with the distinguished politician Cosmo Constantine (Paul Lukas). She also plays matchmaker for her Ivy League assistant Kenneth Gibson (Russell Nype) and the Princess Maria (Galina Talva). Some political enemies of Sally's eventually get her sent back to America, but both couples find true love, so who cares? Irving Berlin's score was one of his best—tuneful, sly, bubbly—but far from political. (The simple ditty "I Like Ike" was about as topical as the songs got.) This harmlessly carefree musical was what passed for political satire in the 1950s, but *Call Me Madam* was first-class entertainment in all categories.

In 1956, the team tried to adapt their comedy *Strip for Action* (1942), about a draftee who convinces the Army to allow a burlesque show on base, into musical form, but it closed on the road in New Haven. Their next effort, the Merman vehicle *Happy Hunting* (1956), did make it to Broadway, where it managed to run a year but still lost money. Philadelphia millionairess Liz Livingstone (Merman) is so miffed at not being invited to Grace Kelly's wedding in Monaco that she decides to show everybody up by marrying her daughter Beth (Virginia Gibson) to a Hapsburg royal, the Duke of Granada (Fernando Lamas). But the elderly duke is more drawn to Liz, so they end up together, and Beth gets the American she wanted to marry in the first place. It was similar to *Call Me Madam* in too many ways but much less fun, and, excepting "Mutual Admiration Society," the songs by Matt Dubey and Harold Karr did not please.

Lindsay and Crouse had much better luck with *The Sound of Music* (1959), the biggest musical hit of their careers. The ailing Hammerstein, who usually wrote his own librettos, turned the writing chores over to the duo so that he could concentrate his dwindling energies on the lyrics for Richard Rodgers's music. The plot is familiar to even the most casual theatregoer, so it need not be repeated, but it should be pointed out that the libretto differs substantially from the popular 1965 film version. Lindsay and Crouse's script uses the rise of Nazism in Europe as a powerful dark cloud overshadowing the more sentimental aspects of the story. For example, the Baroness breaks off her engagement with the Captain because of differing political ideas. The hedonistic Max represents Europe's noncommittal attitude to Hitler, laughing him off and trying to disappear into the status quo. The Captain is not just a moody, romantic fellow looking for a singing partner; he is a proud Austrian nationalist who sees his world crumbling around him. (Maria Von Trapp's autobiography, the basis for the musical, is very political at times.) But the film uses the Nazis merely as background and to add some dramatic suspense in the final reel. The stage libretto is a credit to Hammerstein's ideas about humanity; the movie is a testament to Rodgers's romanticism. Many find *The Sound of Music,* in either version, too treacly and formulaic. It is like an old-fashioned European operetta in many ways, but it is also very well constructed and effectively drawn. All the wonderful songs, children, and lederhosen would not have made for a successful musical without the expert libretto.

Lindsay and Crouse's final Broadway venture, the Irving Berlin musical *Mr. President* (1962), was a sad swan song for all three men. If *Happy Hunting* was a pale version of *Call Me Madam, Mr. President* was downright anemic. President Stephen Decatur Henderson (Robert Ryan) is a genial man who loses his reelection bid when he makes a breach of protocol in Moscow. He is happy to leave politics and return home, but his wife (Nanette Fabray) and the country call him back, and so he ends up running for the Senate. A subplot about the president's daughter and her romance with a Secret Service agent ends happily with few complications. The dull story was complimented by some of the dullest characters in musical theatre memory, and a lackluster score by Berlin didn't help matters. *Mr. President* was competently written and produced but bloodless throughout. Maybe it was the times again: political comedy in the Cold War era never went over well with audiences. But this was also the Kennedy years, and the White House on stage appeared to be a much less exciting place than the real one. *Mr. President* limped along for eight months on the strength of its large advance, but it signaled the end of Berlin's long career, not to mention Lindsay and Crouse's.

In their heyday, Lindsay and Crouse's librettos guaranteed high entertainment value. They usually wrote for stars, and they knew how to serve the particular talents of celebrities. They built their librettos carefully but were not afraid to throw in some outrageous twist if it kept the piece flying. The Broadway musical of the past forty years has moved away from this kind of libretto clowning, and it is our loss. The chances of another *Anything Goes* arriving on Broadway is slim because musicals are not written in that carefree style any more. Yet some of the Lindsay and Crouse scripts are revived with great success. Audiences respond to them because they are audience shows. That is their legacy.

CHARLEY, FLORA, FIORELLO, AND THE YANKEES: GEORGE ABBOTT AND COMPANY

W
hen theatre commentators refer to the Abbott Touch, they usually mean a style of directing. George Abbott staged dozens of plays and musicals with a distinctive touch that involved an urgent and determined pace, bright and bold presentation of character, fast-moving scene changes, and a taut, clear manner of staging. But Abbott also wrote over a dozen plays and librettos, and his famous touch can be found on the page as well. For instance, he perfects the old practical device of writing musical scenes "in one." Shorter scenes involving few characters are played in front of a curtain or backdrop, while a large, more populated scene is set up behind. This not only facilitates scenery changes but also gives a musical an effective pattern that keeps the show lively: the full-stage spectacle is relieved by simple, more intimate character scenes. It is a pattern that can be traced back to the Greek theatre with its alternating episodes and choral interludes. But under Abbott's direction (and plotting), the device reaches its most refined state.

Some the Abbott Touch is so ingenious that it is difficult to determine if the effect was created on the page or in rehearsals. The first act of *New Girl in Town* (1957) ends with the house curtain falling on a stage full of dancing New Yorkers, the music and dance uncompleted. After the intermission, the curtain rose on the chorus dancing to the same song, as if they had been waltzing away the entire interval. The leading man in *The Pajama Game* (1954) sings his ballad "Hey There" alone on stage as his office dictaphone is running. He then switches on the machine and listens to his own singing voice, commenting on the sentiments and eventually singing a duet with himself. Both of these examples are pure Abbott, but whether Abbott the director or the writer is hard to say. Since he often wrote his librettos with collaborators (and doctored others' librettos when he directed them), it is difficult to point to what exactly was written by Abbott. But one knew what was meant by the Abbott Touch when sitting in the theatre and experiencing his indefinable kind of magic.

George Francis Abbott was born in 1887 in Forestville, New York, and was educated at the Kearney Military Academy, at the University of Rochester, and as a member of George Pierce Baker's famous 47 Workshop for playwrights at Harvard. His formal education, particularly his training at military school, influenced his later directing techniques. Yet his brisk, strict approach to theatre was evident in all the areas he pursued. While at Harvard, a play of his was produced on campus and another was presented in Boston. But Abbott chose an acting career instead and appeared in several Broadway plays in the 1910s. Turning to playwriting in the 1920s, his first notable effort was *The Fall Guy* (1925), written with James Gleason. Abbott would go on to pen such celebrated nonmusicals as *Broadway* (1926), *Coquette* (1927), and *Three Men on a Horse* (1935), all written with collaborators. His musical debut was as the director of the mammoth musical extravaganza *Jumbo* (1935) with a score by Rodgers and Hart. Abbott would later write two librettos for the team and stage many of their shows.

The first of these was *On Your Toes* (1936), in which all three men collaborated on the original libretto. Although Abbott was not a choreographer, many of the musicals he staged are celebrated for their innovative use of dance, none more so than *On Your Toes*. George Balanchine choreographed the musical, which included two extended ballet sequences in addition to the usual song-and-dance numbers, but it was still an Abbott show. The libretto is a backstager but about the world of dance rather than Broadway. A down-and-out Russian ballet company is saved by Junior Dolan (Ray Bolger), an ex-vaudeville hoofer who became a music professor. He mixes the foreigners with his song-and-dance pupils, which sets the plot moving and allows for plenty of modern and classical dance pieces. Junior is smitten with the exotic prima ballerina of the troupe, Vera Barnova (Tamara Geva), but ends up in the arms of Frankie Frayne (Doris Carson), a pupil of his who writes songs and manages to save Junior's life in the last scene. Junior takes over for the lead dancer of the "Slaughter on Tenth Avenue" ballet just before curtain, not knowing that two hit men in a theatre box have been hired to shoot the star at the point when he drops to the floor as part of the dance. Frankie passes Junior a note on stage, and he manages to keep dancing (and not dropping from exhaustion) until the police break into the box and arrest the two thugs. A snobbish patron of the arts, Peggy Porterfield (Luella Gear), and a temperamental Russian émigré, Sergei Alexandrovitch (Monty Woolley), were on hand to supply the comedy, though Junior, as played by comic Bolger, was far from straight man in the proceedings. It is an amusing if contrived plot that provides many opportunities for dance, though both the "Slaughter on Tenth Avenue" and the "Princess Zenobia" ballets told a story totally removed from that plot, and no attempt was made to tie the dance stories into the backstage story. *On Your Toes* was a landmark regarding the use of dance in a Broadway musical; as far as the libretto goes, it was just a fun script that worked and still works. (The 1983 Broadway revival, directed by Abbott, proved to be very popular in New York and London.)

Also highly revivable is *The Boys from Syracuse* (1938), which Abbott scripted alone, using only one line from Shakespeare as he adapted *A Comedy of Errors* into musical comedy form. Rodgers and Hart supplied the superior score, and another celebrated "serious" choreographer, Robert Alton, did the dances. But this time the show was not about dance; it was a farce, even a burlesque at times. The twin Antipholuses (Eddie Albert and Ronald Graham) got to sing the pretty ballads, but the two Dromios (Jimmy Savo and Teddy Hart) were the low comics who had the best of the jokes. Although the sets and costumes suggested a stylized ancient world, Abbott's dialogue was delightfully anachronistic and very Broadway. The script was also not afraid to use low puns and outrageous corn. (Luce: "Are you a man or a mouse? Well? Squeak up!") Even Abbott's title was a Broadway joke: the ruling Shubert brothers had come from Syracuse, New York. The libretto may not have the wit or literary panache of some other 1930s musicals, but Abbott knew how to write with the same kind of bravado with which he staged a dozen hits.

Abbott provided uncredited script help on such musicals as *Too Many Girls* (1939) and *Pal Joey* (1940), both of which he directed, but his name would not appear as librettist again until *Where's Charley?* (1948). Working alone again, he adapted Brandon Thomas's 1892 farce *Charley's Aunt* into a lighthearted costume musical with Frank Loesser writing the expert score. Abbott retained the Oxford, England, setting and Victorian period and, for the most part, avoided anachronism in the dialogue, several lines coming right from the original. To make room for the musical numbers and the Balanchine choreography, Abbott needed to shorten and simplify the complicated Brandon plot. The most important change was eliminating the leading character of Lord Fancourt Babberley, who is coerced into dressing up like the aunt, and turning the relatively straight character of Charley Wykeham (Bolger) into the comic lead who must don woman's apparel in order to pass as a much-needed chaperone. While this may seem like rewriting a classic to serve the demands of a star, *Where's Charley?* works very well with the change. In fact, I am among those who find the musical plot an improvement over the original. The libretto is nicely balanced with three pairs of lovers and a comic professor who woos Charley, thinking he is the rich aunt from Brazil. Abbott also skillfully opens up the drawing room comedy: a chorus of university students have a jolly parade, and the action moves through various locations, including a hilarious flashback to Brazil that Balanchine choreographed as a Latin free-for-all. Although *Where's Charley?* got lukewarm reviews (except for Bolger), the musical charmed audiences for two years on Broadway and, a decade later, two years in the West End. It richly deserves a major revival in both venues.

Abbott was usually associated with comedy, so his choice to adapt Betty Smith's bittersweet novel *A Tree Grows in Brooklyn* (1951) into a musical seems atypical. He collaborated with Smith on the libretto, and together they came up with a touching and melancholy musical play. The plot was somewhat familiar to audiences because of the popularity of the book and a 1945 film version. Irish immigrant Johnny Nolan (Johnny Johnston) is a charming dreamer who kids and teases his wife, Katie (Marcia Van Dyke), and their daughter Francie (Nomi Mitty), always promising "I'll Buy You a Star." But Johnny is also a chronic alcoholic who often disappears for periods of time. Katie's unquestioning love for him is both admirable and disturbing. When Katie's sister Cissy (Shirley Booth) comes to stay, she tries to wise Katie up, though Cissy's experience with men is far from practical. She still carries a torch for Harry (Albert Linville), a bigamist who married her and then deserted her. By the end of the musical, Katie is widowed and places all her hopes for the future on Francie. As for Cissy, she realizes how she has been used by Harry when he appears out of the blue once again, so she sends him on his way. It was the kind of tragicomic story that Oscar Hammerstein might have tackled, yet comedy specialist Abbott served the material well. There is a great deal of humor in *A Tree Grows in Brooklyn*, yet it doesn't distract from the underlying sadness of the piece. What did distract audiences was Booth, whose brilliant performance shifted the focus of the tale from Katie and Johnny to Cissy. The poignant score by Arthur Schwartz (music) and Dorothy Fields (lyrics) is also superb in an appropriately low-key manner, capturing the ambiguity of the characters. The musical was well received and ran 270 performances but failed to turn a profit. It has gained something of a cult status over the years, yet is too rarely revived.

Returning to musical comedy, Abbott adapted another novel for Broadway, though Richard Bissell's *7½ Cents* (1953) was not a familiar best-seller. Retitled *The Pajama Game* (1954), the libretto by Abbott and Bissell was about labor relations in the Sleep-Tite Pajama Factory and about a pair of lovers who find themselves on opposite sides of the bargaining table. Sid Sorokin (John Raitt) is the company's new superintendent and must listen to the complaints of union representative Babe Williams (Janis Paige). Although they fall for each other, the relationship is strained by the 7½-cent raise that the union demands. When Sid threatens to fire all the employees who participate in a slowdown, Babe furiously kicks a machine and stops the production line. Sid has to fire her, but, learning from the wily secretary Gladys (Carol Haney) that the company has been overcharging consumers, he gets the workers their raise and wins Babe back. The comic subplot with efficiency expert Hines (Eddie Foy Jr.) trying to overcome his jealousy concerning his flirtatious sweetheart, Gladys, was broad and obvious but played like an old vaudeville routine. For a plot about business and labor, *The Pajama Game* managed to avoid playing favorites by being as simpleminded as it was light-headed. There is no trace of wit or satire in the libretto, only jokes about overworked or oversexed employees. Maybe it was Abbott's conservative political stand and the Red Scare going on in America at the time, but much of the libretto is blandly safe. Yet Bissell's novel was far from an incisive and satirical look at labor relations. The tale was told from Sid's point of view with mostly descriptions about working methods in a garment factory and details about the hero's sex life. The novel is surprisingly undramatic, so it must have been Abbott who made the material stageworthy. Hines is a very minor, very unfunny character in the original, and the wily Gladys needed to be created to give the musical some oomph. All the same, there is something noncommittal and television-like about *The Pajama Game*. Yet it still plays well on stage, and with the marvelous score by Richard Adler and Jerry Ross, it has enjoyed many revivals over the years.

A bit more devilish, in more ways than one, was *Damn Yankees* (1955). Based on another obscure novel, *The Year the Yankees Lost the Pennant* (1954) by Douglas Wallop, the musical was written by Abbott and Wallop with Adler and Ross again providing a crackerjack score. The libretto slightly echoed that very first of all American musicals, *The Black Crook* (1866), in that it concerned a man who sells his soul to the devil. Of course, that premise goes back hundreds of years to the Faust legend, but there was nothing old or worn out about *Damn Yankees*. Middle-aged Joe Hardy (Robert Shafer), an avid fan of the ever-losing baseballers the Washington Senators, exclaims that he would sell his soul for a winning season for the team. The devil, in the form of the smiling Mr. Applegate (Ray Walston), immediately appears and makes a deal with the fan: he will be turned into the youthful slugger "Shoeless" Joe Hardy (Stephen Douglass), who will lead the team to victory over those damn New York Yankees. Joe agrees and is soon a celebrity as the Senators head for the pennant. To keep Joe from getting sentimental about leaving his loving wife (Shannon Bolin), Applegate brings on the funny femme fatale Lola (Gwen Verdon) to seduce the homesick Joe as she has seduced many others throughout history. (Lola even claims to have bedded George Washington.) But Joe's love for his wife is too strong, and Lola ends up helping him outwit Applegate, win the World Series, and return to his old self and his "good old girl." Wallop's novel is only mildly funny and takes the form of science fiction rather than fantasy. (He even sets the story in the future: 1958.) Lola is a minor character and not a comic one at all; in fact, the novel's most serious moments are about her tragic love for Joe. Abbott took the main plot and characters from Wallop and fashioned them into musical comedy. While *Damn Yankees* is not as well plotted as *The Pajama Game* (the final scenes are contrived and even a bit confusing), the former libretto at least has a spark of wit, and there's some subversive fun in it:

> APPLEGATE: I've got too much on my mind. It slipped by me. I'm overworked.
> LOLA: I know, poor dear, elections coming up.

Abbott even returns to the punning kind of blackout-sketch humor of the past:

> TEENAGER: [looking for celebrities] Are you anybody?
> APPLEGATE: Not a soul.

Like *The Pajama Game, Damn Yankees* was a major hit, ran over a thousand performances, and is continually revived. (The popular Broadway mounting in 1994 fiddled with the libretto somewhat, but the spirit of the original was still there.) It has the Abbott Touch throughout: funny, irreverent, and as thrilling as a home run.

Mostly forgotten but oddly thrilling in its own way was *New Girl in Town* (1957). If Betty Smith's novel *A Tree Grows in Brooklyn* was bittersweet, Eugene O'Neill's drama *Anna Christie* (1921), the source material for the musical, was downright bitter. The Pulitzer Prize–winner told of Anna Christie, a former prostitute recovering from tuberculosis, who is reunited with her father, a crusty barge pilot. She finds true love in the arms of a powerful but naive sailor, then sees that love destroyed (temporarily) when he finds out about her past. With the dancing Gwen Verdon playing Anna, the new version was bound to be a lively musical comedy rather than a grim opera-like show. Yet Abbott's adaptation is rather close to O'Neill's play; he discards much of the O'Neill dialogue but keeps the plot, even such unseemly details as Anna's rape by her cousins back on the farm. Abbott also moved the period from post–World War I to the turn of the century to take advantage of the colorful costumes and nostalgic look of the time. Bob Merrill wrote a score that varied from carefree dance songs to disturbing character numbers. Score, book, star, and Bob Fosse's choreography all combined to make a truly unique but unmistakably odd musical that managed to entertain audiences for over a year. Although it would be difficult to revive, there is something fascinating about *New Girl in Town* that makes one want to see it.

Also rarely revived but more yearned for by theatre lovers is *Fiorello!* (1959), a musical that won the Pulitzer Prize and a Tony Award and ran 795 performances, only to disappear from the musical theatre scene. Is the show that dated? Or was it a lucky fluke? Neither, really. The libretto by Abbott and Jerome Weidman is quite accomplished, especially for biography musicals, which tend to be cliché ridden. The subject of the show is Fiorello La Guardia (Tom Bosley), the legendary mayor of New York City from 1934 to 1945. Surprisingly, the authors tell the story of La Guardia *before* he became mayor. They probably supposed that the "little flower" was recent enough history to 1959 audiences that musicalizing his years in office could not compete with newsreels or memories. In the libretto, La Guardia is first seen as a small-time politician who is out to fight for the rights of everyday New Yorkers in the ethnic neighborhoods. When the Tammany Hall politicians need a candidate for district office who is guaranteed to lose so that the status quo is not upset, they choose La Guardia. To their surprise and disgust, the little Italian wins and begins to annoy members of the corrupt administration. With the outbreak of World War I, La Guardia enlists; when he returns from Europe, he runs for mayor but loses to the swank (and well-greased) Jimmy Walker. But the tables turn when the Walker administration is plagued with scandal, and La Guardia sets out to win the mayor seat as the final curtain falls. Romantic relationships and marriages run alongside the story of La Guardia's career, and while there are touching moments here and there, they serve more to humanize the title character rather than to create an engrossing boy-meets-girl tale.

Fiorello! has all the political and social know-how that is lacking in the other Abbott librettos. Both the villains and the heroes are drawn with humor and humanity. There is a curious mixture of both patronizing and satirizing in the script. La Guardia is celebrated but in a very offhand manner.

Like the man himself, the character seems to be utterly ordinary even as he charms you. The librettists also offer an interesting contrast between La Guardia and the character of Ben Marino (Howard Da Silva), a worldly-wise cynic who breathes corruption without ever turning evil. The two politicians have only a few dialogue exchanges in the script, but they often have parallel scenes, showing how each goes about his business in opposite ways. Each man seems to brings out the other's true colors. Here they are arguing about a proposed Draft Act at the outbreak of the war:

> BEN: [an angry outburst] If . . . you really want to keep the boys at home, why do you want to go yelling your head off down there on the floor of the House? Why all this let's pass this Draft Act right away even . . . ?
> FIORELLO: [very quiet] Because when the people of the Fourteenth voted for me, and sent me down here, they changed me a little . . . they made me a little different from themselves. I can no longer think the way they think, as a single individual, a father or mother thinking about a son. I have to think about the whole country, all the people in it, what's best for all of them. I'm not a guy hanging around a political club any more, Ben. I'm a Congressman now.
> BEN: [sore] I wonder how your thinking would go if this Draft Act applied not only to people but also to Congressmen?
> FIORELLO: [quiet] You can stop wondering about that. I enlisted this morning.

Little of this reads like an Abbott script, and one can't help but wonder about the role his co-author played in the show. Jerome Weidman was born in New York in 1913. As a teenager, he worked as an accounting clerk in the garment district, saving his money to pursue a law career. At the same time, he also took up writing, and his first novel, *I Can Get It for You Wholesale*, became a success in 1937. Soon the legal career was dropped, and Weidman wrote several novels before turning to the musical theatre with *Fiorello!* (It was also the first Broadway book show for the composer Jerry Bock and lyricist Sheldon Harnick.)

Weidman and Abbott collaborated again on *Tenderloin* (1960), another musical with Bock and Harnick and one that shared the same milieu (New York City corruption) as their first show together. The librettists started with a 1959 novel by Samuel Hopkins Adams about the real-life muckraker Reverend Parkhurst, who made valiant attempts to clean up the sinful Tenderloin district of Manhattan in the late 1800s. By the time they finished, the libretto was a fictional piece about a Parkhurst-like reformer named Reverend Andrew Brock (Maurice Evans), who battles the den of iniquity from the pulpit and in the press. An enterprising young journalist, Tommy Howatt (Ron Husmann), befriends Brock and pretends to be a fellow reformer but instead helps set up the reverend in a manufactured sex scandal. Brock ends up in court, but Tommy, having a change of heart because he loves the choir singer Laura (Wynne Miller), confesses the truth. By the final scene, Brock has taken his crusade to Detroit, and "little old New York" is as corrupt as ever. Much of the libretto is sly and pointed, showing the self-serving side of both sinners and saviors. But the problem with the script is that neither side is very likable or terribly interesting. Tommy is a smiling and shallow cad, and his redemption seems forced. Brock is full of rhetoric, yet we learn little about the man underneath. Only the prostitutes, led by Nita (Eileen Rodgers), are funny and human. *Tenderloin* suffered from comparisons with *Fiorello!* (though Bock and Harnick's score was just as accomplished) and managed to run only an unprofitable 216 performances.

Weidman took on the libretto duties alone when he adapted his first novel into the musical *I Can Get It for You Wholesale* (1962). The young cutthroat businessman Harry Bogen (Elliott Gould) works his way from small-time strikebreaker to garment district speculator, sacrificing anything and anyone along the way, including the neighbor girl Ruthie (Marilyn Cooper), who loves him. She and Harry's mother vainly try to reform the cheerful but callous wheeler-dealer, and when all his plans go bankrupt, the two women are the only ones left to comfort him. Harry was a dazzling antihero who was much more fascinating on the page than when realized on the stage. He resembled the heel in *Pal Joey* (1940) without the sex appeal and the enterprising Finch in *How to Succeed in Business without Really Trying* (1961) without the whimsy. Harold Rome's score was just as uncompromising as the libretto, and there was a kind of integrity to the whole project that was commendable. *I Can Get It for You Wholesale* received widely mixed reviews and managed a forced run of 300 performances, but never showed a profit. Weidman's subsequent musicals fared even worse. *Cool Off!* (1964) closed before reaching Broadway, and *Poussé-Café* (1966) lasted only three performances once it got there.

Abbott, nearing eighty years old, showed few signs of slowing down, scripting five more librettos and directing many plays and musicals before his death in 1995 at the age of 107. Unfortunately, none of these musicals was a critical or popular success. The most interesting of the lot was *Flora, the Red Menace* (1965), a show that is remembered now mostly as the musical that introduced Liza Minnelli and the team of John Kander (music) and Fred Ebb (lyrics) to Broadway. The libretto, based on a 1963 novel,

Love Is Just around the Corner, by Lester Atwell, was begun by Robert Russell, but Abbott was brought in as co-author and director when the project was floundering. Flora Mezaros (Minnelli) graduates from art school in the midst of the Depression and finds her youthful ambitions dampened by breadlines and unemployment. But she is shown a new world when she starts dating Harry Toukarian (Bob Dishy), a member of the Communist Party who wishes to introduce Flora to sex and leftist politics. She lands a job as a fashion designer but loses it when one of Harry's comrades plants a copy of the *Daily Worker* in Flora's locker. In a refreshing change, boy doesn't get girl, as Flora dumps both Harry and his politics and braves on optimistically alone. With the Red Scare past its peak, it seems that *Flora, the Red Menace* could have made some piquant observations about the Communist threat of the 1930s. But the comrades in the libretto are foolish bumpkins or oversexed opportunists, neither funny nor threatening. Flora is a charming and believable character, moving from wide-eyed naïveté to sadder-but-wiser maturity, and, with Minnelli giving the part her all, the musical almost held together because of her. The Kander and Ebb score is uneven, but when it is good, it soars. *Flora, the Red Menace* is revivable (a revised Off-Broadway production in 1987 was noteworthy) and is the work of some solid if young professionals. For old-timer Abbott, it was a disappointment. Asked at the time by a newspaper reporter if he realized that this was his 105th Broadway show, Abbott responded, "Who cares about statistics? The important thing is whether the show is good or not."

The rest of Abbott's shows were not, all quickly closing. *Anya* (1965) was a musical adaptation of Guy Bolton's 1953 drama *Anastasia* (which was based on an earlier French play by Marcelle Maurette) with lyrics by Robert Wright and George Forrest, set to musical themes by Rachmaninoff. The tale of an orphan who may or may not be the long-lost daughter of the late Czar Nicholas was not without interest, but it was not a story that easily sings, and Abbott (who also directed) solved little of the inherent problems. *Music Is* (1976) was a musicalization of Shakespeare's *Twelfth Night,* a tale that *does* sing. Abbott again adapted and directed, and the score was by Richard Adler (music) and Will Holt (lyrics). Abbott's script was no *Boys from Syracuse* and Adler's music no *Damn Yankees,* but there were many worthwhile things in *Music Is.* Whole sections of dialogue from the Shakespeare comedy were retained, but that sometimes made the transition to the new lines and lyrics jarring. Yet some of the songs are exceptional and do not deserve to be buried with the passage of time. Abbott's last two musicals ran briefly Off Broadway and were also buried: *Tropicana* (1986) and *Frankie* (1989), the second a musicalization of the Frankenstein story.

Whether George Abbott lost his famous touch in later years or the Broadway musical changed and left him behind is debatable. Any one-hundred-year-old man writing and directing a musical is bound to be somewhat out of touch. But Abbott's special talent is much more than a matter of longevity or number of shows. This consummate professional helped shaped the look and feel of the Broadway musical. His librettos are often well-crafted examples of how to tell a story on the musical stage. Practical and pragmatic, Abbott rarely reduced himself to the level of hack writer. He knew the power of a joke, when a dance should come in, how to best present a star, and the ways to keep a musical moving, but he also knew how to best tell the story of boy meets girl. Maybe the Abbott Touch was not so undefinable after all.

CHAPTER EIGHT
THE NEW YORKERS:
THE FIELDS FAMILY

The American theatre has always had its family dynasties, from the Hallams in the eighteenth century to the Booths and the Wallacks in the nineteenth and the Drew–Barrymores into the twentieth. But most of these clans were comprised of actors or producers rather than writers, and although a series of generations may have been involved, few families influenced the theatre for more than three or four decades. But the Fields family was represented on Broadway from 1887 to 1973 and consisted of only two generations. A father and his three children, all writers, had careers that paralleled the growth of Broadway from the early ethnic musical comedies through the jazz-flavored song-and-dance shows to the musical play to the slick Broadway musical after the rock-and-roll revolution. Lew Fields, the patriarch of the family, was known primarily as a performer and producer, but he was also responsible for writing dozens of musical burlesques. His offspring—Joseph, Herbert, and Dorothy—were always behind the scenes, writing librettos for thirty book musicals plus Broadway revues and, in the case of Dorothy, lyrics as well. It is an impressive track record, but the Fields dynasty signifies much more than longevity or numbers. They were instrumental in creating new trends, supporting the finest composers of the day, and bringing a particular kind of comedy to the musical stage.

Lewis Maurice Schoenfeld was born in 1867 in Manhattan's Lower East Side into a poor immigrant family and received very little education. He worked as a soda jerk while still a young boy and by the age of ten was performing under the name Lew Fields in a comedy act at the Chatham Square Museum. His partner was Joe Weber, a neighborhood boy the same age as Fields, and together they wrote and developed a routine as "Dutch" comics. Using an exaggerated German-Yiddish dialect, the tall, thin Fields would give complicated directions to the short, rotund Weber, who always failed to catch on and ended up being choked or beaten by an exasperated Fields. It was a crude but unique act and was so popular that the team was booked on prominent vaudeville circuits. By 1887 they had formed their own company, and by 1897 they took over the Broadway Music Hall and renamed it the Weber and Fields Music Hall. Instead of a variety bill, the Weber and Fields shows consisted of a one-act musical comedy followed by a burlesque version of a popular play of the day. These spoofs were as broad and outrageous as their preceding musicals on the road but also used a wicked sense of satire in their retelling. The drama *Barbara Frietchie* became *Barbara Fidgety* in the hands of the comics, and a new classic like *Cyrano de Bergerac* was turned into *Cyranose de Bric-a-Brac.*

Although Weber and Fields were the main attraction, their shows also offered spectacular scenery, leggy chorus lines, and even some of the biggest stars of the era, from Fay Templeton and Sam Bernard to De Wolf Hopper and Lillian Russell. Since the duo was producing and appearing in each show, the writing chores were eventually turned over to others. Edgar Smith and Harry B. Smith were among the most frequently used librettists and lyricists, and John Stromberg composed many of the scores. Fields usually came up with the plot idea and a list of comic bits to be used, and others put it all together. The two clowns probably contributed to the dialogue since they knew their Dutch characters so well. Fields had coined one of the oldest of all punch lines—"Dat vas no lady. Dat vas my wife!"—back in their vaudeville days, and he probably continued writing one-liners even after he stopped writing his vehicles. But regardless of who the authors were, hit shows like *Hurly Burly* (1898), *Fiddle-Dee-Dee* (1900), and *Twirly Whirly* (1902) were first and foremost Weber and Fields shows.

The team broke up in 1903 and went separate ways, Fields finding more success than his partner. He produced and starred in shows of his own and then later appeared in book musicals written by others. He was a shrewd producer of other artists' works and was one of the first to present Rodgers and Hart's musicals, several of which were written by his son Herbert. By the 1920s, the next generation of Fieldses were making their mark in show business, even though Lew Fields had hoped for them to go into more conventional lines of work. Haunted by the poverty of his youth and trying to be accepted as a respectable man of society, the Fields patriarch watched his children's success with mixed emotions. Joseph was born in New York in 1895 and studied law at New York University. But during military service in World War I, he started writing and performing in skits for servicemen's shows. All thoughts of a legal career were dropped when Joseph was discharged, and soon he was writing sketches for revues and, later, screenplays in Hollywood. With Jerome Chodorov, he wrote such successful Broadway comedies as *My Sister Eileen* (1940) and *Junior Miss* (1941), and his solo effort *The Doughgirls* (1942) was also a hit. He would not turn to the musical theatre until the end of the 1940s.

Herbert Fields was born in 1897 in New York as well and attended Columbia University, where he befriended fellow students Richard Rodgers and Lorenz Hart, the three of them working on original college musicals together. After graduation, he pursued an acting career with modest success, then returned to writing. The trio wrote the play with songs *The Melody Man* (1924), which Lew Fields produced and starred in, but it quickly closed. (The author listed in the playbill program was Herbert Richard Lorenz.) Wide recognition came to Rodgers and Hart for their songs in the revue *The Garrick Gaieties* (1925), for which Herbert wrote some of the sketches. The trio's first book musical on Broadway was *Dearest Enemy* (1925), a sly and romantic piece inspired by an actual event that occurred in New York City during the American Revolution. British General Howe (Harold Crane) and his officers stop at the home of Mrs. Robert Murray (Flavia Arcaro) for some food and drink while marching on the colonist troops. She cleverly detains them for two hours, enough time for the American General Putnam to move his soldiers north and join forces with George Washington's men in Harlem Heights. Herbert Fields's libretto added to history a romance in the Murray Hill home between a Redcoat officer, Captain Sir John Copeland (Charles Purcell), and Mrs. Murray's Irish niece, Betsy Burke (Helen Ford). The two are swept away with each other during the crucial two hours, but part with anger when Copeland believes that it was Betsy who signaled the American troops to escape. Only after the war does he find out the truth and come back to Manhattan to wed her. It is a pleasing libretto that brings history alive by not taking itself so seriously. It also had timely musical comedy touches, such as having Betsy first introduced wearing nothing but a barrel and having the lady friends of Mrs. Murray excited at the prospect of being "compromised" by the British. The Rodgers and Hart score was also highly felicitous, and the show was a hit at 286 performances.

A series of other delightful Rodgers–Hart–Fields musicals followed throughout the 1920s, most of them successes and all of them noteworthy. Several were produced by Lew Fields, such as *The Girl Friend* (1926). Diminutive Leonard Silver (Sammy White) trains for an important bicycle race under the eye of his coach, Mollie (Eva Puck), hooking up his bike to the family churn and making butter while he practices. Leonard has, of course, fallen for his pretty coach, but the romance goes awry when the society gal Wynn Spencer (Evelyn Cavanaugh) goes after him. When Leonard is harassed by gamblers who want him to throw the race, Mollie comes to the rescue, and Leonard wins both the race and his girlfriend. It was a conventional, contemporary musical and slowly grew to become a hit. Herbert Fields's libretto sometimes had touches of the kind of vaudeville humor that his father had made famous:

> LEONARD: I says to the doctor, I says, "[My ankle] ain't broken, doctor."
> PARTY GUEST: And what did the doctor say?
> LEONARD: You musn't say ain't.

On the other hand, the younger Fields captured the tone of the Roaring Twenties rather than the ethnic past. He could also be very innovative in his librettos, as in the case of *Peggy-Ann* (1926). Although it was based on a previous musical, a Marie Dressler vehicle called *Tillie's Nightmare* (1910), the new libretto was bold and imaginative as it explores the world of dreams. Peggy-Ann (Helen Ford) slaves away at her mother's boardinghouse while she waits for her beau, Guy Pendleton (Lester Cole), to finally get around to proposing marriage. To escape from her drudgery, she gets lost in all kinds of fantastical dreams, from being shipwrecked and fighting off pirates to going on a shopping spree on Fifth Avenue to arriving at her own wedding ceremony undressed. Guy's proposal finally comes, and her dreaming can stop. The libretto had many surreal touches (talking animals, props that grew in size, characters with pink hair) and used the Rodgers and Hart songs interestingly (no splashy opening or closing numbers). Herbert even had fun with some of the Freudian clichés of the day. Unlike Moss Hart's later dream musical *Lady in the Dark* (1941), this show never took itself very seriously, and it proved to be another hit for the threesome.

Not all of Herbert Fields's work in the 1920s was with Rodgers and Hart. One of the biggest hits of the decade was *Hit the Deck* (1927) with a score by Vincent Youmans (music), Leo Robin, and Clifford Grey (lyrics). The musical was based on the 1922 play *Shore Leave*, about a sweet New England girl in love with a sailor. Herbert's libretto turned the tale into a dancing musical comedy with a brash Roaring Twenties flavor. Although the sassy LouLou Martin (Louise Groody) runs a coffee bar in Newport, she is really an heiress in disguise who enjoys flirting with all the sailors on leave. She falls hopelessly in love with one of them, Bilge Smith (Charles King), but he is not interested in marriage. When Bilge ships out, LouLou takes some of her inheritance and follows him over the seven seas, ending up in China, where she throws a big party on board for all the Smiths in the Navy. The lovers are reunited, but he is put off when he finds out she is rich. So LouLou signs all her money over to their first-born child, and the couple head for the altar. Youmans provided a terrific score, much of it memorable dance songs, and Fields kept the silly plot afloat with his breezy writing.

Back with Rodgers and Hart, Fields turned a Mark Twain favorite into the musical comedy *A Connecticut Yankee* (1927), all three of them having fun with slaphappy anachronisms in book, music, and lyrics. On the eve of his wedding to the bossy Fay Morgan (Nana Bryant), Hartford citizen Martin (William Gaxton) makes the mistake of flirting with the pretty Alice Carter (Constance Carpenter), so the jealous Fay hits him over the head with a bottle of champagne. Knocked out cold, Martin awakes in the legendary court of King Arthur in Camelot. The stranger is looked on suspiciously by the people, especially the evil magician Merlin (William Norris), who nearly has Martin burnt at the stake. But the clever Yankee, remembering his astronomical calendar, correctly predicts an eclipse of the sun, and suspicion turns to idolization. Martin goes about improving Camelot, introducing telephones, radios, and other modern gadgets and falling in love with Alisandre La Carteloise (Carpenter), who reminds him of Alice. But things get sticky when the villainous Morgan Le Fey (Bryant) goes after the couple, and Martin suddenly awakes to find himself in twentieth-century Hartford. Taking his dream as an omen, Martin breaks off with Fay and pursues Alice. *A Connecticut Yankee* has a daffy yet well-built libretto that pleased audiences for over a year. Fields redid the script in 1943 for a Broadway revival and it is that version, with Martin as a military officer, that is brought back on occasion today.

Later that same season, the trio had a more modest success with *Present Arms* (1928), which recalled *Hit the Deck* more than the previous Rodgers and Hart shows. The story is set in Hawaii, where the gruff marine Chick Evans (Charles King) woos the English Lady Delphine (Flora Le Breton), but is thwarted in his attempts by the attention she is paying to the German aristocrat Ludwig Von Richter (Anthony Knilling). So Chick impersonates an officer to impress Delphine, only to be caught and thrown out of the service. But all is forgiven when Chick rescues the civilians from a yachting accident, and he gets back his rank and his girl. It was all familiar but appealing material. The same cannot be said for the trio's *Chee-Chee* (1928), one of the oddest musicals of the era. In an ancient Oriental court, Li-Pi Tchou (William Williams), the son of the Grand Eunuch, aspires to inherit his father's exalted position but not suffer emasculation because he loves the beautiful Chee-Chee (Helen Ford). The two wed in secret, and Li-Pi nearly gets away with the deception until the couple is found out and banished to the forest. But Li-Pi comes up with a clever plan to appease the court: a friend of his kidnaps the physician assigned to castrate Li-Pi and then substitutes himself in the doctor's place. While the supposed operation is going on, Li-Pi plays dominoes with Chee-Chee and waits to resume his position as Grand Eunuch. It was a daring and highly satirical libretto, and, not surprisingly, audiences didn't buy it. *Chee-Chee* closed in four weeks.

Three months later, Herbert was joined by his father and his sister for a family affair appropriately titled *Hello Daddy* (1928). Dorothy Fields was born in 1904 in Allenhurst, New Jersey, and educated in New York City schools. As a young girl, she performed in some of the fledgling efforts by older students Rodgers and Hart and her elder brother Herbert. Dorothy wrote poetry and lyrics from an early age and turned to writing professionally when she met composer Jimmy McHugh, and they penned songs for Cotton Club revues and the popular "all-Negro" Broadway show *Blackbirds of 1928*. Some McHugh–Fields songs were also to be heard in such Broadway variety productions as *International Revue* (1930), *The Vanderbilt Revue* (1930), and *Singin' the Blues* (1931). Dorothy provided what little book there was for *Blackbirds of 1928*, and she would go on to write librettos for some half dozen book musicals. But her primary talent was for lyric writing. Once proclaimed as one of the finest female lyricists in the American theatre, over the years it has become clear that she was one of the finest Broadway lyricists, period. *Hello Daddy* featured a book by Herbert, songs by McHugh and Dorothy, and Lew as star and producer. Three old friends (Lew Fields, Wilfred Clark, and George Hassell) have each been paying (unwittingly) the same woman for child support for the same boy for many years before the hoax is found out. The child has grown up into the incredibly stupid Noel (Billy Taylor), who is as dishonest as his mother but ends up finding happiness with a girl who has an IQ as low as his. It was a silly libretto that recalled the joke-filled sketches of earlier generations (an extended comic bit revolved around the mispronunciation of the old phrase that kept coming out "a wolf in cheap clothing"), but it was an ideal vehicle for the eldest Fields, pleasing audiences for six months.

Herbert latched onto another bright new songwriter of the 1920s when he teamed up with Cole Porter. His libretto for *Fifty Million Frenchmen* (1929) gave Porter his first Broadway hit, a merry romp in Porter's favorite location: Paris. American millionaire playboy Peter Forbes (William Gaxton) is smitten by the beautiful tourist Looloo (Genevieve Tobin) and bets his friend $25,000 that he can win her heart without revealing his riches.

Peter takes a job as a tour guide and shepherds Looloo and her family around the famous Paris sights. But Looloo's social-climbing parents are setting up a match with the Grand Duke Ivan Ivanovitch (Mannaet Kippen), so Peter has to work fast, which he does. It was Porter's most consistently satisfying score yet, helped by Herbert's fanciful story line filled with eccentric characters. (Helen Broderick played an American abroad who buys copies of James Joyce's banned novel *Ulysses* to send to her kids back home.) The next season, Herbert and Porter came up with *The New Yorkers* (1930), a satirical look at Porter's second-favorite city. The libretto was about the shallow and mildly decadent wealthy who live on Park Avenue, a place where "bad women walk good dogs." Dr. Wentworth (Richard Carle) is not afraid of flaunting his mistress in the presence of his wife (Marie Cahill); she, on the other hand, makes no effort to conceal her gigolo boyfriend from the doctor. Their daughter Alice (Hope Williams) has taken up with Al Spanish (Charles King), a bootlegger who is not against occasional murder when needed. When the whole gang travels down to Miami to vacation, Al finally gets caught by the police—for parking too close to a fire hydrant. Herbert's book was a disjointed but highly stylized affair (the plot took the form of a dream Alice is having) that made room for some prostitutes to advertise "Love for Sale" and allowed gangster Jimmy Durante to do his specialty act. *The New Yorkers* managed a twenty-week run in the darkest days of the Depression, but still lost money.

When Rodgers and Hart returned from a brief foray in Hollywood, they teamed up with Herbert and made fun of the movies with *America's Sweetheart* (1931). Lovebirds Geraldine (Harriette Lake, who later became Ann Sothern) and Michael (Jack Whiting) head for California to become silent-screen stars. Geraldine's pretty face captures the attention of producers, and her career skyrockets while Michael struggles in vain to get noticed. Then Geraldine starts to drift away from her old beau until the positions are reversed: the talkies come in, and Geraldine's lisp destroys her career while Michael's dashing voice makes his. The two are reunited and go to Michael's latest premiere together. The libretto spent as much time lampooning Hollywood as it did on the love story. Idiotic producers try to put Gilbert and Sullivan under contract, remake *Camille* as *Lovey Dovey*, and clamor to present movies based on the Bird of Avon. Herbert even echoed himself when a character proclaimed that a Tinseltown conference room was where "good plays are turned into bad movies." *America's Sweetheart* eked out a 135-performance run, but when Herbert teamed up with the Gershwin brothers, their *Pardon My English* (1933) stumbled badly. Herbert's libretto had a comic lead, a Dresden police commissioner who accidentally arrests two young American tourists as crooks while his daughter gets romantically involved with a real thief. The musical was in so much trouble on the road (Jack Buchanan quit and Jack Pearl took over the leading role) that other writers were brought in, making the story line only more convoluted and less funny. *Pardon My English* was probably doomed in any case. With Hitler rising to power in Europe, the German setting for the show only made audiences uncomfortable. The musical struggled for forty-six performances, then closed on the same day the Reichstag burned in Berlin.

B. G. De Sylva joined Herbert in writing the libretto for *DuBarry Was a Lady* (1939), a show that had more than a passing resemblance to *A Connecticut Yankee, Peggy-Ann,* and other Fields dream musicals. Louis Blore (Bert Lahr) works as a washroom attendant in Manhattan's Club Petite, where he has a crush on the floor-show singer May Daley (Ethel Merman). When Louis wins $75,000 in the Irish sweepstakes, he thinks that May will pay more attention to him, but she is crazy about the newspaper reporter Alex Barton (Ronald Graham), who is already (unhappily) married. The jealous Louis fixes a Mickey Finn to knock Alex out, but Louis accidentally consumes the drink himself and passes out, only to dream that he is King Louis XV and that May is the elusive Madame DuBarry. Louis's luck in France is no better as he pursues DuBarry, his "mistress in name only," but she already has a lover (also played by Graham), so the king throws his rival into the dungeon for writing revolutionary songs. May promises Louis that she'll come to his bedchamber if he will set her lover free. The king agrees, but before he can bed May, his son, the Dauphin (Benny Baker), enters the boudoir and shoots an arrow into Louis's posterior. He awakes to see the error of his ways in reality and in dreamland, gives Alex money for a divorce, pays the rest in taxes, then goes back to cleaning the washroom. Cole Porter wrote the laudable score, though many of the songs did not become popular until years later. The real attractions were Merman and Lahr in the zany story line filled with jokes:

> DUBARRY: Now please, sire.
> KING: Sire! Sire! I'm a hell of a sire. I haven't got any dam.
> DUBARRY: No? You've only got every damn dam in the court.

Louis dispenses with bowing at court by ordering "skip the dip" and outlines plans for building a bridge over the River Seine—lengthwise. Even in pain with the arrow sticking into his royal britches, he exclaims, "I can't go through life looking like a weather vane!" It was that kind of show. It was also a hit, at 408 performances.

Herbert Fields, De Sylva, Porter, and Merman reunited the next year for *Panama Hattie* (1940), which was even more popular but not nearly as skillful. Hattie Maloney (Merman) runs a nightclub in the Panama Canal Zone that caters mostly to sailors. But when the old-money Nick Bullett (James Dunn) arrives from Philadelphia, Hattie is swept off her feet. The biggest obstacle (of many) to their getting married is Nick's young daughter Geraldine (Jean Carroll) from his first marriage. Little "Jerry" must agree to the union, so Hattie has to win over the tyke, which she does. Much of the comedy comes not from the principals but from three sailors on leave looking for girls and from the stuffy Englishman, Vivian Budd (Arthur Treacher). The Porter score was as uneven as the libretto, but again the star carried the day. *Panama Hattie* remains one of Broadway's long runs (501 performances) that has been unrevivable almost from the start.

Dorothy Fields, who had been kept busy in Hollywood writing lyrics for Jerome Kern melodies, returned to Broadway in 1941 and worked with her brother Herbert for the first time as co-librettist. The show was another Cole Porter musical, *Let's Face It* (1941), which was based on the long-running comedy *The Cradle Snatchers* (1925). Three housewives (Eve Arden, Vivian Vance, and Edith Meiser) discover their husbands' philandering ways, so they pick up three service men (Danny Kaye, Benny Baker, and Jack Williams) with the hopes of getting even and having a bit of fun as well. But the soldiers each have a girlfriend, and when the three husbands come on the scene, it turns out that they have been romancing the enlisted men's sweethearts. It was a well-constructed musical farce that balanced story and songs satisfactorily (though Kaye's songwriting wife Sylvia Fine interpolated some specialty numbers for the rising comic). *Let's Face It* was typical wartime fare: bright, fast paced, and eventually forgettable. The same can be said for *Something for the Boys* (1943), in which Porter and the two Fields siblings provided a vehicle, this time for Ethel Merman. Three cousins from New York (Merman, Paula Laurence, and Allen Jenkins) inherit a Texas ranch near a military base and turn it into a home for servicemen's wives. When Blossom Hart (Merman) gets too chummy with airman Rocky Fulton (Bill Johnson), his girl, Melanie Walker (Frances Mercer), gets jealous and declares that the ranch is a front for a brothel, and the cousins' place is put off limits to military personnel. In one of the crazier plot twists of the decade, it is discovered that the fillings in Blossom's teeth pick up radio signals, and she is able to save a distressed plane using her highly communicative mouth. The stunt saves the day and sets the house back in business, and Blossom wins Rocky away from Melanie. *Something for the Boys* was a product of its day (wartime prosperity, escapist shows, brassy stars) and was very successful. Odd to think that the next musical to open on Broadway was *Oklahoma!* (1943), and that it would signal the death knell for shows like this.

But silly, exaggerated musical farce was not dead yet. Porter and the two Fieldses struck gold three times running with *Mexican Hayride* (1944) with comic Bobby Clark as the star. It was even more hectic than *Something for the Boys* and *DuBarry Was a Lady* in that the libretto was one long extended chase. Small-time crook Joe Bascom (Clark) is on the lam, so he goes down to Mexico to hide, something difficult to do when a lady matador named Montana (June Havoc) throws him a bull's ear during a parade and local tradition says that whoever catches the ear is a guest of the government. Joe flees and soon has two countries looking for him as he starts a phony lottery with Lombos Campos (George Givot), a Hispanic hoodlum he befriends. While Joe and Campos disguise themselves as mariachi players, tortilla salesmen, and use other ruses, Montana has a yen for the diplomat David Winthrop (Wilbur Evans). But he suspects that Montana is hiding the two fugitives from justice and cannot commit to his affection for her until Joe and Campos are caught.

It was a door-slamming farce with such exotic settings as the flower-infested gardens of Xochimilco instead of urban interiors. It seemed that Herbert's days of inventive and original librettos were over, but, working with his sister, they were replaced by slick, highly serviceable star vehicles. Yet the two siblings came up with a pleasing musical play for the next season: the charming and understated *Up in Central Park* (1945). With operetta veteran Sigmund Romberg writing the music for Dorothy's lyrics, the musical was as popular as the three light-headed Porter shows that preceded it. Herbert and Dorothy's libretto was about Boss Tweed and the corrupt political machine in New York decades earlier, and there was more than a touch of nostalgia about the piece. (An ice skating ballet on Central Park Lake, which had a distinct Currier and Ives look, was a highlight of the production.) Muckraking journalist John Matthews (Wilbur Evans) is out to expose the graft in the notorious Tweed Ring but finds himself attracted to Rosie Moore (Maureen Cannon), the daughter of one of Boss's cohorts. When John prints some unflattering things about her father in the *Times,* Rosie breaks off with the reporter and marries a man in her father's circle. But John and Rosie make it up and are able to wed when it is found out that her new husband is already married. The plot was more often operetta melodrama than musical play, but the writing was efficient and enjoyable, and the Romberg–Fields songs recalled the glory days of the entrancing operetta scores.

When Rodgers and Hammerstein decided to produce a musical about Annie Oakley with Ethel Merman as their star, they asked Jerome Kern and Dorothy to write the score and for Herbert to co-author the libretto with his sister. But Kern's untimely death in 1945 brought onto the team Irving Berlin, who always wrote his own lyrics, so Dorothy served as librettist only. The result was *Annie Get Your Gun* (1946), the biggest hit of any Fields show. It is also one of their finest. Although based on historical characters, the show is a musical comedy rather than a musical play like so many Broadway entries in those years after *Oklahoma!* Herbert and Dorothy wrote the libretto as a vehicle for Merman (she has the lion's share of the songs and jokes), yet it is a full-fledged story that relies on character rather than comic bits. It is also a sly take on the Cinderella musicals of earlier days. Annie is uneducated, coarse, and funny when she comes out of the backwoods in the early scenes. Yet after she joins Buffalo Bill's Wild West Show, becomes a star, and even gets her heartthrob, the sharpshooter Frank Butler (Ray Middleton), Annie is still the same feisty, uncouth country gal. Her transition is not into a princess but into a more accepted version of her former self, a sort of Eliza Doolittle who retains her Cockney dialect. Berlin's sensational score was justly famous and provided an armful of hits. Yet for the first time in his career, Berlin's songs are character driven. Even the chorus numbers, such as "I Got the Sun in the Morning," stem from the emotions of individual characters. It is not accidental that after forty years of scoring Broadway shows, Berlin suddenly could do this. It was the strong libretto, the best ever handed to him, that made Berlin an integrated songwriter.

Little in the script for *Annie Get Your Gun* has seemed dated despite the efforts of fearful and politically correct producers to hire writers to "fix" the show. (The revised libretto for the 1999 Broadway revival was an embarrassment; the musical was reduced to a camp vehicle and depended on a succession of stars to run.) The Indians are handled with the same comic touch as all the other characters, and Annie's decision to purposely lose the shooting contest in order to win Frank is a potent commentary on the times, not at all an insult to feminism. If the libretto lacks anything, it is a strong subplot. But a secondary comic couple would have been redundant when the leads were so funny, and a more serious pair of lovers, as seen in some of the Rodgers and Hammerstein musicals, would have been inappropriate for this show. What the Fieldses came up with instead is a plot with a firm through line and jokes that kept it moving ahead:

ANNIE: [trying to sell a dead game bird] Look it over, Mister. Look it over keerful. Lift up its wings. See? No buckshot in that bird. Jes' one little hole in his head.

WILSON: Mighty pretty shooting!
ANNIE: Mighty pretty eatin', too. Fer evvy one I get ye, gotta give me two nickels and a dime.
WILSON: Can't hurt to try them. I'll take two dozen.
ANNIE: How many is that?
WILSON: Twenty-four.
ANNIE: [to her brothers and sisters] Who do we know kin count up to twenty-four?

After finding success in Hollywood and on Broadway with comedies, Joseph Fields finally took up the family's talent for musicals, though none of his four efforts was written with his siblings. Joseph's first libretto, *Gentleman Prefer Blondes* (1949), was based on a best-selling comic novella by Anita Loos, and she assisted in writing the musical's script. The original book is arguably the funniest piece of fiction written by an American, yet the libretto is rather mediocre. The show depended on its new star, Carol Channing, and delightful songs by Jule Styne (music) and Leo Robin (lyrics) to come to life and wow audiences for 740 performances. But *Gentlemen Prefer Blondes* is rarely revived now, and the libretto is probably the reason. It is conventional and serviceable, while its source (which had already been turned into a play and a movie) was unconventional and fearlessly outrageous. The 1920s gold digger Lorelei Lee narrates her own episodic tale in the novella, and the libretto retains some of her incongruous commentary as soliloquies and asides to the audience. But many of the plot scenes fall flat, and aside from the deliciously ditzy Lorelei, most of the characters are uninteresting. Lorelei's sugar daddy is Gus Esmond (Jack McCauley), known as the Button King for his family's monopoly on manufacturing buttons for the garment industry. She promises to behave herself when she sails to Paris on the *Ile de France* with her friend and fellow *Follies* girl Dorothy Shaw (Yvonne Adair). But once at sea, Lorelei is attracted to a silly-ass Englishman, Sir Francis Beekman (Rex Evans), because he has the means to buy her a diamond tiara that she lusts after. Once in Paris, complications arise with Beekman's wife finding out about the tiara, and the surprise appearance of Gus. But Lorelei and Dorothy dazzle everyone at the Central Park Casino, all is forgiven, and the two gals each get a wealthy husband. Because Loos's original story was loose and episodic, the librettists had to come up with some kind of plot structure to hold it together. But using a nightclub act to tie up the loose ends was something barely accepted in the 1930s, no less in the late 1940s. Also, the libretto seems to totally ignore the Roaring Twenties flavor of the source material. I suppose my harsh dismissal of *Gentlemen Prefer Blondes*'s libretto stems from disappointment and a lost opportunity. Perhaps, in other hands, this could have been one of the great musical comedies of the postwar years, another *Guys and Dolls* (1950). Instead, we are left with a contrived and flimsy star vehicle. (A 1974 rewritten version of the show called *Lorelei* was even worse.)

Herbert Fields returned to the American Revolution, the setting of his first hit, *Dearest Enemy,* twenty-five years earlier, with *Arms and the Girl* (1950), a musical version of a 1933 comedy called *The Pursuit of Happiness.* He wrote the libretto with Dorothy (and with help by director Rouben Mamoulian), and she provided the lyrics for Morton Gould's music. Patriot Jo Kirkland (Nanette Fabray) is driven from her colonial homestead by the approaching Redcoats, so she disguises herself as a man and joins in the fight. In between uncovering a spy and winning a battle or two, Jo finds time to romance and win the Hessian officer Franz (Georges Guétary), who is only looking for "A Cow and a Plow and a Frau." Both score and book were uneven but had their virtues. Pearl Bailey, as the escaped slave Connecticut (she used to be called Virginia, but she moved), provided the finest comic moments and got to sing the two best songs: "Nothin' for Nothin'" and "There Must Be Somethin' Better Than Love."

Arms and the Girl failed to recoup at only 134 performances, but Joseph Fields had much more luck with *Wonderful Town* (1953), a musical version of the hit comedy *My Sister Eileen* (1940), which he had written with Jerome Chodorov. Born in New York City in 1911, Chodorov made his reputation in Hollywood writing screenplays with Joseph Fields before returning to the East Coast and writing a series of comedies together. The two men collaborated again on *Wonderful Town,* which followed the original play closely. During the Depression, Ruth (Rosalind Russell) and her sister Eileen (Edith Adams) move from their Ohio home to New York City to make their fortune, the acerbic Ruth as a writer and the alluring Eileen as an actress. They find themselves living in a Greenwich Village basement apartment that shakes from the nearby blasts of the construction on a new subway line. While Eileen has no trouble finding amorous admirers, her acting career goes nowhere. Ruth has no luck with men or her writing and is discouraged further when Robert Baker (George Gaynes), an editor at *Manhattan* magazine, turns her down (in more ways than one). Ruth gets a job interviewing a group of Brazilian sailors at the Brooklyn Navy Yard, but it turns into a conga number, and when they all follow her home to the Village, an out-of-control melee results. Eileen slugs a policeman during the brawl and ends up in court, yet she manages to charm everyone and even convinces the cops that she's Irish. The story of the fracas and the trial gets in the newspapers and brings the two girls enough notoriety to launch their careers. The musical was a joyous romp by opening night, but its preparation was very messy. Composer Leroy Anderson and lyricist Arnold B. Horwitt were replaced by Leonard Bernstein (music), Betty Comden, and Adolph Green (lyrics), who provided an exceptional score. The story was a tried-and-true commodity (Russell had already played Ruth in a non-musical film version) and was every bit as enjoyable as the earlier long-running play had been. *Wonderful Town* also has some delectable dialogue that matches the sassy Comden and Green lyrics. (Or was it the other way around?):

> RUTH: [trying to get her stolen typewriter back] Well?
> APPOPOLOUS: Only how do I know this property belongs to you? Can you identify yourself? . . . Have you a driver's license?
> RUTH: To operate a typewriter?
> EILEEN: Now you give that to my sister!
> APPOPOPLOUS: How do I know it's hers?
> RUTH: The letter "w" is missing.
> APPOPOLOUS: Now we're getting somewhere.
> RUTH: It fell off after I wrote my thesis on Walt Whitman . . .
> EILEEN: She's a very good writer—and very original.
> RUTH: Yes. I'm the only author who never uses a "w."

Joseph Fields and Jerome Chodorov came back the next season with *The Girl in Pink Tights* (1954) and had little luck, though it was an intriguing idea for a musical. In 1866, the extravaganza *The Black Crook,* generally thought to be the first American musical, was created by combining a melodrama with a homeless French ballet troupe whose theatre had burnt down. The result was a huge hit, helped no doubt by the fact that the ballerinas wore pink tights that appeared to be sensually flesh colored on stage. Fields and Chodorov took this legendary tale and wrote their libretto, filling it with fictitious characters and original details. The two romantic plots concerned the prima ballerina Lisette Gervais (Jeanmarie) and the melodrama's author Clyde Hallam (David Atkinson) as well as a romance between American producer Lotta Leslie (Brenda Lewis) and the French maestro of the ballet company, M. Gallo (Charles Goldner). Despite its unique premise about the birth of the American musical, the story was a rather routine affair, neither funny nor engrossing enough to please. Sigmund Romberg's music, composed many years earlier (he had died in 1951), ranged from antique operetta to swinging musical comedy. (Leo Robin provided the adequate lyrics.) The critics found praise for only Jeanmarie, and the show struggled on for fifteen weeks.

After writing a superb set of lyrics (but not the libretto) for *A Tree Grows in Brooklyn* (1951), Dorothy Fields provided both for *By the Beautiful Sea* (1954) with Herbert co-writing the book and Arthur Schwartz composing the music. Both shows starred Shirley Booth, who kept the box office alive for eight (unprofitable) months. This time, Booth was Lottie Gilson (a real-life vaudevillian from the turn of the century) who runs a boardinghouse at Coney Island during the warm months when the theatres are dark. She falls into an autumnal romance with Dennis Emery (Wilbur Evans), a down-and-out Shakespearean actor, but can wed him only if she can win the affections of his seventeen-year-old daughter Betsy Busch (Carol Leigh)—a situation paralleling Herbert's earlier *Panama Hattie.* Betsy was a child performer who still acts like a preteen on and off the stage, but when Lottie dresses her like an attractive young adult and Betsy catches the eye of a handsome waiter, the two women become buddies and Lottie gets Dennis. It was a nostalgic but dull tale with a pleasant but unmemorable score. Herbert and Dorothy fared better with another star vehicle, *Redhead* (1959), featuring Gwen Verdon. The show was a curiosity if for no other reason than it is a musical murder mystery set in Victorian London with a Jack the Ripper–like fiend killing off a series of actresses. Essie Whimple (Verdon) works in her aunt's waxworks shop and stumbles onto some clues that point to the red-whiskered Sir Charles Willingham (Patrick Horgan) as the murderer. When music hall strongman Tom Baxter (Richard Kiley) finds his female partner strangled by the mysterious stalker, Essie goes on in her place, and it seems she's the next victim. By the time the police find the real culprit—variety performer George Poppett (Leonard Stone) who donned a red beard to throw suspicion on Sir Charles—Tom and Essie are in love. *Redhead*'s libretto (written by Herbert and Dorothy with Sidney Sheldon and David Shaw) was certainly different, but the popularity of the show rested on Verdon and the inventive dances Bob Fosse devised for her. The score, by Dorothy and composer Albert Hague, is also unusual, ranging from Cockney music hall numbers to Broadway razzmatazz, and the script has a sauciness that is both old hat and refreshing. ("Pearl always wanted to be an oyster so she'd only have to be good from May to September.") Rarely revived, *Redhead* remains an odd and intriguing piece and an atypical swan song for the Fields family.

Herbert died in 1958, nearly a year before *Redhead* opened on Broadway. Joseph contributed to one other musical before his death in 1966, Rodgers and Hammerstein's *Flower Drum Song* (1958), in which he co-wrote the libretto with Oscar Hammerstein (see chapter 3). Dorothy continued to be active on Broadway, though not as a librettist. She wrote the cunning lyrics for *Sweet Charity* (1966) and *Seesaw* (1973), demonstrating a lively dexterity with words that were as young and fresh as those she wrote in the pre-Depression days. In a way, all the Fieldses were eternally young. In his sixties, Lew Fields was still performing on stage with the same farceur flair that had endeared him to audiences back in the Victorian age. Joseph remained a gifted craftsman to the end, and even Herbert's later unsuccessful musicals could hardly be called stodgy or tired. What a rich dynasty of showmen (and showwoman) the Fieldses were! They represented a special kind of musical comedy with roots in the ethnic past and an eye on the current times. The Fieldses were also expert writers of star vehicles, an art form all but gone today. Finally, they were New Yorkers who understood the urban landscape and the world of Broadway.

FLAHOOLEY'S RAINBOW: E. Y. HARBURG AND FELLOW CONSPIRATORS

E dgar Y. Harburg was Broadway's Jewish leprechaun. No one wrote about more controversial subjects, from poverty and racism to women's rights and the atom bomb, than Harburg. Yet he did it with pixie-like glee, using laughter to make his pointed observations about the nightmares of the modern world. More than just a satirist, Harburg had a Shavian view of the world as he burst bubbles and ruffled feathers utilizing the genres of fantasy and comedy. He was not Broadway's only leftist lyricist and librettist, but he was one of the few who understood the power of Swiftian exaggeration and used surreal musical comedy to write about a very real world. Harburg provided hundreds of lyrics for Broadway and Hollywood, but it is in his handful of theatre librettos that his impish insights are best experienced. Only a few of those stage musicals were hits, for it is difficult to be disturbing, funny, and popular all at the same time. Harburg and his fellow conspirators used Broadway as a soapbox. The movies and television were too censored and careful for such ideas. But within the confines of a musical comedy, they could criticize and dream and even entertain.

He was born Isidore Hochburg in Manhattan's Lower East Side in 1896, the son of Russian immigrants, and as a youth he worked as a street lamp lighter and sold newspapers to make ends meet. In high school "Yip," as he was affectionately nicknamed throughout his life, wrote light verse, and his teachers encouraged him to attend City College. While there, he had several pieces published in the *New York World*, the *Tribune,* and other major newspapers. (One of his fellow students was Ira Gershwin, with whom he wrote a column in the college paper.) But after graduation, Harburg went into the electrical appliance business to make a living. He found the work dismal and was more than happy when the crash of 1929 destroyed the business and he was able to pursue writing as a career. Harburg's lyrics were first heard on Broadway in revues such as *The Earl Carroll Sketchbook* (1929), *Americana* (1932), *Ballyhoo of 1932*, the *Ziegfeld Follies* of 1931 and 1934, *Walk a Little Faster* (1932), and *The Show Is On* (1936). A handful of his songs from these shows became popular, none more so than "Brother, Can You Spare a Dime?" which grew to become the unofficial theme song of the Depression. Much of the rest of the 1930s found Harburg in California, where he wrote songs for movie musicals, most memorably *At the Circus* (1939) and *The Wizard of Oz* (1939). Both of these were collaborations with Harold Arlen, the composer most often associated with Harburg.

His first book musical on Broadway was *Hooray for What!* (1937). Harburg plotted out a bizarre story about a scientist (Ed Wynn) who accidentally develops a deadly gas while working on a solution that kills worms in apples. Several nations try to steal the formula, but when one does, it gets twisted, and the result is a laughing gas that brings peace to the world. It was a daffy yet powerful idea, especially in light of the buildup of arms in Europe at the time. But the producers would not risk a novice librettist, so the book was written by Howard Lindsay and Russel Crouse, and by the time Wynn fiddled with the script, the show was much less potent than Harburg's original plan (see chapter 6). But Harburg did get to write the lyrics (with Arlen as composer) and made some piquant comments in songs such as "In the Shade of the New Apple Tree" and "God's Country." He also wrote the lyrics for *Hold On to Your Hats* (1940) with composer Burton Lane and came up with such sassy numbers as "There's a Great Day Coming Mañana" and "Life Was Pie for the Pioneers."

A much more typical Harburg show was *Bloomer Girl* (1944). Although he wrote lyrics to Arlen's music and directed the show, the libretto was penned by Fred Saidy and Sig Herzig. Harburg found in Saidy a kindred spirit, and they went on to collaborate on four more shows. Fareed Milhelm Saidy was born in Los Angeles in 1907 and worked as a journalist before turning to writing film scripts. One of his co-writers in Hollywood was Herzig, and he joined Saidy and Harburg in putting together this Civil War–era musical that was a descendant of the recent *Oklahoma!* (1943) but still very much its own product. Some historic elements were used in the script, primarily the early suffragette Dolly Bloomer, who rebelled against the corseted fashion style of the day and promoted for women the loose-fitting outfits that bore her name. The seeds of the women's rights movement in Seneca Falls, New York, were also evident, as the story takes place in the fictional Cicero Falls, New York, which (like the real upstate New York city) is on the route of the Underground Railroad. Leave it to Harburg and his collaborators to include women's rights, slavery, and a war in one musical. Big business is also touched on as Horatio Applegate (Matt Briggs) manufactures hoopskirts and feels threatened when his daughter, the feisty Evelina (Celeste Holm), takes up with her Aunt Dolly and promotes the advantages of bloomers. Evelina is also an abolitionist, so when her father arranges a marriage with the Southern slaveholder Jeff Calhoun (David Brooks), she is against the match on principle. Yet Evelina is drawn to the dashing gentleman, and it looks like they will wed, until she and Dolly help some runaway slaves on the Railroad, including Calhoun's escaped man Pompey (Dooley Wilson). There is a happy but contrived double ending (Calhoun converts to the Union cause, and Applegate switches his business to the manufacturing of military uniforms and bloomers) but not until several salient points are made. ("Right as the Rain" was the only song to enjoy popularity, but the entire Arlen–Harburg score is excellent.) While much of *Bloomer Girl* played like a musical comedy (there was even a saucy maid played by Joan McCracken, who impatiently waited for sex), the libretto was sometimes in the Hammerstein mold of musical play. A jail full of captured runaway slaves shared their grief and some songs while waiting to be shipped back down to the South, there was a standout Civil War ballet devised by Agnes DeMille, and a cunning scene involved the abolitionists trying to advertise their stage production of *Uncle Tom's Cabin* but getting scattered by the police, while the God-fearing citizens of Cicero Falls dutifully go to Sunday church services. Of course, *Bloomer Girl* was no *Oklahoma!* (as every critic pointed out), but it was very well received and ran two years. Strangely, it has rarely been revived since.

Harburg's first full credit as a librettist on Broadway was *Finian's Rainbow* (1947), which he co-wrote with Saidy and penned a brilliant set of lyrics for Burton Lane's music. The show was audacious, wise, silly, and inspired by a lighter-than-air whimsy. It was also a major hit, which is surprising, because many theatres today are still afraid to revive it. Why? It is a fantasy, which is usually suspicious for adult fare, and it is politically very left of center. Even poverty is handled with a sarcastic laugh, showing what happens when have-nots suddenly have. Finian MacLonergan (Albert Sharpe) steals a pot of gold from the leprechaun, Og (David Wayne) and travels from Glocca Morra, Ireland, to America with his daughter Sharon (Ella Logan) with the idea of burying his gold where the U.S. government buries its gold, Fort Knox, then watching it grow. The two get as far as Rainbow Valley, Missitucky, where Sharon is enamored of Woody Mahoney (Donald Richards). He is a union organizer who is trying to help the black and white sharecroppers in their fight with the bigoted Southern politician Senator

Billboard Rawkins (Robert Pitkin), who is hoping to buy up the whole valley. Og comes in pursuit of his gold, but ever since it has been stolen, he is slowly turning into a human, finding himself romantically and sexually attracted to both Sharon and Susan (Anita Alverez), Woody's mute sister. Using the power that comes from holding the pot of gold, Sharon turns the senator into an African American, and he gets to experience firsthand the horrors of Southern prejudice. Again the ending is happy and contrived: Og turns Rawkins back into a white liberal and gets Susan, Woody and Sharon are united, and Finian continues alone with his wandering ways.

Because of the fantasy premise, the librettists were able to go anywhere they wished with their story, and they often went right for the jugular. Billboard Rawkins was named after two prominent Mississippi politicians of the day, Senator Bilbo and Representative Rankin, and the script had plenty of fun with political double talk. (Senator: "My whole family's been havin' trouble with immigrants ever since we came to this country!") This time the score boasted several song hits, from "How Are Things in Glocca Morra?" and "Old Devil Moon" to "Look to the Rainbow" and the comic gem "When I'm Not Near the Girl I Love." But even with such a marketable score, *Finian's Rainbow* was a risky proposition. (Hollywood took twenty-one years before they attempted a film version, and that was in the permissive late 1960s.) There is something subversive about adult fantasy. One knows it's not real, yet a narrow-minded spectator still finds the humor suspicious. Some of the humor in the musical seems innocent enough:

FINIAN: Here it is on me pink map, witnessed and endorsed by Rand & McNally.
SHARON: I don't know who Rand is, but I could never trust a McNally.

But sometimes the fantasy allows for pointed comic discussions that could not exist in a realistic script:

OG: [to Rawkins, who is now black] What were you hiding from?
RAWKINS: My wife, my people, my friends. You think I want 'em to see me this way?
OG: I see nothing wrong with you.
RAWKINS: You don't? You must be blind. Can't you see I'm black?
OG: Yes, and I think it's very becoming.
RAWKINS: But I'm a white man, damnit, a white man! At least, I was a few weeks ago.
OG: Well, that's a coincidence! I was green a few weeks ago. Don't you find an occasional change of color interesting?

Harburg would play with similar kinds of satire in later scripts, but only in *Finian's Rainbow* is the message tempered with such innocent humor that it never get overbearing. Revived or not, it remains a superior libretto.

More daring and outrageous but also rather overbearing was *Flahoo-ley* (1951), a flop that still has a strong cult following primarily because of the dazzling original cast recording. The Harburg–Saidy libretto is also dazzling but in an audacious way that either thrilled or annoyed spectators. (The show received raves in New Haven and Philadelphia but mixed to poor notices in New York.) The plot is far too complicated to relate in detail, but suffice it to say it involves a mogul toy manufacturer, B. G. Bigelow (Ernest Truex); a laughing doll named Flahooley that is selling like hotcakes; a bunch of Arab spies (including the supposed Peruvian singer Yma Sumac) with a magic lamp that doesn't seem to work; a genie who floods the market with free dolls; a handful of puppets; and a McCarthy-like group of witch-hunters called the Capsul-Anti. The love interest came in the person of doll inventor Sylvester (Jerome Courtland) and his model, Sandy (Barbara Cook), who are brought together by the genie just before the sprite takes up a new job playing Santa Claus. Like *Finian's Rainbow,* it was a suspiciously leftist fantasy, but this time it was not set far away in the South and contained some uncomfortable references to the Cold War and the atom bomb. Those who laughed enjoyed the wicked satire; those who didn't called it unpatriotic. *Flahooley* was probably both. It was Harburg at his most passionate, if a little out of control. When the show was revived as *Jolly Anna* in San Francisco a year later, other authors toned down the satire, and it was a dull musical, even with clown Bobby Clark as Bigelow.

Imperialism, civil rights, Darwinism, and the threat of the atom bomb (again) were major topics in Harburg's next project with Saidy, but by the time *Jamaica* (1957) opened on Broadway, little remained but an alluring star vehicle for Lena Horne. Consequently, it was a hit. The libretto Harburg and Saidy wrote dealt with a black American who leaves the modern world and settles on Pigeon Island, a primitive little isle off Jamaica. There, he and the islanders are invaded by enterprising businessmen from abroad who want to develop the place and bring on all the horrors of the industrialized world. With Harry Belafonte pegged as the star, it was a promising (if also dangerous) musical proposition. Producer David Merrick bought it and then proceeded to do to the script what the businessmen wanted to do to Pigeon Island. The minor role of Belafonte's sweetheart went to Horne, the songs and story were rebuilt around her, and Belafonte was out of the picture. The show was now about the naive islander Savannah, who longs to go to Manhattan and join the sophisticated world where all you have to do is "Push de Button." She is admired by all on the island, especially the poor fisherman, Koli (Ricardo Montalban), who wishes to marry her, but Savannah wants more out of life. Just when it looks like she has found her ticket to America via a city slicker, Joe Nashua (Joe Adams), a hurricane hits Pigeon Island, Koli saves Savannah's little brother, and she comes to her senses, marrying Koli and visiting New York only in a dream ballet. The final product was such a travesty of what he had in mind that Harburg refused to attend the opening night. Yet there are several Harburg touches here and there, particularly in the character of Joe, who is promoting pearl diving in the shark-infested waters and trying to recruit the desperate natives to his plan. And many of the songs (music by Harold Arlen) were still very venturesome. Evolution is ribbed in "Monkey in the Mango Tree," the fleeting nature of fame is lampooned in "Napoleon (Is a Pastry)," and another number warned "Leave the Atom Alone." No one in the audience was upset or disturbed by anything in *Jamaica,* making it a failure in Harburg's eyes but a success for Merrick, Horne, and the box office.

Harburg did not write the libretto for *The Happiest Girl in the World* (1961), but the script was based on his adaptation of Aristophanes' *Lysistrata,* and he directed it and wrote the lyrics, using themes by Jacques Offenbach as his music. It was a literate, bawdy musical about the god Pluto (Cyril Ritchard) stirring up trouble by getting Lysistrata (Janice Rule) and the women of Greece to stop the war with Sparta by withholding sex from their men. The antiwar and antiestablishment issues were pure Harburg, but they seemed to lack punch in the classical setting. Despite some favorable reviews, audiences stayed away. Also literary and unpopular was *Darling of the Day* (1968), for which Harburg wrote the lyrics for Jule Styne's music. At least five writers contributed to the libretto at different times, and Harburg probably contributed to parts of it. But no librettist was listed by opening night, and none offered to take credit for the lifeless show. Based on Arnold Bennett's 1908 novel *Buried Alive,* the musical concerned a famous artist, Priam Farll (Vincent Price), whose valet dies, so Priam escapes from the world by assuming the dead servant's identity and sending out word that the celebrated Farll is dead. Priam's ruse is discovered when he falls into an autumnal romance with the valet's fiancée (Patricia Routledge), but everything works out for the best when Parliament decides to keep up the deception rather than admit that a valet has mistakenly been buried in Westminster Abbey. There is little in the show that recalls the Harburg sparkle, and even his lyrics are more perfunctory than playful. Harburg's last musical project, *What a Day for a Miracle* (1971), tried out at the University of Vermont and died there. Harburg lived another ten years, often being honored for his past work as he outlived most of his contemporaries. The same Harburg mischief that had once ruffled feathers was finally being applauded. Lambasting war, capitalism, nuclear weapons, and male chauvinism was a common and popular pastime in the 1970s. The Jewish leprechaun was finally in vogue.

Harburg's satire is unique in the history of the Broadway musical. George S. Kaufman, Moss Hart, Harold Rome, Lindsay and Crouse, and Ira Gershwin all poked fun at issues of the day in their librettos and lyrics. But those issues were usually safe, their attitudes in sync with public opinion. Rome made fun of Hitler and Mussolini when America was mostly anti-Fascist. Kaufman and Gershwin lampooned politics, always a fair target and graciously accepted even by the opposition. The Hart and Lindsay–Crouse satires were delightful but usually toothless. But Harburg dared go against the mainstream as true satire must. He wrote about racism decades before the civil rights movement of the 1960s. He skewered big business when the stock market was up. By 1960, McCarthy and the hearings of the House Un-American Activities Committee were considered frauds and villains, but Harburg took them to task in 1951. When Harburg's leftist views landed on Broadway, not always the most liberal of locations, the resulting fireworks were fascinating to watch. But there was always more than theatrics at stake. No one (including the man himself) would deny that Harburg and his fellow conspirators had an agenda. They made few efforts to hide their soapbox. But few can deny that there was also inspired brilliance at work in the Harburg shows. The sticky dilemma of art versus politics was never untangled in a Harburg musical. Had they been serious and grim musical dramas, they might have been more admired and more easily dismissed. But because Harburg used musical comedy to assault sacred targets and suggest a better world over the rainbow, he was dangerous. That makes him unique in the American theatre.

CHAPTER TEN
APPLAUSE ON THE TOWN:
BETTY COMDEN AND ADOLPH GREEN

One always knows where one is in a Comden and Green show. The setting may be Coney Island or Neverland or on a train, but we know we are really smack in the middle of Broadway. Their reality is a Broadway reality—not only because all their musicals (save one or two) are bright comedies but because their characters have a Broadway sensibility as well. They seem to exist only in the limelight, and each one is a performer as well as a character. Maybe this comes from the fact that both Betty Comden and Adolph Green were performers first and never totally gave it up. This made them ideally suited to write the librettos and/or lyrics for star vehicles. It also enabled them to create a particular persona for their characters: people as Broadway personalities. Comden and Green began in the musical revue genre, and though they concentrated on book musicals throughout their careers, some of the revue mentality remained. Both characters and plot are sketched quickly, broadly, and clearly. Few of their characters actually grow or develop; they simply *are*. This can be seen as both a weakness in their work and the key to their showmanship.

The American theatre has seen many teams over the years, but no other pairing quite matches their record. Not only did they write librettos, lyrics, and screenplays over a period of fifty years, but they never worked with anyone but each other. Their composer-collaborators changed, but the words were always by Comden and Green. Whenever they penned an article, preface, introduction, or tribute, it was co-written. They often performed together and were nearly always interviewed together. It seemed as though one did not exist without the other. That is truly a team! No wonder so many theatregoers mistakenly thought that they were married to each other. (In 1996, Comden wrote and published a memoir that proved there was a Betty Comden without an Adolph Green and that she actually had a life separate from him.) Working so closely together over so many decades, it would be futile to try to separate their talents and determine who provided what in their work. They are simply "ComdenandGreen."

Both were born in New York City in 1915 (she was born Elizabeth Cohen in Brooklyn), both attended New York University, and both got involved in theatre by way of collegiate productions. In the 1930s, several small theatre nightclubs sprung up in Greenwich Village and in other New York neighborhoods, forming a sort of musical fringe years before the Off-Off Broadway venue existed. Both Comden and Green were hoping to be professional performers, and these clubs were ideal showcases for new talent. The two began working together as part of an act called The Revuers with Judy Holliday in the group and Green's college roommate Leonard Bernstein there to provide encouragement. Comden and Green started writing sketches and songs for themselves, hoping to interest casting agents because their material was fresh and different. This backdoor approach to writing may be the reason why their work would always be so performer oriented and pleasantly unpretentious. By 1938, they were appearing in more prestigious clubs uptown, and producers were impressed by their material if not always their performing skills. The two were asked to write three songs for the Broadway revue *Three After Three,* but it closed in New Haven. It was Bernstein who suggested the team when he and choreographer Jerome Robbins planned to turn their dance piece "Fancy Free" into a full-scale Broadway musical.

There are many accomplishments in *On the Town* (1944), as the project was retitled, that have gone into the musical theatre history books: its innovative use of extended dance sequences, its often-copied premise of servicemen on leave in a place filled with romantic possibilities, its unrealistic yet evocative scenery, George Abbott's brisk and zestful direction, and its vibrant Bernstein score. But it is also worth recalling that *On the Town* was the first Broadway show for Bernstein, Robbins, Comden, and Green. Robbins had danced in the chorus of a few musicals, and Abbott was an old hand at this sort of thing, but, for the most part it was a refreshing and dazzling debut by a group of newcomers. Both Comden and Green appeared in leading roles, another debut for them, and most of the rest of the cast were young unknowns as well. In many ways, the show seemed like a college or summer stock musical that landed on Broadway with all its pluck and charm intact.

The story line was simple enough. The three sailors on twenty-four-hour leave in Manhattan were youth personified. The dreamy Gaby (John Battles) is ripe for love and is smitten by a photograph of "Miss Turnstiles" in the subway and goes off in search of her. She turns out to be the struggling singer Ivy Smith (Sono Osato), who makes ends meet by working as a cooch dancer at Coney Island. The clowning Ozzie (Green) finds a soul mate in the anthropology student Claire de Loon (Comden), both of them the victims of big impulses. Chip (Cris Alexander) is the ardent tourist who wants to see the sights (including some long-gone landmarks) but finds himself chased by the amorous cabbie Hildy Esterhazy (Nancy Walker). The plot is episodic, following each pair of would-be lovers across the Manhattan landscape and taking in nightclubs, the Museum of Natural History, a studio at Carnegie Hall, the subways, and the Brooklyn Navy Yard, where the tale starts and finishes. It is a freewheeling adventure with no other purpose than to celebrate the city and its possibilities for romance and laughs. In addition to such juicy comic songs as "I Can Cook Too," "I Get Carried Away," and "Come Up to My Place," Comden and Green provided the script with sketch-like humor (Hildy: "How do you do? I gave up a concert and a shot-put rally to come and meet you.") and a bittersweet ending, as exemplified in the musical scene "Some Other Time." While the libretto is as thin as the score is full bodied, *On the Town* still works on stage. It breezes along with such innocence and vitality that it probably struck even 1940s audiences as nostalgic. After all, it was wartime, and the sight of military personnel being motivated by romance and sightseeing must have been a comforting idea.

Comden, Green, Robbins, and Abbott reteamed for a more ambitious show, a "Musical Play of the Terrific Twenties" called *Billion Dollar Baby* (1945). This time Morton Gould was the composer, but the score (lyrics by the twosome) was more interesting than likable. Yet the libretto by Comden and Green was better structured and plotted than *On the Town.* Staten Island nobody Maribelle Jones (Joan McCracken) wants to work her way to the top, so she gets involved with bootlegger Jerry Bonanza (Don De Leo) in order to meet Mr. Big himself, the gangster Dapper Welch (David Burns). While she woos Dapper and flirts with the millionaire M. M. Montegue (Robert Chisholm), Maribelle slips into true love with the henchman Rocky Barton (William Tabbert). The speakeasy queen Georgia Motley (Mitzi Green) is Maribelle's chief competition in keeping all these men on a string, but the heroine lands the millionaire, only to have the stock market crash on their wedding day. The script managed to include many of the Roaring Twenties clichés, from Charleston contests to bathtub gin. The 1920s revue series, the *Garrick Gaieties,* were spoofed as the *Jollities,* and Georgia Motley was a thinly disguised re-creation of nightclub favorite Texas Guinan. The farce moved into the ridiculous at times, some characters being rubbed out by the mob, only to reappear and claim "it was only a flesh wound." All in all, it was high-flying nonsense that got mostly favorable reviews. Yet audiences were wary. Twenties frivolity seemed inappropriate during the war years, and the musical could last only seven weeks. (Interest in the 1920s would emerge years later with such shows as *Gentlemen Prefer Blondes*, *Lend an Ear*, and *The Boy Friend*.) Because there was no cast recording, *Billion Dollar Baby* fell into obscurity, though a 1998 Off-Broadway revival was well received, and the score was finally recorded.

Comden and Green's *Bonanza Bound* (1947) with music by Saul Chaplin was Broadway bound but closed in Philadelphia. When the Broadway offers dried up, the twosome headed to Hollywood, where they wrote the screenplays (and sometimes the lyrics) for such musical favorites as *Good News* (1947), *The Barkeleys of Broadway* (1949), *Take Me Out to the Ball Game* (1949), and *Singin' in the Rain* (1952). Back in New York, Comden and Green worked for the first time with the man who would become their most frequent composer-collaborator, Jule Styne, on the revue *Two on the Aisle* (1951). Then they reteamed with Bernstein for the marvelous score for *Wonderful Town* (1953); the libretto was by Joseph Fields and Jerome Chodorov, based on their earlier play *My Sister Eileen* (see chapter 8). *Peter Pan* (1954) opened on Broadway with no librettists credited, but Comden and Green, who wrote half the songs with Styne, contributed to the script for the musicalization of the J. M. Barrie classic. The next year the film musical *It's Always Fair Weather* (1955) was released, the twosome writing the screenplay and lyrics (music by André Previn). It was an ambitious and rather a dark tale about a reunion of three army buddies who realize that their former comradery is dead. In some ways it was a bitter sequel to *On the Town*, and this bitterness pervaded the script and even some of the lyrics. Despite the presence of Gene Kelly, Cyd Charisse, and other stars, the movie was too downbeat to be widely popular. Yet it has some laudable writing in both the script and the lyrics.

Bells Are Ringing (1956), the team's first full-fledged Broadway libretto since *Billion Dollar Baby*, was a vehicle for their former Revuer Judy Holliday. It was a merry romance that entertained audiences for 924 performances. Ella Peterson (Holliday) works for Susanswerphone, a telephone answering service run by Sue Summers (Jean Stapleton). Ella is not above listening in to phone conversations and getting involved with her clients, in particular a floundering playwright, Jeff Moss (Sydney Chaplin), whom she speaks to in a little-old-lady voice as he calls her "Mom." When Jeff sinks into despair after another rejection, Ella goes to him, and the two fall in love (Jeff not knowing that she is Mom). Sue, on the other hand, is romantically involved with the record salesman Sandor (Eddie Lawrence), a client who is secretly using Susanswerphone to take horse racing bets. (For example, an order for Puccini or Tchaikovsky is code for bets at Pimlico or Churchill Downs.) When the police zero in on the racket, the innocent Ella and Sue are suspected, but all ends up happily as Mom becomes Sweetheart. It is a lightweight libretto that relied heavily on the star quality of Holliday, but Comden and Green created an original and charming character for their fellow Revuer. Ella is deliciously naive and yet worldly wise in a cockeyed way:

> ELLA: [to a hung-over Jeff] Well, if you want to drink at this hour of the morning, there must be some work you're trying to avoid doing. I know from my own experience. When I had to do my homework in high school, I'd do anything to escape sitting down to do it. Mostly I'd sharpen pencils—you know—the yellow kind that say "Ticonderoga" on them? I'd sharpen one down to the Ticonderog—then Ticonder—then Ticon— and Tico and, finally, Ti and T—and then I'd have to start on another pencil.

The Styne–Comden–Green score produced two hits, "Just in Time" and "The Party's Over," but all the songs are happy-go-lucky extensions of the thin plot. *Bells Are Ringing* was very conventional and a product of its era; perhaps that is why it is not the easiest show to revive. Lines like "That mustard plaster is so pure, if there's any left over, you can put it on a hot dog" call for an innocence that we no longer have.

After providing lyrics for Styne's music in *Say, Darling* (1958) and *Do Re Mi* (1960), Comden and Green wrote both lyrics and libretto for *Subways Are for Sleeping* (1961), based on a 1957 collection of short stories (under the same title) by Edmund G. Love. All their musical scripts up to this point had been originals, but the source material about wacky and unconventional New Yorkers seemed like typical Comden and Green. It was not an easy adaptation, Love's book being more character stretches than stories. The libretto's main plot about a secretary, engaged to her business tycoon boss, who falls for a society dropout, was rather gritty and (atypical for the team) made some salient points about the modern rat race and the evils of compromising to the establishment. But the story played so poorly out of town that the twosome rewrote the script, softening their approach and turning the tale into a rather uninteresting romance between a well-dressed drifter, Tom Bailey (Sydney Chaplin), and the magazine writer, Angie McKay (Carol Lawrence), who interviews him and eventually falls in love with Tom and his unconventional lifestyle. The secondary comic plot was more fun, if just as insubstantial. Former beauty pageant winner Martha Vail (Phyllis Newman) was once Miss Watermelon, but now she is so hard up for funds that she is being evicted from her hotel room and runs around Manhattan clad only in a towel. Charlie Smith (Orson Bean), a drifter friend of Tom's, woos the alluring destitute, and the two end up opening a coffee-vending service together. While the libretto had its enjoyable scenes, most of the show came down to watching do-nothings do nothing. Some of the songs (music by Styne) remain tunefully pleasant, but the musical is a very unlikely candidate for revival. Today, homeless New Yorkers can be the subject of a tragicomic piece like *Rent,* not escapist musical comedy like *Subways Are for Sleeping.*

Comden and Green drew on their Hollywood experiences (and plenty of Tinsel Town clichés) for their libretto and lyrics for *Fade Out—Fade In* (1964). It was set in the 1930s, and the story recalled the broad kind of Hollywood satire that the team had provided for the film *Singin' in the Rain.* Movie usherette Hope Springfield (Carol Burnett) dreams of film stardom but has worked her way up only to chorus girl in screen musicals. Yet through a bureaucratic mistake by a bumbling studio executive, Hope is starred in a feature film. When the executive in charge finds out, heads roll, and the print is hidden away in a vault until one of the film mogul's nephews, Rudolf (Dick Patterson), takes a shine to Hope and has the film released. Of course it's a hit, Hope becomes a real movie star, and she and Rudolf literally walk off into the sunset. Much of the show was built around the considerable talents of Burnett, but there was room also for some playful satire in the persons of the dashing but plastic screen idol Byron Prong (Jack Cassidy) and the lecherous Louis B. Mayer–like Lionel Z. Governor (Lou Jacobi):

> GOVERNOR: [on the phone] Hello, Mathews . . . I got Prong here. I need him! So finish the picture—now—without him. So he won't rescue the girl. . . . He's killed by a bolt of lightning. That's right. . . . There's no clinch at the end—they don't kiss . . . instead a close-up of her kissing his picture. . . . Fade Out. The End. . . . What do you mean it's not satisfying? I'm satisfied! Look, it's booked into seven hundred theatres already. The public will like it whether they like it or not!

Although the story was clearly plotted, much of *Fade Out—Fade In* came down to a series of memorable scenes, a Shirley Temple–Bill Robinson spoof by Burnett and Tiger Haynes being the one most fondly recalled. Again Styne wrote the music, and again the score was admirable, though no hits emerged from it. With the right kind of star, the musical might play very well today.

While Comden and Green contributed lyrics only (again with composer Styne) to the ambitious 1967 musical *Hallelujah, Baby!* (see chapter 15), they found themselves writing libretto for only *Applause* (1970), adapting the film classic *All about Eve* (1950) into musical form. The celebrated plot (originally a short story by Mary Orr) concerns Broadway star Margo Channing (Lauren Bacall), who befriends the seemingly innocent Eve Harrington (Penny Fuller), only to see the conniving Eve take over her role, her playwright (Brandon Maggart,) and almost her director-lover (Len Cariou). Eve successfully claws her way to the top of her profession, but Margo gets her man and learns to balance her career with the more important things in life. Told in the form of a flashback, it was a story that cried out to be dramatized, and Comden and Green musicalized it with a sure and steady hand. They made the wise choice of keeping Margo a Broadway actress rather than a musical star because the real star, Bacall, was neither a singer nor a dancer. Yet Bacall had a half dozen songs, all of which were character and plot numbers rather than show-within-a-show pieces. The librettists made no attempt to soften or romanticize the characters, and they even took a few swipes at the theatre profession:

> BUZZ: [the playwright] The play is actor-proof!
> MARGO: Actor-proof! If you knew the bits, the schtick, I have to dredge out of the vaudeville trunk to give the illusion that something amusing is going on . . .
> BUZZ: You empty-headed, conceited bass fiddle! You're just a body and a voice! Don't ever forget—I'm the brain!
> MARGO: Till the autopsy, there's no proof!

Two of the most memorable characters from the film were dropped: George Sanders's acid-tongue critic and Thelma Ritter's equally acid dresser. But both characters were so strongly identified with those unique film performers that it would have been foolhardy for other actors to try to eclipse them. (The Ritter role was turned into a gay hairdresser played by Lee Roy Reams—a cliché now but a rather bold choice for the time.) The vivacious score by Charles Strouse (music) and Lee Adams (lyrics) was efficiently integrated into the libretto, even such group numbers such as "But Alive" and the title song being offstage celebrations in theatre folk hangouts rather than on-stage pieces. (The former was performed in a gay bar, another interesting choice.) *Applause* was such a hit that Broadway producers raided the Hollywood repertoire looking for other film-to-musical possibilities. Many followed, but few were as well crafted as the Comden–Green adaptation.

After the team supplied some new lyrics for *Lorelei* (1974), a revised and inferior version of *Gentlemen Prefer Blondes* (1949), they wrote another commendable adaptation, *On the Twentieth Century* (1978). Comden and Green supplied both lyrics (to Cy Coleman's music) and libretto for the mock operetta based on the 1932 farce *Twentieth Century* by Ben Hecht and Charles MacArthur. It was another Broadway backstager but this time set on a train, the luxury streamliner of the title that sped passengers between New York and Chicago in the days of the great railways. Impoverished theatre producer Oscar Jaffee (John Cullum) books a compartment next to the movie star Lily Garland (Madeline Kahn) in the hopes of wooing her, during the trip to New York, into appearing in one of his shows, thereby guaranteeing backers' money and boffo box office. Since Lily and Oscar were once lovers who broke up when she went to Hollywood, the relationship is a bit touchy. Add to that Oscar's melodramatic ego and Lily's diva personality, and the love story was more rambunctious than your typical musical. The librettists opened the story up by showing a few flashbacks and a production number that was solely in Lily's imagination. The minor character of a male religious zealot in the original play was expanded into the wacky heiress Letitia Primrose (Imogene Coca), who battles smut and offers to back Oscar's play if it is about Mary Magdalene. Also fleshed out was Lily's handsome fiancé played by newcomer Kevin Kline, whose expansive clowning was right in keeping with the bigger-than-life show. The libretto recalls Comden and Green's high-flying exaggeration of *Singin' in the Rain* and captured the frenzy and sarcasm of the 1930s. The Coleman–Comden–Green score was a wonderful pastiche of operetta bombast, and Robin Wagner's sleek art deco train was roundly applauded. But *On the Twentieth Century* had trouble appealing to 1970s audiences. Despite some glowing reviews and a handful of awards, it managed to run only 460 performances and showed no profit. In many ways it was a musical wrong for its time but one that remains immensely enjoyable when revived.

Comden and Green's next libretto was their least typical, a dark musical play called *A Doll's Life* (1982), which ventured to guess what happened to Nora after she left her husband in Henrik Ibsen's 1879 landmark drama *A Doll's House*. The libretto takes the form of an odyssey as Nora (Betsy Joslyn) searches for fulfillment, first with lawyer Johan (George Hearn), then with composer Otto (Peter Gallagher), and then with the elderly businessman Eric (Edmund Lyndeck), whom she sleeps with in order to gain better working conditions for his factory employees. Nora also embraces early feminism before going into business for herself, becoming wealthy and independent enough that she can return to her husband and children in the end. The tale was as humorless as it was ambitious, yet it boasted a subtle but powerful score with the duo providing the lyrics for Larry Grossman's engaging music. Like *Applause,* the show took the form of a flashback: a modern-day rehearsal of Ibsen's play prompts the actress playing Nora to consider the character's fate. But the libretto never returned to the present, which might have given the meandering plot some unity. The character of Nora herself was not terribly interesting, though some of the men in her life were. And Harold Prince's moody and theatrical staging was sometimes more effective than the story being told. The critics trounced *A Doll's Life,* and it closed after five performances, the biggest flop of the twosome's career. But it remains a fascinating failure and a curious accomplishment in the career of Comden and Green.

The team adapted their *Singin' in the Rain* screenplay into a Broadway musical in 1985. Although it had been a hit in London, the show struggled for a season in New York and lost money. It was a weak adaptation, its changes not being for the better and its original scenes not playing as well on stage as they had in the film. Critics blamed the inappropriate choreography by Twyla Tharp and the lackluster, starless cast, but much of the musical's failure rested on the book. Comden and Green had not found a way to rethink the piece for the stage, and too often the script fell flat. (Subsequent productions of *Singin' in the Rain* adapted by others fared better.) Sadly, it was their last libretto. They did write a competent set of lyrics for Cy Coleman's music in *The Will Rogers Follies* (1991), and that biomusical (book by Peter Stone) was a long-running hit (see chapter 16).

At their best, the Comden and Green librettos were bold, playful, and entertaining. Each one can also be seen as a vehicle. Whether a star was employed or not, the script was usually a performer's script. Depth of character may have been sacrificed for charm, heart, or even laughs, and the plot sometimes twisted and turned to fulfill a particular performing bit. But Comden and Green were always highly professional in their writing and understood how to create honest charm, heart, and laughs. The sketch-like tone of their librettos may limit them in terms of plot and character, but it rarely kept the twosome from coming up with proficient entertainment values. Betty Comden and Adolph Green are show business personified; no one writes that way anymore. Some see this as an advancement in the musical theatre, but we lost something when we lost that animated kind of writing.

ON A CLEAR DAY:
ALAN JAY LERNER

What a dazzling career librettist-lyricist Lerner enjoyed: after two promising works, he had thirteen years of back-to-back hits. Yet what a sad career he suffered after that: twenty-two years of back-to-back flops. Because most of Lerner's successes were collaborations with composer Frederick Loewe, one might assume that it was the teaming of the two men that was responsible for those marvelous musicals. Yet looking over Lerner's list of failures, it is clear that his lyric ability never waned. There are radiant lyrics in even his most dismal musicals. The answer more likely lies in the Lerner librettos. He always wrote the books for his musicals, and it is in these librettos that one sees the decline that made his later career so unfortunate.

Alan Jay Lerner was one of the very few Broadway musical writers to be born to wealth. His family owned and operated the prosperous chain of garment stores called the Lerner Shops. He was born in New York City in 1918 and, from his earliest days, received the highest pedigree education possible: exclusive private schools in America and Europe and college studies at Harvard and Oxford. Not even Cole Porter had such a prestigious (and unlikely) background for a career in musical theatre. In Lerner's mind, there was no question of what he wanted to do with his life. He eschewed the idea of continuing in the family business and decided to be a Broadway writer. At Harvard, he wrote for the Hasty Pudding theatricals, and after graduation he gained professional experience scripting radio shows. It was while writing revues for the Lambs Club that he met Frederick Loewe, the German-born immigrant who had been a child prodigy in Europe but was then a struggling composer with few prospects. Loewe had written some unsuccessful musicals in America with Earle Crooker, and when one of them called *Patricia* was retitled *The Life of the Party*, Lerner was brought on as libretto doctor. The 1942 show closed without getting any closer to

Broadway than Detroit, but Lerner and Loewe, despite their very different temperaments, liked working together and would continue to do so for nearly twenty years.

Many of Lerner's librettos over the years would be original scripts not based on previous works. Such was the case with *What's Up?* (1943), the team's first full collaboration. Arthur Pierson and Lerner wrote the odd libretto, an old-fashioned piece of comic operetta that had more than a few touches of the ribald wartime shows that were so popular in the 1940s. The U.S. Air Force is flying the Sultan of Tanglinia (Jimmy Savo) to America for an official visit, but the plane must make an emergency landing near Miss Langley's School for Girls. Since the school is quarantined because of measles, the Sultan must stay there for the duration of the epidemic. The short, leering little Sultan found an American equivalent to a harem, but the misadventures that followed were more naughty than lecherous. Despite its farcical premise, little in *What's Up?* struck critics as very funny except for Savo. The highlight of the show was a George Balanchine ballet in which Savo had to keep standing on a chair to reach high enough to dance with an Amazon chorine. The Lerner and Loewe score was as quickly forgotten as the musical itself, which managed to linger on for eight weeks because of Savo's admirers.

Much more promising was *The Day Before Spring* (1945), another original that Lerner scripted alone this time. Peter (John Archer) and Katherine Townsend (Irene Manning) return to their alma mater Harrison University for their tenth reunion, where Katherine is reunited with the novelist Alex Maitland (Bill Johnson). Ten years earlier, Alex and Katherine had tried to elope together, but their car broke down, and she ended up marrying Peter. She has never forgotten her former suitor, and after some fond reminiscing and a few love songs, the twosome decide again to run off together. But again their automobile fails, and again Katherine ends up with Peter. It was the kind of plot that Guy Bolton might have devised for a Princess musical, but Lerner's writing was still rather clumsy, and *The Day Before Spring* was more intriguing than satisfactory. The Lerner and Loewe score, on the other hand, was highly polished and offered such minor gems as "God's Green World," "I Love You This Morning," and "A Jug of Wine." This time their musical lasted twenty-one weeks.

The musical *Brigadoon* (1947), the team's next project, not only established Lerner and Loewe as Broadway's next Rodgers and Hammerstein but also was biggest hit of the season and has enjoyed many revivals over the years. Lerner's original libretto, about a dreamy Scottish town that appears only once every one hundred years, was a romantic fantasy very unlike Hammerstein's more earthbound scripts, but there was no question Lerner was learning his character and construction skills from the older writer. The romantic couple Laurey and Curly of *Oklahoma!* (1943) became American Tommy Albright (David Brooks) and Scottish lassie Fiona MacLaren (Marion Bell) in *Brigadoon,* and the secondary couple of Will Parker and Ado Annie turned into the lackadaisical Jeff Douglass (George Keane) and the man-hungry Meg Brockie (Pamela Britton). There was even a Jud-like villain, the jealous lover Harry Beaton (James Mitchell), who threatens the just-married couple, Charlie Dalrymple (Lee Sullivan) and Fiona's sister Jeannie (Virginia Bosler), and dies accidentally by the hand of the hero. And Agnes DeMille's dance sequences brought the musical a lyrical, dream-like quality. Despite all these parallels, *Brigadoon* is pure Lerner. His longtime fascination with J. M. Barrie, Scotland, and magical folklore fed his imagination, and his growing skill as a writer allowed him to tell a very fragile and wisplike tale in the format of a big Broadway musical. When critic George Jean Nathan later accused Lerner of stealing his plot from an 1852 German story called *Germelshausen,* the librettist was adamant about the musical's originality. But the triumph of *Brigadoon* is the handling of the material, not its source. Lerner finds a poetic form of dialogue that is never cloying, and he uses it to gently lead into the highly romanticized lyrics:

> FIONA: Ye see, I dinna want to jus' get married. I think ye should only do it when ye an' your lad want to stay together fiercely an' gettin' married is the only way ye can do it that's proper.

This flowing kind of prose is purposely punctured by the hard, modern sounds of the American characters:

> MR. LUNDE: [a wise old Scot] Two hundred years ago the Highlands of Scotland were plagued with witches; wicked sorceresses who were takin' the Scottish folk away from the teachin's of God an' puttin' the devil in their souls. They were indeed horrible destructive women. I dinna suppose ye have such women in your world.
> TOMMY: Witches?
> JEFF: Yes, we still have them. We pronounce it differently.

This contrast is never more jarring than when Tommy returns to New York City and the harsh sounds of his fiancée, Jane Ashton (Frances Charles), make the lilting voices of *Brigadoon* all the more sweet. Whereas Fiona

121

muses that "I dinna know anythin about ye, but from the little ye've said I'm quite certain that everythin' ye think I think differently about," Jane can only complain about how "antisocial" Tommy and Jeff are behaving and how "everybody is bored to death" with them. The audience has no trouble empathizing with Tommy and his yearning to return to a simpler yet more poetic world. They buy into Lerner's fantasy because it is so appealing. *Brigadoon* remains a stage favorite because of this and for its famous score ("Heather on the Hill," "It's Almost Like Being in Love," "Come to Me, Bend to Me," and others) that is supported by an equally adroit libretto.

Lerner's next project was perhaps his most inventive one, and interestingly it was not with Loewe but with another German composer, the Americanized Kurt Weill. Lerner subtitled *Love Life* (1948) a "musical vaudeville," but commentators many years later would label it one of the early "concept" musicals. Sam (Ray Middleton) and Susan Cooper (Nanette Fabray) are wed in 1791, and we follow their marriage over the years, each day of their lives taking up a decade or so of historical time. This *Brigadoon*-like conceit allows the Coopers to experience the various stages of marriage (honeymoon bliss, children, infidelity, separation, reconciliation, compromise) as they live though the industrial revolution, the Roaring Twenties, the Crash, and the war years. The episodic plot was punctuated with vaudeville acts that paralleled the plight of the Coopers' marriage, from magician's tricks to a Punch and Judy battle to a minstrel show. It was a bold, expansive idea that was too unwieldy to work all the time. But there was much to recommend in *Love Life*, from the scintillating Weill–Lerner score ("Green-Up Time" was the only song to come close to being a hit) to the expressionistic Boris Aronson sets to the fine performances throughout. (Two decades later, Joe Masteroff would use the same concept with better results in *Cabaret*.) Yet Lerner's foolhardy experiment managed to run 252 performances on mixed reviews. One cannot help but ponder on what future Weill–Lerner projects might have been like had Weill not died in 1950.

Slightly more successful but far less innovative was *Paint Your Wagon* (1951), Lerner and Loewe's frontier musical that boasted such hit songs as "I Talk to the Trees" and "They Call the Wind Maria." Despite such a fine score, the show is little revived today because its traditional libretto just isn't traditional enough. Widower Ben Rumson (James Barton) discovers gold on his land and watches his property become a boomtown. His newfound wealth prompts him to remarry and to send his daughter Jennifer (Olga San Juan) to a finishing school in the East. Although Jennifer is in love with a dashing Mexican prospector named Julio (Tony Bavaar), she leaves the growing Rumson Town for school. But soon the gold mine fades, the towns goes bust, the new wife deserts Ben, and the lonely prospector quietly dies dreaming of his first wife, Elisa. Jennifer returns to find Julio a disenchanted man, ready to give up pipe dreaming and willing to settle down and become a farmer with Jennifer as his bride. It is a well-crafted story (another Lerner original), and the characters are well drawn. But *Paint Your Wagon* was a bit too somber without being a serious musical play. The score fluctuated between the lyrical and the rousing, but the libretto was consistently ponderous. Years later Lerner rewrote the story as a farce for the failed 1969 film version. The original was much better but still not good enough.

About the same time as *Paint Your Wagon*, Lerner tried his hand at screenwriting and wrote the book and lyrics for *Royal Wedding* (1951). That same year his screenplay for *An American in Paris* (1951) won him an Oscar. Lerner would return to Hollywood for such projects as *Gigi* (1958) and *The Little Prince* (1974), writing script and lyrics for each as well as the film versions of most of his stage musicals.

As admirable as much of the Lerner and Loewe shows had been up to this point, nothing in them suggested that the team was capable of *My Fair Lady* (1956), a musical project that was given to them after practically every other songwriter in town had either turned it down or given up on it in frustration. The musical is so well known and beloved today that it is often forgotten how unlikely a prospect it was in the first place. George Bernard Shaw's *Pygmalion* (1914) is a talky drawing room comedy with little romance and few opportunities for song and dance. It is also so unfalteringly British and concerned with such non-American issues as language and class hierarchy that any Broadway producer would question its likeliness for success on Broadway. Yet *My Fair Lady* has become, in the opinion of many, the Broadway musical by which all others are judged. The music and lyrics are so tightly integrated with character and plot that it seems the whole musical was born of a piece and by one brilliant mind. But like all musicals good and bad, *My Fair Lady* was a collaboration, and one cannot credit its success without mentioning Shaw's original play and even Moss Hart's astute direction along with Lerner and Loewe. It was Lerner's first musical based on another source, and it remains his (as well as anybody else's) finest adaptation. Lerner did not so much musicalize *Pygmalion* as to reimagine it in terms of a musical. Shaw's witty exposé on language and class was antiromantic; Lerner turned it into an appealing Cinderella tale but (most importantly) without discarding any of Shaw's original intentions. It is one of Broadway's most literate musicals, not because it retained much of

Shaw's dialogue but because it used Shaw's genius as a springboard for the equally literate libretto and lyrics. *My Fair Lady* is not improved Shaw—it is Shaw redefined in musical terms.

One has only to look at the failed Shaw-based musicals after *My Fair Lady* to realize what a masterful job Lerner did in writing the libretto. The play had been opened up a bit by Shaw himself when he wrote the screenplay for the 1938 film version of *Pygmalion*. Lerner goes further in the process, following Alfred Doolittle (Stanley Holloway) to his usual haunts to illustrate his music hall–like world and briefly includes the embassy ball that is spoken of in the original play. Lerner also opens up the tale in two areas that give depth to the both the characters and the plot. First, in a series of blackout sketches and song fragments, he shows exactly how Eliza (Julie Andrews) is transformed from a howling Cockney into a genteel lady. In Shaw's comedy, we see Eliza before and after this transformation. Lerner gives us glimpses of the process and lets it climax in song ("The Rain in Spain"). It is a rousing and illuminating moment. Professor Higgins (Rex Harrison) has succeeded in teaching her the externals; what he doesn't realize is that he has also allowed the "fair lady" inside Eliza to grow. Lerner's other major contribution in opening up the story for the musical stage is the scene at the Ascot races. In Shaw's version, Higgins decides to test out his new creation at his mother's "at home," an Edwardian version of open house or calling hours. How much more interesting (and dramatic) for Eliza's debut to be at such a public and high-society function as the opening day at Ascot. Lerner first sets up the scene with a wry chorus number ("Ascot Gavotte"), then brings on the major characters for a merry display of the superficial class system at work. Eliza's expletive of "not bloody likely" in *Pygmalion* would mean little to American audiences, but her "Come on, Dover! Move yer bloomin' (arse)!" in *My Fair Lady* does the trick perfectly. As for the so-called happy ending of the musical as opposed to Shaw's less hopeful conclusion in the play, one should remember that Shaw himself rewrote his last scene for the 1938 film version. Perhaps there was a streak of romanticism (or shrewd practicality) in the old Irishman after all. Regardless, the muted but warm "Eliza? Where the devil are my slippers?" is an apt ending for *My Fair Lady*.

It is obvious that Lerner was able to keep up with Shaw when one examines the superb lyrics in the musical, many of which were suggested by an idea or a phrase in *Pygmalion*. But there is also evidence in the libretto that Lerner could echo Shavian humor when he had to. Neither of the following samples of dialogue from *My Fair Lady* are to be found in Shaw's original:

ELIZA: [reciting with her mouth full of marbles] "With blackest moss, the flower pots . . ." I can't! I can't!

PICKERING: I say, Higgins, are those pebbles really necessary?

HIGGINS: If they were necessary for Demosthenes, they are necessary for Eliza Doolittle. Go on, Eliza.

ELIZA: "With blackest moss, the flower pots were thickly crusted, one and all . . ."

HIGGINS: I cannot understand a word. Not a word.

ELIZA: [with anger] "With blackest moss, the flower pots . . . !"

PICKERING: I say, Higgins, perhaps the poem is too difficult for the girl. Why don't you try a simpler one, like: "The Owl and the Pussycat"? Oh, yes, that's a charming one.

HIGGINS: [bellowing] Pickering! I cannot hear the girl! [Eliza gasps, then takes the marbles out of her mouth] What's the matter? Why did you stop?

ELIZA: I swallowed one.

HIGGINS: [reassuringly] Oh, don't worry. I have plenty more. Open your mouth.

PICKERING: [on the phone to Scotland Yard] Yes, this is her residence. . . . Between three and four in the morning. . . . No . . . No . . . No . . . No relation at all. Let's just say a good friend. [a troubled look clouds his face] Now, see here, my good man, I'm not at all pleased with the tenor of that question. What the girl does here is our affair. Your affair is to get her back so she can continue doing it!

Everything came together for Lerner in *My Fair Lady*, from his love of British comedy of manners to his delight in acerbic characters caught up in the battle of the sexes to his own highly romantic sensibility. These had been glimpsed in his earlier librettos, but this time they all flourished in one magnificent package.

Two years later, Lerner and Loewe enjoyed a similar triumph in Hollywood with their film musical *Gigi*, a Gallic version of some of the ideas in *My Fair Lady*, including an irascible hero who takes a young innocent under his charge and ends up falling in love with her. But the movie was far from a rehash of their Shavian musical and deserves praise for its own merits. When the team returned to Broadway with many of the same *My Fair Lady* talents (including star Julie Andrews and director Moss Hart) for *Camelot* (1960), anticipation was high. Few musicals could be a satisfying follow-up to *My Fair Lady*, and this one was so fraught with problems that it is a miracle it ended up in the black. T. H. White's novel *The Once and Future King* (1958) is a long, elaborate Arthurian fantasy that mixes folklore, philosophy, legend, and romance together in an epic form. It is easy to see why it appealed to Lerner. The stories, characters, and ideas in the book are oversized and theatrical. The magic of *Brigadoon* is there as well as plenty of adventure and one of the world's great love stories. White's chronicle could easily provide fodder for several musicals. (In 1963, the Disney studios made a full-length animated movie of the book's first section called *The Sword in the Stone*.)

Lerner decided to concentrate on the love triangle among Arthur (Richard Burton), Guenevere (Andrews), and Sir Lancelot (Robert Goulet) and retained the noble ideas of the Knights of the Round Table and the utopian dream of Camelot. He kept Merlin and Morgan Le Fey for their magical aspects, but neither was woven very well into the increasingly realistic libretto. Much of the first act ended up light and almost fairy tale–like; the second act, dealing with adultery and treachery, was heavy and humorless. Despite continual cutting before and during rehearsals, the show was still way too long, even after the opening scenes and songs were rearranged or cut. *Camelot* also suffered a notorious preopening history with Hart suffering a heart attack (that killed him a year later) and both Lerner and Loewe being carted off to hospitals at different times. What finally opened in New York was a huge, beautiful, lopsided musical with something for everyone but not enough to totally please most critics and audiences. The initial disappointment was overcome by word of mouth, including President John F. Kennedy endorsing it as his favorite musical. After the young president's death in 1963, *Camelot* took on a mythic quality of its own as a symbol for the Kennedy years and enjoyed more popularity with the passing years. Today the musical is regularly revived and highly regarded, though it still is long and difficult when not staged with efficiency and prudent pruning.

Since the Lerner and Loewe score is splendid throughout, much of the problem with *Camelot* has been blamed on Lerner's libretto. Yet looking at it carefully and comparing it to its giant source material, one cannot but admire what Lerner tried to do. Frankly, the task was beyond him; it was probably beyond the talents of any of Broadway's writers. The libretto has some of Lerner's finest moments, but it also suffers from some weak sections that do not do him justice. Arthur is a complex and stirring character, but both Guenevere and Lancelot often come across as types. Most of the supporting roles, such as Pellimore, Mordred, and Merlin, are too cartoonish for the rest of the piece. Some scenes are charming and move along nicely, such as the initial meeting of Arthur and Guenevere, while others are drawn out and tedious, such as those featuring the knights Lionel, Dinadan, and Sagramore. The joust scene, a medieval sort of Ascot, is curiously unexciting, and aside from the lovely songs, most of the love scenes between Guenevere and Lancelot are rather inert. Where Lerner seems to be at his best is when he departs from White's novel and creates his own dramatic moments, such as Arthur's soliloquy at the end of the first act or the show's final scene between Arthur and the youth Tom of Warwick. Perhaps *Camelot* remains popular because its riches outweigh its drawbacks.

After the difficult birth of *Camelot*, Frederick Loewe retired from the theatre. His only compositions in the future would be a few new songs for the Broadway version of *Gigi* in 1973 and a handful of numbers for the film *The Little Prince* (1974). Lerner, on the other hand, was far from ready to retire and worked with various composers on seven more musicals before his death in 1986. He wrote the librettos and lyrics for all of them. On occasion he also produced and even directed the productions. Soon a Lerner show didn't seem like a collaboration at all, always a dangerous sign.

The best of the post-Loewe musicals was *On a Clear Day You Can See Forever* (1965), which began as a collaboration with Richard Rodgers. The announcement of Broadway's greatest living composer teaming with the highly regarded Lerner sounded too good to be true. In essence, it was. Neither man liked the other, and after a few months the venture was called off. Lerner continued the project with Burton Lane providing the music, and the resulting show boasted a superior score but a problematic book. It was Lerner's first original libretto since *Paint Your Wagon* fifteen years earlier and his first contemporary script since *The Day before Spring* ten years before that. The librettist's fascination with extrasensory perception fueled the story: kookie New Yorker Daisy Gamble (Barbara Harris) is blessed and cursed with the powers of ESP. Not only does she know when the phone is about to ring but she talks to flowers and encourages them (successfully) to grow. Daisy is also a heavy smoker and wishes to kick the habit in order to impress her fiancé's prospective boss. So she asks the psychiatric lecturer Dr. Mark Bruckner (John Cullum) if he can cure her addiction by hypnosis. Once she is in a trance, the doctor discovers that Daisy is a reincarnation of an elegant eighteenth-century London lady called Melinda Wells, who lived a scandalous life in high society, took up with a raffish painter, abandoned him when he was unfaithful, then ran off and drowned while on a ship traveling to America. Melinda is as alluring and sophisticated as Daisy is scatterbrained and funny, and Dr. Bruckner soon finds himself keeping company with the latter in order to spend time with the former. Once the doctor's findings are leaked out, Daisy is furious with him, and he loses his job. But the twosome are drawn together when her ESP warns him about boarding a plane that is going to crash. Much of *On a Clear Day* is bright and playful, but few of the characters are very interesting except for Daisy/Melinda, and the plotting is often more complicated than necessary. But again there is much to enjoy in both the libretto and the score. The musical received mixed notices and managed a run of 280 performances, not enough to show a profit.

Running a bit longer but still losing money was *Coco* (1969), a musical bio about French fashion designer Gabrielle "Coco" Chanel that brought Katharine Hepburn to the musical stage for the first and only time. Lerner's libretto centered on the designer's return to prominence after World War II, with flashbacks to earlier times and past successes. It was far from a gripping plot, and its climax (the French rebuke Coco's comeback, but American buyers from Orbach's, Sach's Fifth Avenue, and Bloomingdale's sign on the dotted line) was limp. The nonsinging Hepburn held together the overproduced show, in which the subplots were boring and even the costumes (by Cecil Beaton) were disappointing. No hits came from the score by Lerner and composer André Previn, though much of it was quite good, especially Lerner's lyrics. Returning to adaptation again, Lerner tried to musicalize Vladimir Nabokov's notorious 1955 novel *Lolita* into a dark tuner called *Lolita, My Love* (1971). John Barry wrote the music for Lerner's lyrics, but the venture was going so poorly that it closed in Philadelphia. Lerner even had trouble adapting his own film *Gigi* into a Broadway musical in 1973. The wonderful movie score was augmented by some inferior new numbers by the original songwriters, and a top-notch cast (Alfred Drake, Maria Karnilova, Daniel Massey, Agnes Moorehead, and Karin Wolfe as the title heroine) was selected to re-create the memorable film personages. But Lerner's libretto failed to rethink the screenplay in terms of the stage, and what was pure gold on the screen became molten lead on Broadway. The production limped along for 103 performances and lost a bundle. Ironically, because of a quirk in the American Theatre Wing's voting rules, *Gigi* won a Tony Award for Best Score.

The biggest disaster of Lerner's career (he later referred to it as "the *Titanic*") was *1600 Pennsylvania Avenue* (1976), an expensive and ambitious musical about the history of the American presidency from George Washington to Theodore Roosevelt. Composer Leonard Bernstein, returning to Broadway for the first time in twenty years, was Lerner's collaborator, and the mammoth score (twice the number of songs as the ordinary Broadway musical) they came up with was filled with laudable songs (many still being discovered today). But Lerner's libretto was a shambles as it flew through the decades, Ken Howard playing all the presidents, Patricia Routledge portraying all the first ladies, and Gilbert Price as the African American servant,

Lud, who does not seem to age any faster than Mr. and Mrs. Cooper did in *Love Life*. Slavery and other issues dotted the endless book in rehearsals, but by the time *1600 Pennsylvania Avenue* was trimmed and revised, it ended up being about nothing more than "A Musical about the Problems of House-keeping," as its subtitle foolishly proclaimed. The show was gone in a week, and the score still cries out to be recorded in full.

More conventional and mildly more entertaining was *Carmelina* (1979), which Lerner co-wrote with Joseph Stein, the first and only time he used a libretto collaborator since *What's Up?* Although Lerner would not acknowledge it, the premise for the musical came from a 1968 film, *Buona Sera, Mrs. Campbell*, in which Carmelina Campbell (Gina Lollobrigida) claimed to be an Italian war widow whose daughter was fathered by a brave but deceased American GI. In truth, the child was illegitimate, and she has been receiving money from three distant Americans, each thinking the off-spring is his. When the three former GIs return to the Italian village for a seventeen-year reunion, the so-called widow's secret is out. The *Carmelina* libretto retains this plot, adding an elderly admirer for the heroine, and turns the film farce into more serious romantic comedy. (Lerner claimed that he got the idea for the musical from a newspaper clipping, not the 1968 screenplay; though both film and musical have details that are remarkably similar.) Georgia Brown gave a valiant performance as the deceiving widow, and Cesare Siepi was in fine voice as her autumnal suitor, but critics complained of the show's lifeless and old-fashioned quality. The score, with music by Burton Lane, was much better than the libretto; at times it was first rate, as in the songs "Someone in April," "Why Him?" and "One More Walk around the Garden." Again, some of Lerner's lyrics are masterful. But it wasn't enough, and *Carmelina* closed in two weeks.

That was about two weeks more than Lerner's final offering ran; *Dance a Little Closer* (1983) closed on opening night. Charles Strouse was the composer on hand, and he and Lerner came up with a delightful score, some of the songs finding admiration years later. The source material was promising: Robert Sherwood's dark comedy *Idiot's Delight* (1936) about patrons at a mountain resort in the Austrian Alps with the world on the brink of war. Lerner unwisely updated the tale, setting it on the eve of World War III and trying to make the piece more timely by adding a Henry Kissinger–like diplomat, references to NATO and the Cold War, and a gay couple. Despite its title, there was very little dancing. There was also too little charm, comedy, or drama. What might have been a thought-provoking yet entertaining musical became a vanity production. (Lerner not only wrote the libretto and lyrics but also produced and directed the show and cast his wife, Liz Robertson, in the leading role.) Such a sad end to such an illustrious career.

At the time of his death, Lerner was working on a musicalization of the film classic *My Man Godfrey* (1936). Again it sounded promising (the few completed lyrics are quite expert), but given Lerner's pattern over the past decade or so, it is unlikely that it would have amounted to much. Not long before he died, Lerner was asked by Andrew Lloyd Webber to write the lyrics for his planned musical of *The Phantom of the Opera* (1986). Since the operetta-like piece was to be sung through, it meant Lerner would in essence be the librettist as well. Given the strong story line of the original novel, Lerner might have pulled off a hit at the end of his career. (In any case, his lyrics would have been a vast improvement over those finally used.) But Lerner was so ill that he graciously turned Webber down.

Alan Jay Lerner always insisted he was a playwright rather than a librettist. Ironically, his lyrics (especially in his later shows) are often more satisfyingly dramatically than his librettos. He was a born dramatist who knew how to create vivid scenes and memorable characters. His ear for dialogue, whether it be rural Scottish or urban London or crusty frontier talk, was quite accomplished. But Lerner's structure and plotting were the downfalls of his later musicals. Interesting characters singing commendable lyrics is not enough for a book musical after World War II; how the story unfolds is the key to making the people and the songs come alive. Yet when Lerner's musicals came alive, they shone like few others. His uncanny ability to mix lush romanticism with intelligent talk cannot be underestimated. Lerner was an incurable romantic (anyone who gets married eight times is a thorough romantic), yet he rarely wallowed in sentiment in either his lyrics or his librettos. He found ways to be ardent and passionate without turning giddy or brainless. This quality can be found in few musical writers before him or since. Lerner may be considered the last of the great romantic Broadway writers, but he is also part of the new postwar movement toward more literate librettos. When his vision was clear and his story unclouded, one felt as though you could indeed see forever.

CHAPTER TWELVE
FLYING HIGH, TAKING A CHANCE: B. G. DE SYLVA AND OTHERS IN THE 1930s AND 1940s

The 1930s was a golden age for the musical revue. Of the 175 shows to open on Broadway that decade, sixty-three of them were revues. Most of these were not lavish *Follies*-like extravaganzas as in previous decades. Neither were they the retrospective shows filled with old favorites that pass as Broadway revues today. The Depression-era revue was a sharp, satirical, timely, and original program of songs, dances, and sketches. These sketches were not librettos, but some of the finest librettists of the era often wrote them. George S. Kaufman, Morrie Ryskind, Moss Hart, E. Y. Harburg, and other writers already discussed provided sketches as well as librettos for Broadway. Two other names, Howard Dietz and B. G. De Sylva, deserve some attention also.

With his composer-partner Arthur Schwartz, Dietz wrote some of the finest revue scores in the history of the genre. Such fondly remembered shows as *The Little Show* (1929), *Three's a Crowd* (1930), *The Band Wagon* (1931), and *Flying Colors* (1932) defined the Broadway revue, and Dietz wrote lyrics and sketches for all of them. Yet Dietz and Schwartz never found success together whenever they turned to book musicals. The team who wrote some of Broadway's finest scores would see their work revived only in the movies and on Tin Pan Alley. Howard Dietz (1896–1983) was born in New York City and educated at Columbia, where his classmates included Oscar Hammerstein and Lorenz Hart. Dietz wrote for the college shows and saw his light verse published in recognized newspaper columns. About the time he started writing lyrics for Broadway, he began his parallel career as a publicist. Dietz would rise to an executive position at MGM and stayed there for many years, all the time contributing lyrics and sketches for Broadway.

Dietz and Schwartz's first attempt at a book musical was *Revenge with Music* (1934), an operetta based on an antique Spanish tale by Pedro de Alarcon titled *El Sombrero de Tres Picos (The Three-Cornered Hat)*. The three

131

corners consisted of a lusty provincial governor, Don Emilio (Charles Winninger); the lovely Maria (Libby Holman), whom he hopes to bed on her wedding night; and Maria's fiancé Carlos (Georges Metaxa), who takes his revenge by wooing the governor's wife. Dietz's libretto was efficient, stageworthy, and even charming at times. And the score produced two standards, "If There Is Someone Lovelier Than You" and "You and the Night and the Music." But the operetta format was problematic in the Depression years, and *Revenge with Music* managed an unprofitable run of only 158 performances. Even less successful was the team's *Between the Devil* (1937). Dietz's libretto was again a three-cornered affair and was also based on an old farce plot. When his wife is lost at sea and presumed dead, Englishman Peter Anthony (Jack Buchanan) disguises himself as a Frenchman and marries a French girl. But, of course, the first wife survives and arrives on the scene for predictable plot complications and lots of jokes about bigamy:

NATALIE: You admit you're a bigamist. Why, you might even have three wives!
PETER: Oh, no! That would be trigonometry!

The only unfamiliar aspect of Dietz's libretto was the ending: unable to satisfactorily resolve the triangle, the characters told the audience that it was up to them to provide their own conclusion. Again the score had some timeless gems ("By Myself," "I See Your Face before Me," and "Triplets"), but the book format once again eluded Dietz and Schwartz. (In 1961, the team came up with a superior character-book score for *The Gay Life*, but the problematic libretto was by Fay and Michael Kanin, and it failed to run.) Schwartz would find some success writing musicals with Dorothy Fields, and Dietz would provide expert lyrics with other composers, but no other librettos by Dietz would reach Broadway. Although he was one of the era's sharpest writers, Dietz's playwriting skills were limited to sketches now long forgotten.

B. G. De Sylva (1895–1950) was born George Gard De Sylva in New York City, but he was raised in California as "Buddy," as he was called the rest of his life. De Sylva's father was in vaudeville but didn't want his son to have to go into show business, so Buddy was educated at the University of Southern California. But while at college, De Sylva started writing lyrics and sketches. After graduation he moved to Manhattan, where he provided lyrics for Al Jolson and collaborated with such prominent composers as George Gershwin and Jerome Kern. But resounding fame came to De Sylva when he was teamed up with lyricist Lew Brown and composer Ray Henderson and the trio wrote a series of revues and book musicals in the 1920s and 1930s. It was a true team, each of the triumvirate contributing to both story and songs, but De Sylva was the principal librettist for the shows. After writing sketches for some De Sylva–Brown–Henderson revues, most memorably *George White's Scandals of 1926,* De Sylva scripted his first hit book musical, *Good News!* (1927), one of the few shows from the 1920s that is still revived today.

Good News! wasn't the first (or last) of daffy musical comedies set on a college campus, but it remains the best of the genre. De Sylva collaborated with Laurence Schwab on the libretto, a predictably enjoyable yarn about footballer Tom Marlowe (John Price Jones), who is the hero of Tait College but will soon be kicked out if his grades don't improve. Co-ed Connie Lane (Mary Lawlor) takes on the task of tutoring him, and the two fall into the quintessential collegiate romance, despite the fact that Tom is engaged to a snooty society gal. Most of the supporting characters are in the farcical vein, especially the clownish Bobby (Gus Shy) and the fast-and-loose flapper Flo (Zelma O'Neal), who leads the cast in "The Varsity Drag." Other hits from the score include "The Best Things in Life Are Free" and "Lucky in Love," but it is the libretto's lighthearted nonsense that keeps *Good News!* on the stage today. Nearly as popular in its day (though seldom revived) was De Sylva–Brown–Henderson's *Hold Everything!* (1928), in which De Sylva (with co-author John McGowan) turned from college football to pro boxing. Welterweight "Sonny Jim" Brooks (Jack Whiting) is caught between sweetheart Sue (Ona Munson) and wealthy dame Norine Lloyd (Betty Compton). He also has to deal with a boxing ring contender and some behind-the-scenes bribery and corruption. As in *Good News!* the laughs came from a duet of sidekicks: inebriated cook Nosy Barlett and punch-drunk boxer Gink Schiner, played by the beloved clowns Victor Moore and Bert Lahr. Dietz's libretto is far from inspired, but it allowed for plenty of song and dance ("You're the Cream in My Coffee" was the standout number) and hilarious situations for its comic stars.

Three months later, De Sylva was represented on Broadway with yet another hit musical about sports: *Follow Thru* (1929) featuring golf and the De Sylva–Brown–Henderson standard "Button Up Your Overcoat." Collaborating with Schwab again, De Sylva penned the silly libretto that was subtitled "A Musical Slice of Country Club Life." Lora Moore (Irene Delroy) and Ruth Van Horn (Madeline Cameron) are in competition for both the Bound Brook Country Club's women's golf championship and the heart of golfer Jerry Downs (Jack Barker). The audience could see from the start that Lora would win both, but the fun came from the reticent son of a chain store mogul, Jack Martin (Jack Haley), who is being pursued by the flighty Angie Howard (Zelma O'Neal). There were the requisite golf jokes along the way

("The trouble with your game is that you stand too close to the ball—after you've hit it!") and a merry score that kept the slight show bouncing for 403 performances. Nearly as successful was *Flying High* (1930), the last De Sylva–Brown–Henderson book musical. The late 1920s saw Charles Lindbergh, Admiral Byrd, Amelia Earhart, and other aviators in the news, so De Sylva (with Brown and McGowan) cobbled together a musical about flying. Broadway legend has it that the cast went into rehearsals with only a score and a rough outline for a libretto; the resulting script is a haphazard mishmash of a show but one that clearly had its selling points. The musical opens unconventionally—not with a chorus number but with wealthy but lonely socialite Eileen Cassidy (Grace Brinkley) singing a lament on her penthouse terrace. Soon mail pilot Tod Addison (Oscar Shaw) parachutes into her life, and the main romantic plot begins. The secondary couple consists of Rusty Kraus (Bert Lahr), Tod's airplane mechanic, and the hefty Pansy Sparks (Kate Smith), who pursues him and stops the show with a red hot rendition of "Red Hot Chicago." Lahr was in top form and became the focal point of the musical with all the best lines. When he must take a urine test as part of a preflight medical examination, Rusty fills the vial with Scotch whiskey:

DOCTOR: Nationality?
RUSTY: Scotch by absorption.

Even the ending of *Flying High* was an old joke, one copied from *Going Up!* (1917): Rusty sets a world's endurance record for air time because he doesn't know how to land a plane.

De Sylva collaborated on one notable libretto after the team of De Sylva, Brown, and Henderson broke up, the backstager *Take a Chance* (1932), with lyrics by De Sylva and music by Richard Whiting, Nacio Herb Brown, and (later) Vincent Youmans. Under the title *Humpty Dumpty*, the show had bombed in Pittsburgh, but Schwab (the producer), Sid Silvers (the star), and De Sylva did some fast play doctoring and brought a hit into Manhattan two months later. The plot centers on two crooked backers, Silvers and Jack Haley, who invest in a Broadway revue satirizing American history that Harvard grad Kenneth Raleigh (Jack Whiting) is producing. Kenneth falls in love with the backers' friend, Toni Ray (June Knight), but later suspects (wrongly) that she is a shyster too when the two crooks are discovered. Only a few of the musical's songs were from the revue being staged, but they were the showstoppers, and Ethel Merman participated in all three: "Eadie Was a Lady," "Rise 'n' Shine," and "You're an Old Smoothie." Like *Flying High*, *Take a Chance* was an agreeable mess and managed to please audiences in the darkest days of the Depression. Perhaps De Sylva never developed much beyond a revue sketch writer, but he did contribute to some of Broadway's most farcical librettos just before and after the Crash.

Musical comedy took on a slightly more satirical edge with the two musicals scripted by the husband-and-wife team of Sam (1899–1971) and Bella (1899–1990) Spewack. Both writers were born in Europe (he in Russia, she in Bucharest), emigrated to America in their youth, and worked as journalists before turning to playwriting. They penned such popular comedies as *Boy Meets Girl* (1935) and *My Three Angels* (1953), but also came up with two superb librettos for Cole Porter: *Leave It to Me!* (1938) and *Kiss Me, Kate* (1948). The former is little known today but in its day was a topical and wily piece of musical theatre. Based on the Spewacks' 1932 comedy *Clear All Wires*, the libretto drew on the couple's experience as foreign correspondents in Russia. Mrs. Alonzo P. Goodhue (Sophie Tucker) has contributed so much money to FDR's reelection campaign that the president appoints her meek, befuddled husband "Stinky" (Victor Moore) as the U.S. ambassador to Russia. The publishing tycoon J. H. Brody, who wanted the ambassadorial post for himself, sends the brash journalist Buckley Joyce Thomas (William Gaxton) to Moscow to try to sabotage Goodhue's work. But the unhappy Goodhue, who just wants to go back to America, is already doing everything he can to get sacked, from kicking the Nazi ambassador to accidentally shooting a counterrevolutionary in Red Square. Mrs. Goodhue has brought a chorus line of girls to add culture to the backward country, and Brody's girlfriend, Dolly Winslow (Mary Martin), also shows up and demonstrates, in a famous striptease, that "My Heart Belongs to Daddy." While Buckley is falling for the alluring Colette (Tamara), Goodhue starts to enjoy his job and proposes a plan for international peace. Ironically, Goodhue's previous blunders were looked on as good foreign policy, but his peace plan upsets all the world's leaders, and he is recalled to Washington.

While *Leave It to Me!* is far from the pointed satire of Kaufman and others in the 1930s, there is a likable screwball quality to it that is still enjoyable. Goodhue, trying to talk to his Russian chauffeur, requests that he take him to the "Americansky Embassky." The comedy also has plenty of cockeyed logic to it:

> GOODHUE: I just ran into Brody . . . well, we had a chat . . . and he said to me, "How much do you spend a week on newspapers?" And I said, "Oh, about fifty cents." And he said, "Why not buy your own newspaper and save money?" That kind of got me.
> BUCKLEY: You bought the World-Tribune?

The political satire in *Leave It to Me!* was not very daring, but with the buildup of arms in Europe, even innocent frivolity about international affairs was tricky. The first act closed with Josef Stalin leading a big dance number. By the time the musical went on tour, Stalin had made his pact with Hitler, and America's feelings shifted against Russia. The Stalin number was cut, and disclaimers were put in the program stating that the show had nothing to do with current events. Talk about weak-willed satire!

A decade later, the Spewacks came up with a better libretto. In fact, it remains one of the finest of all Broadway librettos. *Kiss Me, Kate* is so familiar to audiences from revivals and Porter's score is so much a part of Broadway legend that one sometimes forgets what an accomplished libretto the musical boasts. A musical adaptation of Shakespeare's *The Taming of the Shrew* might have turned into a belabored costume show or perhaps succeeded in using the Bard merely as an outline, as in *The Boys from Syracuse.* But *Kiss Me, Kate* uses the Shakespeare original as a springboard for a totally new show. There was nothing unique about backstage musicals, but the Spewacks' libretto was unusual in that it told both the onstage and the backstage stories equally well. Audiences feel as though they have observed the entire *Shrew* musical while in fact only key scenes are shown. The parallels between the Elizabethan couples and the modern lovers are not forced, and the goings-on behind the scenes are not restricted by the limitations of Shakespeare's plot. Porter came up with his greatest score because, for once, he had a superior libretto to write songs for. And, while the Spewack dialogue may not sparkle like a Porter lyric, it comes pretty darn close, particularly in the mouths of the two gangsters:

> FIRST MAN: Miss Vanessi, you have been my ideal for years. I married my wife because in a certain light, when it's kinda dark, she might pass for your sister. . . . Your glorious voice has been an inspiration to me in my work.
> SECOND MAN: What a trouper!
> FIRST MAN: What a personality!
> SECOND MAN: Is it true, Miss Vanessi, that you're contemplating quitting this high-type entertainment?

As intricately plotted as the book is, the musical seems breezy and effortless. It can be revived with no apologies. It also has that quality that few Broadway musicals possess: it does not seem to be a product of its time. The backstage story may look and sometimes sound like the late 1940s, but there is something timeless about the world of theatre it creates. *Kiss Me, Kate* takes the slaphappy fun of the pre-*Oklahoma!* musical comedies and puts it into the form of the Rodgers and Hammerstein musical play. What a joyous combination it turned out to be! If the Spewacks represented the writers who helped audiences laugh through the Depression, the more serious side of the coin can be seen in the works of Marc Blitzstein, Paul Green, and Maxwell Anderson. All three writers took on weighty issues in their musical librettos and saw Broadway as a platform for political and social ideas rather than a refuge from an unhappy world. Marc Blitzstein (1905–1964) was born in Philadelphia and received formal training in music in New York and Berlin. His dream was to write modern, relevant operas, and though most of his works were first performed on legit stages, they all can be described as operas of some kind. The circumstances surrounding his controversial "Play in Music, *The Cradle Will Rock* (1938), is more remembered than the show itself. Because of its inflammatory nature and the recent cuts in their budget, the Federal Theatre Project canceled the production at the last minute and even put an injunction on the actors and musicians that they were not allowed to perform it on stage. But director Orson Welles, producer John Houseman, and composer-lyricist-librettist Blitzstein led the audience to an empty theatre where the actors delivered their lines from the house and Blitzstein played the score by himself on a rehearsal piano. Never less than a propaganda piece, *The Cradle Will Rock* mesmerized its first-night audience, and the musical was eventually presented for 108 performances.

That historic first performance was one of the American theatre's most electric nights. But later revivals of *The Cradle Will Rock* have been of only passing interest. The truth of the matter is, Blitzstein's piece was a bold but unexceptional curiosity. Inspired by the recent mobilization of various trade unions under the leadership of John L. Lewis, the libretto celebrated the power of the common man over a capitalistic society. Mr. Mister (Will Geer) and his family run Steeltown with an iron fist and with pockets full of corruption. Union organizer Larry Foreman (Howard da Silva) leads the workers in revolt, not just against the factory but in defiance of every level of society that hopes to control the populace. A prostitute plies her trade with unsentimental frankness; but Blitzstein reveals other levels of the "sellout" in the press, the church, education, medicine, and even the arts. The characters are all broad stereotypes with expressionistic names like President Prexy, Reverend Salvation, Dr. Specialist, and Editor Daily. There is some eloquence in some of Blitzstein's driving lyrics but little in the script itself. *The Cradle Will Rock* made no efforts to be subtle; it also made few concessions to being entertaining. But it was the most politically charged piece of theatre of its era and the work of a dedicated and gifted artist.

Blitzstein's subsequent works were more polished and satisfying, though rarely popular. He adapted Lillian Hellman's 1939 drama *The Little Foxes* into the quasi-opera *Regina* (1949), again providing music, lyrics, and libretto himself. It is a sensible and tame adaptation of the play that comes truly alive only in some of the vibrant songs. Blitzstein musicalized whole scenes, something still rather rare on the Broadway stage at the time, and at least with greedy, determined Regina Giddens (Jane Pickens) he created a vivid musical theatre character who breathed both words and music. But *Regina* was too much like opera for the average theatregoer and not grand enough for opera lovers. It received mixed notices and closed after fifty-six performances. Just as accomplished but also a box office failure was *Juno* (1959), in which Joseph Stein wrote the libretto (see chapter 16). Blitzstein's other music-theatre pieces either closed on the road or were given limited runs outside New York. Ironically, his most lasting work was not his own creation but his expert adaptation of Bertolt Brecht's libretto and lyrics for *The Threepenny Opera* (1954). A failure when first presented on Broadway in 1933, the Kurt Weill–composed piece from Germany was given a loose but effective new version by Blitzstein, who was very close to the piece musically and philosophically. Some of Brecht's harshness was toned down into a more sly kind of theatricality, and lyrically some of the songs became more romanticized in the adaptation. There have been many translations since Blitzstein's, most claiming to be more faithful to the German original, but the 1954 version still strikes me as the most exciting.

Paul Eliot Green (1894–1981) was born and educated in North Carolina and wrote many plays based on Southern folk tales and the history of the region, including his Pulitzer winner, *In Abraham's Bosom* (1926), and the long-running outdoor drama, *The Lost Colony* (1937). He wrote only one Broadway libretto, but *Johnny Johnson* (1936) is a one-of-a-kind musical and deserves looking at. A statue to peace by sculptor Johnny Johnson (Russell Collins) is being dedicated in his hometown in 1917, and all the citizens agree that the situation is Europe is wrong until news arrives that President Wilson has led America into a war "to end all wars." Pacifist Johnny is not convinced, but through the prodding of his sweetheart Minny Belle and her widowed mother, he enlists and is soon in the trenches in France. There he preaches peace to his fellow soldiers and even his commanding officers. In one bizarre scene, he uses laughing gas on the generals, and they happily agree with his peace plans until the gas wears off and Johnny is arrested. Sent back to the States, Johnny is confined to a psychiatric sanitarium because of his "peace monomania," and there he is put to work making toys. Years later he is released and makes his living as a street peddler who sells toys. One day he spots Minny, now married to a wealthy industrialist, and her young son who wants to buy a toy; but Johnny doesn't sell toy soldiers, so mother and son walk away, and Johnny is left singing his song of peace. Where *The Cradle Will Rock* is harsh and obvious *Johnny Johnson* is lyrical and dreamy. It is an allegory like the Blitzstein musical, but it uses expressionism in a fanciful manner. At one point the Statue of Liberty sings to Johnny how she is weary of men using her as inspiration for their own selfish plans, and later German cannons issue the sounds of a lullaby to the sleeping soldiers on both sides of the trenches. Green's libretto is as poetic as Weill's haunting music, and both are disturbing in a way that Blitzstein's shouting could never be. *Johnny Johnson* was Weill's first score for Broadway; he would go on to collaborate with other major writers, but there is something indelible about this first work with Green. While it ran only sixty-eight performances, the musical has not disappeared. In fact, it was later popular in eastern European countries.

Weill's other famous collaborator was Maxwell Anderson (1888–1959), one of Broadway's most popular playwrights from the 1920s through the 1940s. Anderson was born in Atlantic, Pennsylvania, and educated at the University of South Dakota and Stanford University. After working as a teacher and a newspaperman, he turned to playwriting and had his first hit with *What Price Glory?* (1924), a brutally realistic drama about World War I that he wrote with Laurence Stallings. Dozens of dramas followed, many of them written in verse and several exploring difficult issues (the Sacco and Vanzetti case) and complex historical figures (Elizabeth I, Joan of Arc, and others). He scripted only two Broadway librettos, and both are unique and admirable.

Knickerbocker Holiday (1938), with music by Weill, was a musical comedy set in the early days of New Amsterdam. But Anderson's libretto and lyrics are far from escapist. Both are filled with bittersweet commentary on American values and, less subtly, on the current state of affairs in the United States and Europe. While Washington Irving (Ray Middleton) is writing his history of New York, he is transported back to seventeenth-century New Amsterdam, where the new governor, Pieter Stuyvesant (Walter Huston), is overreaching his powers and taking away freedoms from the Dutch citizens. The radical youth Brom Broeck (Richard Kollmar) is thrown into jail because of his call for anarchy (and because he wishes to marry above his station and to a girl that the governor fancies himself). Brom is about to be hanged, but a sudden Indian attack turns him into a hero. Irving advises Stuyvesant to think of how history will re-member him, and the governor releases Brom and lets him get the girl. The parallels to FDR's current administration were obvious; one of the old Dutch council members was even named Roosevelt and kept insisting, "I vould vant to know who done something!" Anderson's script is filled with inflammatory speeches and disturbing ideas about the role of total power in a democracy. Stuyvesant states that "a government is always a group of men organized to sell protection to the inhabitants of a limited area at a monopolistic price." But Brom, who calls himself the "First American," ar-gues that the perfect government is "the delicate balance between personal liberty and the minimum of authority which is necessary for the free growth of ideas in a tolerant society." Some saw *Knickerbocker Holiday* as an attack on FDR's New Deal, while others found it a thought-provoking comedy that raised questions about totalitarianism. Either way, the show was neither a critical nor a commercial success. But it did boast a winning performance by Huston as a lovable dictator, and his rendition of "Sep-tember Song" is one of Broadway's fondest memories. (Anderson wrote the lyrics for the score, and they are quite accomplished.)

His libretto skills were better honed in *Lost in the Stars* (1949), a deeply moving music drama that goes far beyond political argument. Working again with composer Weill, Anderson adapted Alan Paton's 1948 novel *Cry, the Beloved Country* about South Africa into a theatre piece that had the height-ened power of an opera but managed to use a musical theatre format effec-tively. The story follows the plight of two fathers, the black preacher Stephen Kumalo (Todd Duncan) and the white landowner James Jarvis (Leslie Banks), who live in the same South African village. Both have sons who go off to Johannesburg, where they meet with tragic ends. Stephen's son Absa-lom gets involved with criminals, is caught in a robbery scheme where he ac-cidentally shoots a white man, and is condemned to die. Jarvis's liberal son Arthur tries to help the black residents of the city, but he is the one killed by Absalom in the robbery attempt. The two fathers ought to be bitter enemies, but by the end of the story they are drawn together, both grieving parents rather than members of different races. It is a beautifully written libretto with little preaching or sentimentality and an amazing amount of restraint in the storytelling. Despite its difficult subject matter, *Lost in the Stars* was a critical success and managed to run an impressive (but not profitable) 273 perform-ances. Again Anderson's prose and lyrics are superb, and later revivals have shown the musical to be just as potent as when it was first presented.

It is not possible to leave the 1930s and 1940s without looking briefly at five exceptional musicals by various librettists not yet discussed. Two of

B. G. DE SYLVA AND OTHERS IN THE 1930s AND 1940s

these were also composed by Kurt Weill. Humorist S. J. Perelman and wily poet Ogden Nash collaborated on the script for the musical comedy *One Touch of Venus* (1943), a daffy fantasy about a meek barber who is pursued by a statue of Venus come to life. The show is mostly remembered for Mary Martin's whimsical performance as Venus, but there is delicious comic writing in the musical that must be mentioned. Nash (who also penned the lyrics) and Perelman set their satirical eye not only on mythology but on the modern art world and contemporary American life as well. (When Venus realizes that marriage to the barber means she'll have to live in the suburbs, she wishes to be turned back into a statue.) The dialogue is both breezy and wicked:

VENUS: I've come to stay with you.
RODNEY: You can't do that—it's against the law!
VENUS: What law?
RODNEY: The—the law against men and women rooming together.
VENUS: You mean to say they've got around to regulating that?

One Touch of Venus found an audience for 567 performances, and the song "Speak Low" became a standard. Oddly, neither Perelman nor Nash ever turned to libretto writing again. The other Weill musical, *Street Scene* (1947), was quite different in subject and tone. This musical version of Elmer Rice's 1929 drama of the same name was closer to opera as it explored the disappointments and broken dreams of a group of residents in a Manhattan apartment building. Rice devised the libretto, and Langston Hughes wrote the penetrating lyrics, the result being an engrossing musical drama. It was more a critical than a box office hit, but *Street Scene* would enjoy many revivals over the decades, usually by opera companies.

Similar in subject but more oversized in its emotions and music was *Porgy and Bess* (1935), which Du Bose Heyward adapted from the 1927 play *Porgy* by his wife Dorothy Heyward and himself. The Gershwins' monumental score (Heyward also wrote some of the lyrics) has been justly proclaimed over the years, but too little has been said about the libretto. Although *Porgy and Bess* is generally considered an opera today, its script is indeed Broadway. Some revivals use the extensive recitative so that the libretto is sometimes shortened to song cues, but the power of the story holds the magnificent score together. Each of the characters is a vivid individual; even the villains, Crown and Sportin' Life, are written with distinction. Porgy's innocent optimism and Bess's streetwise weariness are

141

both fully realized. Everyone is familiar with their soaring duets together, but even their dialogue is ripe with honesty and insight:

> BESS: Plenty of de mens ask me [to go to the picnic]. But I don't hear none of de ladies say nuttin'.
> PORGY: Bess, you can put on my lodge sash an' be as good as any woman in dat crowd.
> BESS: Yo' an' me know it take more'n sash.

Like *Street Scene*, *Porgy and Bess* has been revived mostly by opera companies, but its libretto is more theatrical than operatic; it is the score that keeps it in the opera house.

The score by Harold Arlen (music) and Johnny Mercer (lyrics) for *St. Louis Woman* (1946), on the other hand, is pure Broadway, and its infrequent revivals have been in theatres. Arna Bontemps and Countee Cullen collaborated on the libretto, based on Bontemps's novel *God Sends Sunday*. Like *Porgy and Bess*, it also deals with African Americans and a love triangle that ends tragically. Racehorse jockey Little Augie (Harold Nicholas) is on a winning streak and is the talk of St. Louis, so he starts to win the affections of the beauty Della Green (Ruby Hill). But Della is the property of Biglow Brown (Rex Ingram), a jealous bar owner who beats Della when he suspects she is unfaithful. Augie plans to get his revenge against Brown, but the brute's rejected mistress Lila (June Hawkins) shoots the barman before Augie can have it out with him. The experience shatters Augie and his winning streak, so Della leaves him. Unlike the unlucky couple in *Porgy and Bess*, Augie and Della are reunited by the final curtain. The writing is not as lyrical as Heyward's, but it is well plotted and has some vivid characterizations. Today *St. Louis Woman* is remembered mainly for its score, which includes such favorites as "Any Place I Hang My Hat Is Home," "Come Rain or Come Shine," and "I Had Myself a True Love."

Bontemps, Cullen, Heyward, and some others mentioned did not return to the Broadway musical, which is unfortunate. The fact that John O'Hara did not is a downright shame, as his libretto for *Pal Joey* (1940) is one of the finest Broadway ever saw. His source was his own *New Yorker* stories about a heel named Joey, who wrote (in fractured spelling and grammar) of his misadventures in the world of seedy nightclubs. In a series of letters (signed "pal Joey") to his "pal Ted," Joey related his latest brush with the law, dames, money, and show business, his narration often revealing his cynical and even fatalistic view of life. The letters have few recurring characters, so O'Hara had to draw from minor personages to people his libretto.

The many women in Joey's life were represented by the young and naive Linda English (Leila Ernst) and the middle-aged, worldly-wise socialite Vera Simpson (Vivienne Segal). Joey (Gene Kelly), a singer in a tacky Chicago nightclub, woos and wins Linda, then soon discovers the more useful Vera, becoming her kept man and even letting her build a nightclub of his own for him. By the time blackmailers threaten to tell Vera's husband, she is getting tired of the self-serving Joey and sends him on his way. Even the innocent Linda wises up and dumps him, leaving Joey to pursue a new female as the curtain falls. Here was the boy-meets-girl formula turned on its side, with none of the characters particularly likable. (Even the good-hearted Linda acts too stupid to engage the audience's sympathy.) Yet *Pal Joey* is a fascinating musical, an adult show far ahead of its time (this was three years before *Oklahoma!*) and smarter than many theatregoers wanted to see. The dialogue had the sass of a 1930s musical but the sting of a much later kind of comedy of manners. Consider Joey and Vera's first encounter:

> VERA: Are you a Chicagoan? . . . Oh, you're going to be difficult. Secretive.
> JOEY: Sure. If I give it to you all at once you wouldn't come back.
> VERA: You're about the freshest person I think I've ever met. What makes you think I care enough to come back?
> JOEY: Lady, you can level with me. You'll be back.
> VERA: [to one of her gents] Shall we go? I don't like this place.
> JOEY: Wait a minute. I'm liable to get the bounceroo if you walk out like this.
> VERA: You worry about that.

The Rodgers and Hart songs are as sardonic as O'Hara's writing, and the show is still too tough for many; its revivals have been few and far between. But *Pal Joey* remains one of the highlights of the Broadway musical. It goes places few musicals would dare venture until the cynical 1970s.

CHAPTER THIRTEEN
HALLELUJAH, GYPSY!
ARTHUR LAURENTS

There are perhaps two writers named Arthur Laurents. One is a conventional author of well-constructed, sometimes old-fashioned, but sturdy plays, musicals, novels, and screenplays. Then there is Laurents the creator of bold, experimental, even foolhardy ventures in the theatre. Both writers have had their hits and flops, and both have raised eyebrows and surprised audiences on occasion. A third Laurents is a notable director on Broadway, staging both his and others' works. Put them all together, and you have a man of the theatre who provided audiences with thought-provoking projects for over forty years.

Arthur Laurents was born in Brooklyn in 1918, the son of an attorney and a teacher. He was educated at Cornell University and, after graduation in 1937, began his writing career. He was first represented on Broadway with the drama *Home of the Brave* (1945), a powerful look at anti-Semitism during World War II. The play received mixed reviews and failed to make money, but Laurents was picked up by Hollywood to write the screenplays for some unusual and hard-hitting films. He tackled such ambitious subjects as Leopold and Loeb–like murderers in *Rope* (1948), state mental institutions in *The Snake Pit* (1948), and prostitution in *Anna Lucasta* (1949). Back on Broadway, Laurents had his greatest nonmusical success with the romance *The Time of the Cuckoo* (1952), but he continued to write for the screen as well. His most memorable films to follow were *Anastasia* (1956), *The Way We Were* (1973), based on his own novel, and *The Turning Point* (1977). Among his other nonmusical plays were *A Clearing in the Woods* (1957) and *Invitation to a March* (1960).

Laurents's first libretto assignment came from choreographer Jerome Robbins, who had the idea of resetting *Romeo and Juliet* in contemporary New York City, the two lovers kept apart by families of differing religions. Robbins and composer Leonard Bernstein began working on the project in

1949 when it was called *East Side Story* and dealt with a Jewish–Catholic rivalry in Manhattan. The subject had been previously handled in the long-running comedy *Abie's Irish Rose* (1922), but Robbins and Bernstein had a very different, very serious musical in mind that would involve extended dance sequences and a gritty plot that remained faithful to the tragic nature of the original Shakespeare play. But *East Side Story* was delayed because of both Robbins's and Bernstein's demanding schedules. By the time they got back to it in the mid-1950s, they soured on the Jewish–Catholic idea but saw a more potent equivalent to Shakespeare's Montagues and Capulets in the rival street gangs springing up on Manhattan's West Side, particularly between young Puerto Rican immigrants and the "native" youths in the city's dilapidated neighborhoods. It was at this point that Laurents was brought into the project as the author who would transpose a lyrical Renaissance tragedy into a contemporary, streetwise musical. It was a task that could make or break a librettist's career.

How the music, lyrics, and choreography of *West Side Story* (1957) so beautifully handled this transposition is well known and well documented. But none of those wonderful aspects could have made *West Side Story* work without Laurents's libretto. It is far from a perfect piece of writing, and some of it has dated poorly over the decades, but Laurents possessed the courageous audacity to write a libretto that was not afraid to go where musicals rarely went before. Bernstein and lyricist Stephen Sondheim devised Latin and jazz sounds and phrases to tell the story, and Robbins used dance to create moods not yet seen on a Broadway stage; but Laurents had to write a script that bridged the gritty realism with a musical mentality and make it all palatable for a 1950s audience. We have little trouble accepting the conceits of *West Side Story* today, but how disturbing most of those ideas were in a year that saw the successful musicals *The Ziegfeld Follies, Jamaica,* and *The Music Man.* Characters had died in musicals before, but when had a Broadway show ended its first act with two dead bodies lying in an alley and the roaring of police sirens providing the only musical finale? Laurents dropped Shakespeare's double suicide, which would have seem far fetched in a modern context, and rewrote the end of the story with the hero murdered and the heroine having to live with her grief. It is a melodramatic ending rather than a classically tragic one, but it is a more effective conclusion for the musical stage. Finding contemporary parallels for the Nurse and Friar Laurence presented difficulties. The lusty Puerto Rican Anita (Chita Rivera) and weak-willed candy store owner Doc (Art Smith) may not figure into the plot as fully as their Elizabethan counterparts, but both are fully realized characters who act as confidants to the hero and heroine.

Riff (Mickey Calin), the leader of the Jets, is not as fully developed a character as the brazen, over-the-top Mercutio is, but he too is well written and is an interesting compromise between the reluctant Tony (Larry Kert) and the other hyperactive gang members. For the most part, the characters in *West Side Story* manage to spring to life without competing with the Shakespeare originals.

Just as the harsh, discordant tones in Bernstein's music and the nightmarish aspects of Robbins's choreography reached for a terse and unpretty kind of storytelling, Laurents's dialogue is often raw and unpoetical. The adult characters have the grittiest lines:

> SCHRANK: Clear out, Spics. Sure; it's a free country and I ain't got the right. But it's a country with laws: and I can find the right. I got the badge, you got the skin. It's tough all over. Beat it!

The gang members speak in a staccato, rap-like language that seems so contrived today but still manages to turn street talk into rhythmic music:

> RIFF: I say I want the Jets to be Number One, to sail, to hold the sky!
> DIESEL: Then rev us off. [a punching gesture] Voom-va voom!
> ACTION: Chung! Chung!
> A-RAB: Cracko, jacko!
> SNOW BOY: Riga diga dum!
> BABY JOHN: Pam pam!
> RIFF: O.K., buddy boys, we rumble!

Only the lovers, Tony and Maria (Carol Lawrence), are allowed to become flighty in their dialogue. Competing with Shakespeare's verse is a futile exercise, but Laurents comes up with his own pattern that allows the lovers to kid themselves at times:

> MARIA: You cannot come by. My mama . . .
> TONY: Then I will take you to my house—
> MARIA: Your mama . . .
> TONY: She will come running from the kitchen to welcome you. She lives in the kitchen.
> MARIA: Dressed so elegant?
> TONY: I told her you were coming. She will look at your face and try not to smile. And she will say: Skinny—but pretty.
> MARIA: She is plump, no doubt.
> TONY: Fat!

In revival, *West Side Story* has its difficult patches in the libretto. There are a few too many "daddy-o"s and "womb-to-tomb"s for today's audiences, and Maria's final speech ("We all killed him; and my brother and Riff. I too. I can kill now because *I* hate now!") is a very difficult one to deliver effectively without moving into melodramatics. But Laurents's libretto is still a wonder. One has only to look at all the unsuccessful attempts to turn a serious classic into a musical play to realize the many accomplishments of Laurents's script.

Robbins and Sondheim worked with Laurents again on *Gypsy* (1959) with Jule Styne providing the music this time. One of the best musical backstagers in Broadway history, *Gypsy* was loosely based on burlesque queen Gypsy Rose Lee's 1957 memoir of the same name. It is a very conventional show in many ways, a rags-to-riches "fable" with well-balanced doses of comedy, pathos, spectacle, and charm. Yet the libretto is unconventional in other ways. The tale is about the slowly rising star Louise (Sandra Church), but the spine of the play is her funny, scary, pushy mother, Rose (Ethel Merman). The plot is episodic with very few recurring characters, yet it builds beautifully and holds together with every piece of the puzzle firmly in place. The romance in the script (and score) is muted, as if everyday and commonplace emotions rather than love must give way to bigger ones in Rose and Louise's life. *Gypsy* is about show business, but it spends as much time belittling vaudeville and burlesque as it does celebrating the theatre itself. When Merman sang "There's No Business Like Show Business" in *Annie Get Your Gun* (1946), it was playful and sincere. When she sang "Everything's Coming Up Roses" in *Gypsy,* there was a desperation, a dark subtext suggesting that show business may be the last refuge of life's losers.

This dark and knowing subtext runs throughout Laurents's libretto. The dialogue is even richer than that for *West Side Story* with humor used effectively to agitate as well as entertain. Laurents echoes the comics in vaudeville and burlesque in some of his backstage banter:

> ROSE: We happen to be headliners from the Orpheum Circuit. We were booked into this theatre by mistake.
> TESSIE: [a stripper in a burlesque house] Weren't we all? [reaching for a costume Rose has unpacked] Say! Who made that?
> LOUISE: I did. I make all our costumes.
> TESSIE: My! Look at them ladylike little stitches! That miserable broad who makes my gowns must be usin' a fish hook!
> LOUISE: What do you pay her?

TESSIE: Twenty-five bucks a gown and I provide the material.
ROSE: Thirty.
TESSIE: She's new in the business!
ROSE: Thirty.
TESSIE: Who're you? Her mother?
ROSE: Yes.
TESSIE: Thirty.

But the dialogue sometimes moves into dangerous territory with Spartan economy and few embellishments:

ROSE: Herbie . . . why does everybody walk out?
HERBIE: Maybe Louise won't.
ROSE: Don't leave, Herbie . . . I need you.
HERBIE: What for?
ROSE: A million things.
HERBIE: Just one would be better. Good-bye, honey. [kisses her on the top of her head] Be a good girl.
ROSE: You go to hell!

If Laurents's words come to life more in *Gypsy* than in *West Side Story*, it may be because he has more complex characters to write for. Shakespeare's characters sometimes came down to types in the modern version, but Rose, Louise, and Herbie are living and breathing individuals. All three change over the course of the years and the miles traveled, even the seemingly consistent Rose. Early in the script, Herbie (Jack Klugman) describes her as "a pioneer woman without a frontier," and this desperation and hopelessness disguised by bravado is what makes Rose one of Broadway's most penetrating characters. Sondheim's skillful lyric for her emotional breakdown number "Rose's Turn" is the climax of the show, but it builds on all that Laurents has given her in the previous scenes. Like only the most inspired characters, Rose is open to different interpretations, and several actresses have mined the mother lode that is Rose and come up with solid gold performances. Merman was outstanding, but it is Rose on the page that gave birth to and allows Rose to live on the stage year after year.

Laurents the experimenter never got more audacious and cockeyed than when he teamed with Stephen Sondheim for a third time, and they came up with *Anyone Can Whistle* (1964). This bold and innovative musical is more typical of the many challenging Sondheim shows, so it is discussed in chapter 15. Also with Sondheim but at the other end of the spectrum was *Do I Hear a Waltz?* (1965), the Richard Rodgers musical based on Laurents's

1952 play *The Time of the Cuckoo*. Laurents had already successfully adapted the Broadway hit into a popular movie called *Summertime* (1955), so returning to the stage with it as a musical may have seemed like a sure thing. But much went wrong in *Do I Hear a Waltz?*, from the unfortunate casting to the ill-chosen director. Laurents's libretto is curiously inert. The New York secretary Leona Samish (Elizabeth Allen) arrives alone in Venice for a holiday, a spinster ripe for romance but also a practical and somewhat hardened woman who looks at everything around her with suspicion. She is wooed and temporarily won by the handsome antique shop owner Renato Di Rosi (Sergio Franchi), who, she later learns, is already married. They part with few regrets, though Leona has learned that being correct about the weakness in others is not a very satisfying pastime. The libretto follows both the play and the film closely, with few attempts to open up the story and add a chorus or additional characters. It is a chamber piece and ought to have been quite appealing on a small scale. But there seems to be little of the heart and charm of the earlier versions in the libretto, and Leona too often comes across as cold and calculating. The character seemed to warm up only in some of the songs, always a questionable sign in a libretto. (Despite the antagonism that arose between Rodgers and Sondheim, most of the score is excellent.) With some slight revision and a more cohesive production, *Do I Hear a Waltz?* might someday prove to be the shining little jewel of a show it was meant to be.

Laurents wrote his first original libretto with *Hallelujah, Baby!* (1967), a musical that echoed *Gypsy* in its episodic plotting and show business milieu. Long interested in writing about different forms of prejudice and being a white liberal championing the civil rights movement in America, Laurents tried to put it all together in another "musical fable." It was a tall order, to say the least, and he went through many rewrites before and during rehearsals in his efforts to make the unwieldy project work. The central character, the ambitious would-be performer Georgina (Leslie Uggams in a role originally intended for Lena Horne), lives through the twentieth century but hardly ages, her youth bringing her from World War I up through the World War II years. Alan Jay Lerner had used a similar conceit in his experimental musical *Love Life* (1948) to show a marriage that paralleled American history. Laurents used the gimmick to chart the plight of African American performers through the years. It was an exciting concept that offered many adventurous possibilities—too many, in fact: Laurents never got all the elements of the story to congeal.

The plotline that Laurents ended up with was perhaps a little too pat. Scrubbing the floors of her modest family home, Georgina dreams of a better life and plans to marry the Pullman porter, Clem (Robert Hooks). But when he loses all their money in a crap game, Georgina heads to New York City, where she gains the amorous favors of the white businessman Harvey (Allen Case), who gets her into the chorus line of a nightclub show. During the Depression she waits on bread lines and does ethnic theatre for the WPA. Entertaining the troops during the war, Georgina achieves stardom and in the 1950s is featured in ritzy supper clubs catering to wealthy whites. But she starts to question her values when the turbulent 1960s arrive, and she discovers her own ethnic pride, leaving Harvey and matching up with Clem, who is now an ardent civil rights worker. Some audiences (and critics) found the musical challenging and uplifting; others deemed it trivial or patronizing. Uggams got rave reviews, and the musical itself won the Tony Award in a lean season, but by then the show had closed and has rarely been heard of since. The admirable score by Jule Styne (music), Betty Comden, and Adolph Green (lyrics) was perhaps too bright and entertaining for a show that had such lofty aspirations. Or perhaps it was a no-win situation. *Hallelujah, Baby!* was a product of its time and also a victim of its time.

Laurents's directing career, which had begun with the musical *I Can Get It for You Wholesale* (1962), occupied much of his time after 1970. He staged successful Broadway revivals of *Gypsy* in 1974 and 1989 and the hit musical *La Cage Aux Folles* (1983). He also collaborated on the screenplay versions of *West Side Story* and *Gypsy*. But his libretto career faltered, and his last two musicals fared poorly. A show he co-wrote with actress Phyllis Newman called *My Mother Was a Fortune Teller* came to Broadway in 1979 as *The Madwoman of Central Park* and found few takers. The one-woman musical featured Newman in an autobiographical reminiscing of her career. A more embarrassing failure was *Nick and Nora* (1991), a highly anticipated musical based on Hollywood's *The Thin Man* films and the original Dashiell Hammett stories. Charles Strouse (music) and Richard Maltby Jr. (lyrics) provided the agreeable score, and Laurents directed his own libretto. Park Avenue sleuths Nick (Barry Bostwick) and Nora Charles (Joanna Gleason) visit friends in Hollywood, where a film producer's mistress (Faith Prince) is murdered one night. Nick doesn't wish to get involved, but Nora pursues the case, eventually solving it after several reenactments of possible solutions are displayed. For the most part, the libretto lacked wit and charm, the story being neither an engrossing thriller nor a satisfactory romance. Many also faulted the direction, a double blow for Laurents. After nine weeks of desperate previews, *Nick and Nora* opened to scabrous reviews and closed in a week.

CHAPTER THIRTEEN

Still writing nonmusicals into the mid-1990s, Laurents kept up his energy, publishing his memoir, *Original Story*, in 2000. His contribution to the Broadway musical may have been far in the past, but it remained a significant contribution all the same. When one considers that only a small portion of Laurents's career was dedicated to libretto writing, he made quite an impact. His handful of musical scripts include two classics, *West Side Story* and *Gypsy*, and two significant failures, *Anyone Can Whistle* and *Hallelujah, Baby!* His librettos inspired superior work by Jule Styne, Leonard Bernstein, Richard Rodgers, and Stephen Sondheim. He also created some of the most memorable characters of his era. All in all, Broadway is fortunate that one of those men named Arthur Laurents wrote scripts for the musical theatre.

CHAPTER FOURTEEN
GUYS AND DOLLS AND STOCKINGS: ABE BURROWS AND OTHERS IN THE 1950s

One of the reasons why the 1950s are considered a golden age for the American musical is the happy coincidence that so many of Broadway's giants were active during that period. Cole Porter and Irving Berlin may have been past their prime, but Rodgers and Hammerstein, Lerner and Loewe, Frank Loesser, Leonard Bernstein, Jule Styne, Comden and Green, Dorothy Fields, and others were still going strong. Then there were such newcomers as Adler and Ross, Meredith Willson, Stephen Sondheim, and Bock and Harnick to add to the mix. It was a fertile time for musicals, and many of our most revived shows come from that decade. Most of the important 1950s musicals have already been discussed in the previous chapters, but there are some librettists and musicals not yet considered that cannot be overlooked.

Abe Burrows (1910–1985) was born Abram Solman Borowitz in New York City and entered show business late in life. He worked first as an accountant and then as a commercial broker before turning to acting. Burrows's writing career began on radio, but he later moved to film and television. In the late 1940s, he had his own talk show on CBS radio. His first theatrical venture came about when the producers of *Guys and Dolls* (1950) were dissatisfied with the libretto written by Jo Swerling. They asked Burrows to go back to the Damon Runyon stories and come up with a completely new libretto, which he did with great success. (Swerling's name remains as co-author, though it is generally acknowledged that little of his original libretto remains.) Although it is the product of a man who had never written a play, *Guys and Dolls* is beautifully structured in the traditional musical comedy model: two couples (one romantic and the other comic), a big opening production number, a rousing eleven o'clock number ("Sit Down, You're Rocking the Boat"), and so on. Frank Loesser's marvelous score is rather traditional (except maybe for the pseudofugue for the bookies) but well integrated into the story and filled with variety. What is unusual about the show is how the two love stories are equally interesting. Sky Masterson (Robert Alda) is the romantic lead, but he gets plenty of comedy bits. Even the staid Sarah Brown (Isabel Bigley) gets to finally cut loose and play some daffy moments rarely given to the ingenue lead. As for the story line with Nathan Detroit (Sam Levene) and his long-suffering fiancée, Adelaide (Vivian Blaine), it is one of the funniest comic romances Broadway has ever seen:

> ADELAIDE: Well, Nathan, this is something I never told you before, but my mother, back in Rhode Island—she thinks we're married already.
> NATHAN: Why would she think a thing like that?
> ADELAIDE: I couldn't be engaged for fourteen years, could I? People don't do that in Rhode Island. They get married.
> NATHAN: Then why is it such a small state? . . .
> ADELAIDE: Then, after about two years . . . we had a baby . . . it was a boy. I named it after you, Nathan.
> NATHAN: Thank you.
> ADELAIDE: You're welcome. . . . He's in boarding school. I wrote Mother he won the football game last Saturday.
> NATHAN: I wish I had a bet on it.

Burrows brings the Runyon New Yorkese to the script with ease, and the whole libretto has a cockeyed language unlike any other musical:

> HARRY THE HORSE: Is he got a place for his crap game? I'm loaded and looking for action. I just acquired five thousand potatoes.
> NICELY-NICELY: Where did you acquire it?
> HARRY: I collected the reward on my father.

Guys and Dolls is continually revived by all kinds of theatre groups; it is practically indestructible. It refuses to date because Runyonland has its own kind of reality.

Burrows had to start from scratch for his libretto for *Can-Can* (1953), a period musical about the scandalous dance of the title, and this time his two couples are a rather uninteresting group. La Mome Pistache (Lilo) runs the Bal du Paradis in Montmartre, where the illegal cancan is performed every night without trouble from the police. When the self-righteous judge, Aristide Forestier (Peter Cookson), decides to act and visits the dance hall himself, he falls for Pistache and, after a series of mishaps, ends up disbarred. His efforts to clear himself in public include becoming Pistache's partner in a new club, the two of them dragged into court, where they make speeches about art and obscenity. The secondary story is a comic triangle involving the dancer Claudine (Gwen Verdon) and her two suitors, a no-talent artist and an oversexed art critic. It was mildly enjoyable entertainment enlivened by a evocative Cole Porter score and some memorable dancing, particularly by Verdon, who became a star with this show. Although *Can-Can* was greeted with mixed notices, it ran a very profitable 892 performances. But revivals are infrequent, and it remains a show that sounds better than it actually is.

With *Silk Stockings* (1955), Burrows had a better story line and another top-notch Porter score, but the result was even less satisfying. George S. Kaufman and Leueen McGrath adapted the classic screenplay of *Ninotchka* (1939) into musical form and updated the tale from prewar to Cold War times. It was a fatal error. Making fun of our humorless Russian allies was one thing; lampooning Communists during the 1950s was uncomfortable comedy. *Silk Stockings* was faltering on the road, and Burrows was brought in to rewrite it. Much of the Porter score was redone, and some subplots not in the original film were added. But the result was very unsatisfactory, and only Porter's reputation allowed *Silk Stockings* to run a year. Burrows would contribute to several other musicals (sometimes as collaborator, other times as uncredited play doctor), such as *Make a Wish* (1951), *Three Wishes for Jamie* (1952), *Say, Darling* (1958), *First Impressions* (1959), and the infamous *Breakfast at Tiffany's* (1966), all of them failures. But he did write another Broadway favorite near the end of his career.

How to Succeed in Business without Really Trying (1961) was based on a humorous guidebook by Shepherd Mead that came out in 1952. The book is a droll, tongue-in-cheek look at big business, and while it has no plot per se, it is filled with the various character types that an eager executive would meet on the way up (and down) the corporate ladder. Willie Gilbert and Jack Weinstock updated the material to the early 1960s but fumbled with trying to make a cohesive story out of all the comic episodes. Again Burrows was called in, and, as with *Guys and Dolls*, he fashioned a superb libretto. What is remarkable about *How to Succeed . . .* is how it avoids any romantic or sentimental moments. The hero, J. Pierrepont Finch (Robert Morse), is not a villain or a heel, but he is totally self-serving and self-centered. His relationship with secretary Rosemary is perfunctory at best, and he sings the show's big love song ("I Believe in You") to himself in the mirror. The people he bamboozles on the way up are unsympathetic oafs, and even the musical's happy ending is dishonest:

> ROSEMARY: Darling, I don't care if you work in the mail room, or you're chairman of the board, or you're President of the United States, I love you.
> FINCH: Say that again.
> ROSEMARY: I love you.
> FINCH: No, before that.

Yet Burrow's libretto is very likable and never so satiric as to not be entertaining. Frank Loesser's score actually takes a back seat to the libretto in *How to Succeed*... (though it is an expert score all the same), and audiences actually get involved with the cartoonish goings-on. The dialogue sometimes has the same kind of colorful jokes that punctuate *Guys and Dolls*. (BIGGLEY: "I keep hiring men who are supposed to have brilliant ideas, and not one of them will ever do what I tell them.") But much of the humor is more subtle and sly:

> BRATT: We're not hiring anyone today.
> FINCH: Well, I was just speaking to Mr. Biggley . . .
> BRATT: J. B. Biggley himself? You were speaking to him?
> FINCH: Yes, sir. I just bumped into him.
> BRATT: Ah, is he a friend of yours?
> FINCH: Sir, I don't think a man should trade on friendship to get a job.
> BRATT: Very well put, young man. Well, if you step into my office, I think we could work something out.

It is a unique, difficult-to-explain kind of musical but one that works even as it breaks so many of the rules. Burrows remained on Broadway for several more years, often as a director of other writers' work, both comedies and musicals. He came to the theatre late but quickly became of one its top professionals and put his mark on dozens of productions.

Starting on Broadway even later in life was composer-lyricist-librettist Meredith Willson (1902–1984). He was born in Mason City, Iowa, where his mother was the piano teacher, and he started music lessons as a young boy. While still a teenager, he landed a job as flautist in John Philip Sousa's famous band and later played for the New York Philharmonic. Willson became one of the busiest conductors and arrangers in show business, working on radio and television and composing musical soundtracks for a handful of movies. He even had a few hit songs on the charts before turning to Broadway with *The Music Man* (1957). Willson had little trouble writing the score, filling it with marches, ballads, character songs, and other traditional musical numbers. But he also wrote such unusual pieces as barbershop quartets, rhythmic patter songs, a duet set to practicing scales, and a march that could be slowed down into a lullaby. It was a bold and original score and remains as unique today as it was nearly half a century ago. But Willson had a difficult time with the libretto, rewriting the tale dozens of times as he tried to fit the many character types he recalled from turn-of-the-century Iowa into a workable story. Finally, he had to enlist the help of Franklin Lacey, who organized the material and gave it a solid structure. (The show's credits list Willson as composer, lyricist, and librettist, "based on a story by" Lacey and Willson.)

The Music Man is one of those timeless musicals that captures an era so beautifully that the date of its creation cannot be detected in the work itself. Willson's approach in both the libretto and the score is one of wry amusement. He finds the small-town locals naive and narrow minded, but he writes about them with such humor and affection that the show never slips into parody or camp. We know Professor Harold Hill (Robert Preston) is a con man, yet he mesmerizes the audience as completely as he dazzles the residents of River City:

HAROLD: That spread of the little finger! It's hereditary!
MAYOR SHINN: Oh it is—what does that mean?
HAROLD: It means that your son's little finger is perfectly situated to operate the spit-valve on a B flat flugel horn!
SHINN: Is that good?
HAROLD: Good! It means that America has at last produced an artist who can flugel the Minute Waltz in fifty seconds.
SHINN: How could I get one of those horns?
HAROLD: Sign here, Mr. Mayor. That'll be seventeen dollars import fee.
SHINN: [signing] Yes sir. Just think, I coulda' missed this whole— [stops suddenly] I haven't any son!

Like the later J. Pierrepont Finch, Hill is dishonest, yet we root for him to succeed even before he has a change of heart. The heroine, the piano teacher Marian Paroo (Barbara Cook), has more gumption than most Broadway ingenues, and her transformation is as delightful as the Professor's. The libretto has one of the finest collections of character types of any musical, each one funny and lovable. They speak in a down-to-earth form of Broadway Americana that is more eccentric than *Oklahoma!* but just as sincere. Everyone in *The Music Man* is interesting and funny, a claim few musicals can make. The show remains a staple on stages across America, and it is not difficult to see why.

After all his libretto problems with *The Music Man,* Willson turned the script chores over to Richard Morris for *The Unsinkable Molly Brown* (1960). Neither score nor libretto worked as well as in his first musical, but both have their moments. Willson handled his own script for *Here's Love* (1963), a lackluster musicalization of the film *Miracle on 34th Street* (1947), which was based on a story by Valentine Davies. The libretto is competent but uninspired, and despite the popularity of the film and its story each Christmas, the musical version is rarely revived. Willson's last musical, *1491* (1969), got no closer to Broadway than Los Angeles. Perhaps Willson had only one story in him, but he told it so well in *The Music Man* that his place in American musical theatre is secure.

Before leaving the 1950s, there are four musicals that must be looked at. All four are atypical of the decade's musicals in that they are all satirical and eschew the warm, sentimental kind of show that reigned at the time. *Li'l Abner* (1956) was based on Al Capp's popular comic strip at the time and retained its political cartoon mentality throughout. Screenwriters Norman Panama and Melvin Frank wrote the libretto, putting all the major Capp characters into a far-fetched story that was practically anarchy itself. While the overromantic Daisy Mae (Edith Adams) chases the layabout Li'l Abner (Peter Palmer), the U.S. government makes plans to use the "totally useless" town of Dogpatch as the testing ground for a new nuclear bomb. A corrupt general tries to steal Mammy Yokum's secret formula for super health, the creepy Earthquake McGoon tries to steal Daisy from Abner, and the sex bomb Appassionata von Climax tries to steal Abner from Daisy. The libretto is a wacky and untidy affair, but one that works in the cartoonish context. There is even a forced W. S. Gilbert–like ending with the town and the citizens saved because it is discovered that Abe Lincoln once declared Dogpatch a national shrine. The vigorous score by Gene de Paul (music) and Johnny Mercer (lyrics) is as farcical as the shenanigans of the plot, and the show still has great appeal, even though modern audiences are much less familiar with Capp's characters.

More tame but also more charming is *Once upon a Mattress* (1959), a musicalization of a classic fairy tale told with a modern sensibility. Jay Thompson, Marshall Baer, and Dean Fuller collaborated on the libretto, using the Rodgers and Hammerstein format. The primary couple, the unladylike Princess Winifred (Carol Burnett) and bumbling Prince Dauntless (Joe Bova), are the comedy duo, while the ballads are given to the secondary love story between Lady Larken (Anne Jones) and Sir Harry (Allen Case). The whole tale is nicely plotted with such nice touches as a soft-shoe jester and a king struck mute until the final scene. The tale is well constructed, going through the requisite character and charm songs with ease. The jester's narration frames the story as in children's theatre, but the writing maintains a literate and gently mocking tone. Much of the libretto has the breezy feeling of an old Rodgers and Hart show:

DAUNTLESS: Mama, look! She's all wet!
WINIFRED: Actually, I swam the moat. But never mind. If I just stand right here, there's a nice draft. I'll be dry in no time.
QUEEN: You swam the moat?
KNIGHT: We tried to stop her, but she wouldn't wait for the drawbridge.
QUEEN: You swam the moat?
KNIGHT: She seemed determined to arrive as soon as possible.
ANOTHER KNIGHT: We had to get a rope and pull her out.
QUEEN: You swam the moat?
WINIFRED: All right, I was a little anxious.

The songs by Mary Rodgers (music) and Baer (lyrics) are memorable in a quiet way; the same can be said for the show itself. Never a blockbuster, *Once upon a Mattress* continues to be appealing, its wry commentary on fairy tale romance still entertaining audiences.

Satire of a different kind can be seen in *Little Mary Sunshine* (1959), a spoof of American operetta that manages to please even those who are not familiar with *Rose-Marie, Sally, Naughty Marietta, Music in the Air,* and its other targets. Rick Besoyan wrote the music, lyrics, and libretto, and all go beyond mere parody. Besoyan seems to have had great affection for the old operetta form, and his spoofing is filled with admiration. The libretto captures the comic characters of the original models quite well, and Besoyan even finds ways to keep the lovers lively without totally burlesquing them:

CAPTAIN JIM: Captain Big Jim Warrington at your service, Miss Mary.
LITTLE MARY: Welcome, Captain Jim. How sorry I am that I wasn't here to greet you on your arrival but I was in the garden saying "hello" to my flowers.
CAPTAIN JIM: Think nought of it, Miss Mary.

A long-running hit Off Broadway, *Little Mary Sunshine* still holds the stage well. Modern audiences may laugh at the outdated operetta tricks, yet they soon find themselves enjoying the music and the way the old-time musical still pleases us. Besoyan returned to the operetta genre for his spoof *The Student Gypsy, or The Prince of Liederkranz* (1963), but as on target as the songs were, the libretto aimed at too many classic shows, and the result was a disjointed and rather ineffectual musical. His musicalization of *A Midsummer Night's Dream* called *Babes in the Wood* (1964) fared even worse. But Besoyan got it right with *Little Mary Sunshine*, and it remains one of the best pastiche musicals.

Less often revived but possibly the best of these musical satires is *The Golden Apple* (1954), a spoof of Homer's *The Iliad* and *The Odyssey* that quickly turns into a knowing commentary on American music and attitudes. John LaTouche wrote the lyrics and the libretto; the two tasks were actually combined since *The Golden Apple* was sung through, one of the first such experiments in the American musical theatre. LaTouche resets the classic tale in Angel's Roost in the state of Washington soon after the Spanish-American War. The seducer, Paris (Jonathan Lucas), is a traveling salesman who woos Helen (Kaye Ballard) and then takes her away to the rival town of Rhododendron. Their masculinity threatened, Ulysses (Stephen Douglass) and the other men in Angel's Roost follow in hot pursuit. But in this version, the Trojan War turns into a boxing match that Ulysses wins. As in antiquity, his journey home is filled with adventures. The crushing rocks of Syclla and Charybdis become dishonest stockbrokers, Calypso is a high-society hostess, and the alluring sirens are nightclub chorines with a seductive South Seas number. Eventually Ulysses ends up back in the arms of his faithful wife Penelope (Priscilla Gillette), and the satiric look at America's macho sensibility ends in domestic harmony. Jerome Moross composed the splendid music, which aped various musical styles, just as LaTouche's sly lyrics managed to be silly and captivating. There is very little prose in the musical, yet LaTouche finds a way to put exposition, character scenes, and plot developments into verse without slipping into recitative or rhymed doggerel. As in a Gilbert and Sullivan comic operetta, the chorus is used extensively throughout to echo the principal characters and comment on the action. (They tell us that Ulysses is "smarter than Nick Carter" and that Helen's chief attribute is that she's "always willin'.") Sung-through musicals would be commonplace by the end of the 1980s, but few of those creators would understand lyric storytelling like LaTouche did. *The Golden Apple* is a musical satire that sustains itself throughout and remains as enthralling as it is clever. Although it was a hit Off Broadway, the musical failed to find an audience once it transferred to Broadway. It is too rarely produced today and still waits for a major revival to bring it the recognition it deserves.

TO THE FORUM, IN THE PARK, INTO THE WOODS: STEPHEN SONDHEIM'S COLLABORATORS

Stephen Sondheim, the most important creative force in the American musical theatre for over three decades, has worked with a variety of librettists who are as different and unpredictable as the Sondheim shows themselves. Sondheim's musicals are often innovative, always intriguing, and only sometimes popular, and have challenged librettists more than other Broadway works, each one an experiment of sorts. This handful of writers often were saddled with the blame when these experiments were less than satisfactory and, in the eyes of the critics, always took a back seat to Sondheim's dazzling music and lyrics. But the Sondheim musicals have also given Broadway some of the most adventurous librettos in the history of the genre.

It is puzzling that Sondheim has never attempted to write his own libretto. Before he broke onto the Broadway scene with his lyrics for *West Side Story* (1957), he wrote television scripts for *Topper* and other series. He would later co-author the screenplay *The Last of Sheila* (1973) and the Broadway whodunit *Getting Away with Murder* (1996), both of which drew on his years of experience writing crossword puzzles in *New York Magazine*. Some of Sondheim's lyrics often take the form of an effective little one-act play, and many others can be viewed as musicalized dialogue. But Sondheim has always found stimulation in the art of collaboration. Having another person as the librettist opens up the field, allows for new ideas, and gives the lyricist the foundation he needs to explore. Sondheim usually writes his songs based on scenes provided by the librettist. Sometimes the scene is totally enveloped into the lyric, and that part of the book is no longer needed. Also, in most of the Sondheim musicals, the line between book and score is invisible, making it impossible at times to determine where the librettist leaves off and the songwriter begins. This implies a close and detailed collaboration between the book writer and the lyricist. Sondheim has rarely been brought in to score a show that is already completely written; he is usually an active participant from the very beginning. One may go so far as to say that his involvement in the writing process has encouraged and even pushed librettists to go where they may not have ventured on their own. For most of the librettists discussed in this chapter, it can be said that they did their finest work with Sondheim.

A Funny Thing Happened on the Way to the Forum (1962) was the first produced musical in which Sondheim wrote both music and lyrics, and, atypical as it might seem for this very atypical songwriter, it is pure Sondheim. Larry Gelbart and Bert Shevelove wrote the libretto, one of the rare instances where the book got more attention from the press than the score. The show won six Tony Awards, including ones for best musical and libretto, but Sondheim's score was not even nominated. It seemed an inauspicious debut for the composer-lyricist but a fair indication of the high-quality libretto that the Sondheim shows would usually boast. Larry Gelbart, one of America's most successful comic writers, has worked in every medium, from radio and television to Broadway and Hollywood. Born in Chicago in 1923, he began writing sketches as a teenager, and his work was heard on the radio as early as 1939. His radio and television credits include *Duffy's Tavern;* sketches for Jack Parr, Bob Hope, Sid Caesar, and others; and the long-running series *M*A*S*H,* which he created and wrote many of its episodes. Gelbart's Hollywood career began with *The Notorious Landlady* (1960), and subsequent screenplays included *The Wrong Box* (1966), *Oh, God!* (1977), *Movie, Movie* (1981), and *Tootsie* (1982). His theatre career began in 1950 with a nonmusical called *My L.A.,* but Gelbart's first major Broadway assignment was writing the libretto for *The Conquering Hero* (1961), a musicalization of the film classic *Hail, the Conquering Hero* (1944). The experience was not a happy one, the out-of-town tryouts being particularly grueling and the show opening in New York without a director or choreographer listed in the program. Gelbart's comment at the time has become Broadway legend: "If Hitler's alive, I hope he's out-of-town with a musical." Ironically, Gelbart's book was quite proficient, turning the Preston Sturges screenplay into a workable libretto by remaining faithful to it, yet finding possibilities for musical numbers. The tale of a GI (Tom Poston) released by the Army for asthma and mistaken for a hero in his hometown was fertile musical comedy material. But the pedestrian score by Moose Charlap (music) and Norman Gimbel (lyrics) and the superb but lengthy ballets by Bob Fosse seemed to erode at the intended satire. *The Conquering Hero* closed in a week, but Gelbart had his first taste of libretto writing, even if it was a bitter taste. Bert Shevelove was born in 1915 in Newark, New Jersey, and studied theatre at Brown University and Yale. During the war he served as an ambulance driver, then pursued a career in professional theatre after he was discharged. Known mostly as a director, Shevelove staged his first musical in 1948, the Broadway revue *Small Wonder,* and would go on to direct such shows as *Hallelujah, Baby!* (1967) and the 1971 revival of *No, No, Nanette.* Shevelove's first libretto was for *A Month of Sundays* (1951), a musical about a crusty boat pilot who decides to take his excursion tug and all its passengers to the West Indies. The script was an adaptation of Victor Wolfson's popular play *Excursion* (1937) with music by Albert Selden, but the offbeat tale didn't translate, and the musical closed during its out-of-town tryouts.

Shevelove had adapted a Roman comedy by Plautus into a musical while at Yale and thought the idea worth pursuing. Sondheim, Shevelove, and Gelbart read all of Plautus's twenty-six extant plays and tried to fashion a single plot out of the wealth of material. After five years and several different drafts, Shevelove and Gelbart came up with a complicated farce held together by the conniving slave Pseudolus (Zero Mostel), who is trying to buy his freedom. Titled *A Roman Comedy,* the script seemed slapdash and carefree but, in fact, was an intricate mating of different plots and characters from the various Plautus works. *A Funny Thing Happened on the Way to the Forum,* as it was eventually titled, is remarkable in that it does not seem like an anthology or a potpourri at all. The tight construction; the rapid, burlesque dialogue exchanges; and the skillful way the songs enter into the story are still a marvel. While most musicals burst into song and dance because the drama or passion in the book needs a release, *Forum* relies on the score to relieve the audience from the nonstop jokes and hectic goings-on. It is also one of the few musicals to remain faithful to the unities of time, place, and action. The single setting on a Roman street (the standard location for Roman comedies), the lack of scene breaks, and the three-way action coming from the three houses on stage all keep *Forum* one of the most economic of Broadway librettos. Even taking an act break seemed to go against the temperament of the show, so the authors contrived to have Pseudolus halt the action, request one word from Captain Miles, and then shout "Intermission!"

Because the script borrowed heavily from vaudeville and burlesque (both of which owed more than a passing nod to Plautus), *Forum* contained the kind of crisp, comic dialogue that had not been heard on Broadway since the days of the great comics. It is a jokey kind of dialogue that makes no attempt to be natural or conversational. Instead, it has a rhythm that seems to create its own patter music:

> LYCUS: [grabs him] What is the news?
> PSEUDOLUS: What news?
> LYCUS: The news from Crete.
> PSEUDOLUS: I heard it. Tragic.
> LYCUS: Pseudolus! [shakes him]
> PSEUDOLUS: You force me to tell you! Crete is ravaged by a great plague. People are dying by the thousands.
> LYCUS: But this girl is healthy. She goes smiling through the day.
> PSEUDOLUS: She doesn't! I thought you knew. When they start to smile, the end is near.
> LYCUS: No!
> PSEUDOLUS: Yes! I am told it is lovely now in Crete. Everyone lying there, smiling.
> LYCUS: Is it contagious?
> PSEUDOLUS: Did you ever see a plague that wasn't?

While the characters in *Forum* are all comic types, ranging from the clever slave to the braggart soldier to the domineering shrew of a wife, they are very specific types whose consistency keeps the plot flowing. Hysterium (Jack Gilford), for example, is as frantic and worrisome as his name. Yet it is these qualities that bring both complications to the plot (he threatens to expose Pseudolus's matchmaking to Hero's parents) and resolutions as well (he agrees to play the dead Philia to abate Miles's anger). Every character in the musical is an important piece of the intricate plot. There are no extraneous people or scenes as the exposition, foreshadowing, and complications tumble forward to a tidy ending filled with long-lost relatives rediscovered and couples reunited.

While few would call *Forum* daring or innovative, it is surprisingly courageous. Musical farces are hard to come by and for good reason. The pattern of farce is such a delicate thing that the presence of a score threatens to waylay it. But Shevelove and Gelbart juggle all the elements so skillfully that *Forum* remains indestructibly stageworthy and popular. Sondheim's score eventually found favor, and today the show is more highly thought of than during its initial successful run. Shevelove would write only two other librettos before his death in 1982: a new, anachronistic version of Aristophanes' *The Frogs* with a Sondheim score that was performed in a swimming pool at Yale in 1974, and the short-lived *Happy New Year* (1980), a musicalization of Philip Barry's 1928 comedy of manners, *Holi-*

day, with old songs by Cole Porter as the score. The first was a delightful curiosity, the second a leaden flop.

Gelbart, on the other hand, would go on to write comedies such as *Sly Fox* (1976) and *Mastergate* (1989), returning to the musical form with *City of Angels* (1989), which he wrote with Cy Coleman (music) and David Zippel (lyrics). A spoof of hard-boiled private eye films of the 1940s, *City of Angels* is an original libretto but is indirectly based on several Humphrey Bogart films and Philip Marlowe stories. It also reminds one of *Kiss Me, Kate* (1948) in that two stories are being enacted side by side; the Cole Porter musical moved from backstage to on stage, while *City of Angels* travels from the soundstage to the silver screen. Pulp author Stine (Gregg Edelman) goes to Hollywood, where they are making a film version of one of his novels featuring the tough-as-nails private dick Stone (James Naughton). Characters in the novel parallel people in the movie business, often the same actor playing both characters. To keep the audience from getting too confused, the real-life scenes are in color (both sets and costumes), while the fiction events of the novel are in black and white, as they will be seen in the movie version. The Stone story is a familiar tale about a beautiful but dangerous wife with a much older millionaire husband who appeals to the detective for help in finding her wayward sluttish daughter. The Stine plot concerns the difficulties in making the movie, mostly because of the eccentric Sam Goldwyn–like producer, and the author's apprehensions about selling out to Hollywood. *City of Angels* is so intricately plotted and has such fun stereotypic character types that it doesn't seem to matter much that both plots are rather frail and forgettable. In fact, the whole idea of a pulp fiction writer searching his conscience because Hollywood might corrupt his art is too inane even to be funny. When Stine and Stone start to confront each other in a Pirandellian manner, the only result is that both come across as rather unlikable guys.

Gelbart's dialogue is delicious throughout, especially when it echoes the pulp style: "She had the kind of face a man could hang a dream on, a body that made the Venus Di Milo look all thumbs, and only the floor kept her legs from going on forever." He also had fun with Hollywood doubletalk, particularly with the producer Buddy Fidler (Rene Auberjonais): "Sweetheart, I'm your biggest fan. I've read every synopsis of every book you've ever written. With a little mustard on some rye, every word is a meal. But nothing was ever hurt by being improved." *City of Angels* was popular on Broadway and on tour but has seen little life since. The difficulty in producing the show is certainly a factor (after all, it has the cast, sets, and costumes of two musicals), but I suspect that the musical is too unfeeling for many. In *Forum*, every character is funny and likeable; in *City of Angels*, every person, real or fiction, is funny and unlikable. Perhaps that's the price you pay when you present a film noir musical.

Arthur Laurents, whom we looked at earlier in chapter 14, reteamed with Sondheim for *Anyone Can Whistle* (1964), arguably the most bizarre musical either of them ever presented. The two had worked together previously on *West Side Story* (1957) and *Gypsy* (1959), Laurents providing reputable books and Sondheim writing expert lyrics. But those two shows were no foreshadowing for the left-wing, audacious *Anyone Can Whistle*. In a financially destitute town run by the wealthy and corrupt mayoress, Cora Hoover Hooper (Angela Lansbury), the city officials create a lucrative tourist attraction by faking a miracle: water springs from a rock where the saintly brat Baby Joan sits and bestows blessings. When Nurse Apple (Lee Remick) brings a group of inmates from the local "cookie jar" to partake of the waters, the smiling lunatics escape and mix with the tourists, forcing the mayoress and her cronies to call on psychiatrist Dr. J. Bowden Hapgood (Harry Guardino) to separate the sane from the insane. But the radical doctor only raises questions about sanity in the modern world and succeeds in creating chaos rather than right-wing stability. Hapgood falls in love with Apple, who has disguised herself as a French femme fatale in order to investigate the so-called miracle, and reveals to her that he is no doctor but just a new recruit for the cookie jar. Eventually, both the fake miracle and the fake doctor are exposed, the tourists rush off to a nearby city where a new miracle has been discovered, and Hapgood and Apple find a genuine miracle in their love for each other.

As much as this plot might appear to be in the boy-meets-girl format, nothing in *Anyone Can Whistle* was formulaic. One of the last three-act musicals ever written, Laurents's script approached each cockeyed situation with impudent glee. One of Cora's backroom strategy sessions took the form of a multiple message treatment, the balcony of the local hotel lowered itself to bring the lovers together, English subtitles flashed overhead when Apple spoke in her drooling French, and the first act ended with the cast sitting in theatre seats facing and ridiculing the audience. This time every aspect of the show, from the impertinent script to Sondheim's quirky score to Herbert Ross's mocking ballets, *was* bold and innovative. But just how successful the whole effect was is another matter. The privilege of nearly thirty years of hindsight reveals that much of *Anyone Can Whistle* was indeed ahead of its time. But it is also quite clear that much of the libretto is preachy and exasperating. The script's central premise, that crazy people are the only sane ones in a world run by conservative and corrupt authority figures, was making the rounds in the 1960s. The next season's *Man of La Mancha* (1965) and the film *King of Hearts* (1966) would find more success promoting the same theme. Yet Laurents's soapbox rhetoric contains the libretto's weakest writing. Cora and her henchmen are loud and decadent cartoons that still amuse, but the heroes' preachings, such as Hapgood's encouraging one to ignore the signs and to walk on the grass and Apple's argument to view her "cookies" as the only unspoiled human beings left in society, undermine the intelligence of much of the book. A brave experiment if there ever was one, *Anyone Can Whistle* did open some doors and test the waters for innovative libretto writing. It was certainly the beginning of an exciting new phase for Sondheim. But the show itself did not work, and scattered revivals over the years have not done any better. Many theatre lovers are nostalgic about the musical, but their nostalgia is secondhand. Only a few critics saw anything in the musical, and the show ran only nine performances. The radiant original cast recording has led many to declare *Anyone Can Whistle* a neglected masterpiece. Much of the score has proved to be superior, but the libretto continues to fail. Yet it was an illustrious failure and, perhaps, a necessary one.

Some of Laurents's experimentation would resurface in George Furth's libretto for Sondheim's *Company* (1970), a revolutionary show that *did* work. George Furth was born in Chicago in 1932 and educated at Northwestern University, where he became interested in theatre. He moved to New York to pursue graduate study in acting at Columbia, and soon after graduation found himself an often employed character actor. Ironically, little of Furth's work was on the stage. Instead, he became a familiar face in various television series and on film with hundreds of credits to his name by the time he was forty. His first attempt at writing was a series of eleven playlets about life in contemporary New York City. He showed the script to Harold Prince, and the producer-director immediately pictured it as a musical with Sondheim doing the score. The three men reorganized the material, retaining three of the playlets and Furth writing two new pieces, tying it all together by creating the character of Bobby (Dean Jones), a thirty-five-year-old bachelor who is facing up to the lack of commitment in his life. The pattern was similar to *Forum* in that it was another series of plays held together by a central character. But *Company* was far from the cause-and-effect plotting of the Roman musical.

Bobby's closest friends are five urban couples who illustrate both the pleasant and the unpleasant aspects of married life. The bachelor is grateful to be single and free, yet he envies the five duos. His own romantic relationships, as seen in three of his former girlfriends, have fared poorly, causing Bobby to retreat further into a protective shell. Only by realizing that he needs the pain as much as the "company" of another person does Bobby begin to understand himself. The story, such as it can be called that, does not follow any sequential order, each episode popping into Bobby's head, overlapping, and sometimes even playing out simultaneously. The score was often a complicated jumble of voices and observations, and Furth's libretto echoed this at times. Bobby's three ex-lovers, for example, probably never met each other, but in his head they are a trio, singing together and each playing scenes with him while the other two watch and make comments. Furth's most telling idea was using Bobby's birthday party as a leitmotif. The musical begins with his friends waiting in his apartment to surprise him with a cake; later we see the party in progress; finally, at the end of the show, we realize that the party has never taken place. The recurring image in Bobby's mind is only in his mind. Instead of confusing or annoying the audience, the use of the party helped everyone maneuver through this, the first successful concept musical. The term is often used to describe *Company* and other shows that are more concerned with ideas and manner of presentation than with plot or even content. But audiences did not need to understand conceptual musicals to know that they liked this one.

Much of the fun in *Company* was provided by the sometimes dysfunctional but usually likable characters and their high-strung, urban way of talking. Some are frantic and feverish in their speech ("I am just so glad we're not having a Catholic wedding because next year when I get a divorce I won't be a sinner."), others jaded or naive ("He was born in New York so *nothing* really interests him."), and still others wistfully philosophical ("A person like Bob doesn't have the good things and he doesn't have the bad things. But he doesn't have the good things."). The caustic Joanne (Elaine Stritch) gets most of the best lines, staring and observing as she takes deep drags on her cigarette: "That's the best. Better than Librium. Smoking may be the only thing that separates us from the lower orders." There is no question that television writing creeps into Furth's script on occasion, but there are few gratuitous jokes, and there is a gritty subtext in the humor that was rarely found on the tube. Most of the book scenes in *Company* are rather short, but Furth makes every moment count:

ROBERT: Whew! It's very drunk out tonight. What are you looking at, Joanne? It's my charisma, huh? Well, stop looking at my charisma!
JOANNE: [still staring; no change in position or voice] When are we gonna make it?

ROBERT: [a pause] I beg your pardon?
JOANNE: When're we gonna make it?
ROBERT: [making light of it] What's wrong with now?
JOANNE: [slowly, directly, sultrily, quietly, and evenly] There's my place.
It's free tomorrow at two. Larry goes to his gym then. Don't talk. Don't
do your folksy, Harold Teen with me. You're a terrifically attractive man.
The kind of man most women want and never seem to get. I'll—take care
of you.
ROBERT: [a pause; he's been looking down; he looks up] But who will I
take care of?
JOANNE: [a big smile] Well, did you hear yourself? Did you hear what
you just said, kiddo?

Company was bolder, more daring, and less compromising than *Anyone
Can Whistle*, but it was also less off-putting and more satisfying. A critical
and popular hit, *Company* ushered in a new era that accepted the Broadway
musical in nontraditional forms. Not only the subsequent Sondheim shows
but also *A Chorus Line* and other musicals that departed from the causal
plot would benefit from *Company*. And although the show is not as often
revived as many other hits of its era, its craftsmanship has not diminished.
Today, *Company* is a difficult musical to produce. It is so set in the 1970s
mentality that it cannot be satisfactorily updated or revised. Furth was so
concerned with writing a contemporary comedy that many of the script's
ideas were out of date a few years later. The straight-laced couple trying
marijuana, the kookie New Yorker who thinks Fourteenth Street is the center of the universe, the couple who enjoy living in sin more than legal mat-
rimony, the bride who fears becoming a conventional housewife, the sophisticated matron who despises society clones, and Bobby himself—a man
trying to enjoy the sexual revolution while yearning for old-fashioned
affection—are all products of their time. When the musical is presented today, audiences sometimes see the characters as cold and unfeeling and ask
themselves if Bobby is a latent homosexual. We bring too many questions
with us to *Company* now and forget that this is the show that first asked
questions. The score, also very 1970s in temperament, is rightfully considered a milestone. But we accept a song that sounds like the past; we are
skeptical of a libretto that speaks in a bygone tongue. *Company* may be the
greatest of unrevivable Broadway musicals.

Furth's later libretto endeavors were not happy experiences for him or
Broadway. His script for the Liza Minnelli vehicle *The Act* (1977) was a
slight affair about a movie star trying to make a comeback in a Las Vegas
act after a messy divorce. The critics trounced the troubled show (it had

gone through director, cast, costumer, and title changes) with only Minnelli and some of the John Kander–Fred Ebb songs finding favor. To be fair to Furth and some of the others involved, the musical that opened on Broadway was not what they had started with. During the lengthy pre-Broadway tour, the directors, film helmer Martin Scorsese and then Broadway wizard Gower Champion, cut scenes, songs, costumes, and characters until all that was left was a nightclub act. Judging by the deleted songs later recorded by others, *The Act* was supposed to be much more than what they ended up with. But what Broadway saw was as "cold as a stripper's behind," to quote one of Furth's more unfortunate lines.

Furth would reteam with Sondheim for *Merrily We Roll Along* (1981), a massive flop that, like *Anyone Can Whistle*, has gained a cult following over the years. George S. Kaufman and Moss Hart's 1934 play of the same name was not one of their runaway successes, yet it had found an audience for 155 performances. It told the story of two artists, a painter and a playwright, who were close friends in their youth but had ended up bitter enemies as the writer sold his talent cheap and compromised everything and everyone along the way. This somewhat familiar tale was given a twist by having the order of the scenes presented in reverse, the play starting with the bitter middle-aged characters and then working backward, ending up in the days when they were optimistic youths. Furth retained the basic plot (and the backward gimmick), changing the friends to a songwriter (later a Hollywood producer) named Franklin Shepard (Jim Walton) and a lyricist called Charley Kringas (Lonny Price), and built up the part of their female friend, turning her into a forever-stalled novelist named Mary Flynn (Ann Morrison). The story begins in 1980 and works back to 1957 with even Sondheim's score going in reverse. (Some songs are given a brief reprise *before* they are later "introduced" in toto.) It was ambitious writing on both Furth's and Sondheim's parts, and director Prince added to the adventure by casting young unknowns in all the roles save one. After a troubled and long preview period, *Merrily We Roll Along* opened, got the worst reviews of any Sondheim show, and closed in two weeks.

Furth has tinkered with the script over the years for various revivals (including a highly praised production in London in 2001), but the premise of the show, that of telling a story backward, has never changed. Some feel it is what makes the musical so powerful; others are convinced that it is what keeps *Merrily We Roll Along* from succeeding. Reviews for the original Kaufman and Hart play (which used adult actors and had them play *down* for the youthful scenes) pointed out the problem early on. Meeting a group of jaded and cynical characters after they have lost all their ideals is not the best way to capture the audience's empathy. By the time we see the more noble and hopeful kids that they were, it is too late. Furth, Prince, and Sondheim were most interested in the process by which idealism is compromised and destroyed; audiences were not. Had the story been told in chronological order, the result would have been a very conventional and safely satisfying show. But those are not the words to describe any Sondheim musical, and one must admire Furth for writing such an unrelenting script. What is harder to admire is Furth's dialogue, a weaker version of the urban angst of *Company*. Perhaps he was intimidated by trying to compete with the Kaufman and Hart wit (many of the 1934 play's slyest, most cutting lines were not used in the musical) because the dialogue moved even closer to television writing. This was more disappointing because Sondheim's lyrics are at his most scabrous. Every librettist for a Sondheim show has the unenviable task of trying to write dialogue as potent as the lyrics. In *Merrily We Roll Along,* Furth was not up to the challenge. Plotting and characterization were subject to the backward notion of the musical, but whether in reverse or in forward motion, much of Furth's dialogue flounders. He would go on to write a series of nonmusicals—*Twigs* (1971), *The Supporting Cast* (1981), *Precious Sons* (1986), and, with Sondheim, *Getting Away with Murder* (1996)—most in a sitcom style and most quick failures. But none of that diminishes the fact that Furth was a vital part of the creation of *Company* and, therefore, played no small part in the development of libretto writing in America.

James Goldman had collaborated with Sondheim on a television musical called *Evening Primrose* in 1966, and they reteamed for *Follies* (1971), a glorious failure and the queen of cult musicals. Goldman was born in Chicago in 1927 and had ambitions to become a music critic. He studied at the University of Chicago and was pursuing a postgraduate degree at Columbia until he was drafted into the Army. By the time he was discharged, Goldman had decided he wanted to be a writer like his brother William. The two collaborated on the Broadway comedy *Blood, Sweat and Stanley Poole* (1961), and *A Family Affair* (1962), a broad musical comedy about a Jewish wedding. (The music was by a young John Kander, who had not yet teamed up with Fred Ebb.) Both brothers would find success as novelists and Hollywood screenwriters, and James received recognition on Broadway for his comedy-drama *The Lion in Winter* (1966). *Follies* started as a musical mystery called *The Girls Upstairs* that Goldman and Sondheim began working on long before *Company*. After changes in concept and producers, the story started to take its final form. Just as *Company* uses a birthday party to gather the characters and then explore their current lives, *Follies* uses a theatrical reunion to reconvene its late middle-age characters who were literally haunted by their past. The ghosts involved were the younger versions of themselves, and instead of traditional flashbacks, the script put past and present on stage together, climaxing when the two collided in a spectacular but painful showcase of all their personal "follies." This was not safe writing by any stretch of the imagination. Add to the complex plotting a large cast of characters and twenty-two Sondheim songs, and *Follies* became what was cited as "an overabundance of riches." Even those critics who disliked the show had to admit that there was some kind of brilliance going on here. From sterling performances to unforgettable sets and costumes to the fluid staging by Prince and Michael Bennett, there was something for even the most disgruntled naysayer. Some dismissed Sondheim's score as clever pastiche, and most blamed Goldman's book for the reason that they did not have a good time. But more than any of the sparkle or fireworks, *Follies* is about the book and score, and the two work powerfully together.

It was quite clear from the opening image (a ghostly chorus girl standing in a decaying theatre) that this was not going to be musical comedy on an escapist level. It was a ghost story, but the thrills were going to be ugly. The libretto is about people drowning, some hanging onto the past to keep their sanity, others haunted by the past mistakes they had made. The four main characters were dismissed by many as "dreary," but people on the edge of a breakdown were bound to be tiring. The character of Ben Stone (John McMartin) is a successful author and diplomat who has been finessing his way through life as if it were a Cole Porter musical. While performing his "follies" number, "Live, Laugh, Love," he falls apart, unable to remember the lines and incapable of lying anymore. Buddy Plummer (Gene Nelson) is a smiling salesman, a man who tries to keep his wife and his mistress laughing so that no one will notice that their lives have turned into a burlesque sketch. His wife Sally (Dorothy Collins) puts on a brave front and fantasizes about her lost love for Ben; she sees herself as a tragic Helen Morgan–like figure, but she knows she's just another dowdy and discontented housewife. Ben's wife Phyllis (Alexis Smith) is a smarter, cooler version of *Company*'s Joanne. She is perhaps the most disturbing of the foursome because she is so clear headed about her situation:

PHYLLIS: Bargains, Buddy. That's the way to get through. One makes bargains with one's life. That's what maturity amounts to. . . . I learned to be an artist with my life. I constantly select, as if each day were a painting and I had to get the colors right. We're careful of our colors, Ben and I, and what we've made is beautiful. I had a lover once. His name was Jack,

I think. He played the drums and had long hair and no command of language . . . I have a birthmark under my left breast, just here—my only flaw. I think he loved that in me most of all. He was so tender touching it, and when he kissed me there, one found it difficult to breathe. I thought it answered everything, but these things pass, and I have thirty thousand dollars worth of Georgian silver in my dining room.

What one calls dreary might be intriguing drama in someone else's book, and I contend that Goldman's work in *Follies* is superior libretto writing. Just as it took time for his play *The Lion in Winter* to be fully appreciated, it has taken *Follies* years to finally get a fair shake. It is not a tight and perfect little script like *Forum*, and it never could be; it looks down too many paths and considers too many ghosts to be tidy and neat. Goldman and Sondheim made changes in *Follies* for the London and other productions, and further cuts were made by others for the 2001 Broadway revival (many of which were more damaging than helpful). The musical is like *Show Boat* in that the libretto is too much for any one stage, and each generation must revive and revise it as they see fit. *Follies* is so ambitious, so out of control in its beauty, that it offers more rewards than many a "better" show.

Hugh Wheeler would prove to be one of Sondheim's most productive collaborators, although he did not begin writing librettos until he was sixty-one years old and completed only four musicals before his death in 1987. Wheeler was born in London in 1912 and educated at the Clayesmore School and the University of London. He began his writing career as the author of detective novels using the pen names Patrick Quentin and Q Patrick. Wheeler served in the U.S. Army medical corps during World War II, becoming a naturalized citizen in 1942 and remaining in America, where he wrote screenplays for some dozen films. His first play was the Broadway comedy *Big Fish, Little Fish* (1961), a modest success, and his adaptation of Shirley Jackson's *We Have Always Lived in a Castle* (1966) enjoyed popularity in regional theatres. Wheeler's first musical assignment was reworking the script of the British hit *Half a Sixpence* (1965) for Broadway. Harold Prince knew Wheeler from working together on the film *Something for Everyone* (1970) and brought him on board when he and Sondheim wanted to turn the Ingmar Bergman film *Smiles of a Summer Night* (1955) into an operetta. Wheeler would prove to be a master adapter of material for the stage, all his subsequent librettos based on well-known but difficult sources.

Bergman's film is a deft comedy of manners but very foreign in tone and rather small in scale. *A Little Night Music*, as the musical version was eventually was titled, was written like a chamber opera filled with romantic triangles that led to duets and quartets in both song and dialogue. The middle-aged lawyer Fredrik Egerman (Len Cariou) has tried to recapture his youth by marrying the young Anne (Victoria Mallory), but he is drawn to his old flame, the actress Desiree Armfeldt (Glynis Johns). Fredrik's son Henrik (Mark Lambert) is torn between a religious vocation and his appealing virgin of a stepmother, Anne. Desiree's lover Count Carl-Magnus Malcolm (Laurence Guittard) neglects his wife Charlotte (Patricia Elliott) and is jealous of his mistress's interest in Fredrik. Observing and commenting on all the triangles is the aging courtesan, Madame Armfeldt (Hermione Gingold), herself torn between nostalgia and regret for her scandalous past. Wheeler's script keeps all the plot elements floating in the air (the original film is mostly realistic and rather earthbound), and the light, nimble dialogue commingles with Sondheim's waltzing score beautifully. *A Little Night Music* was Sondheim's most traditional work since *Gypsy*, and both critics and audience had no trouble embracing it. More than one review labeled the operetta "adult" because of its elegant sophistication. But what were *Company* and *Follies*—adolescent? It seems one doesn't mind confused, frustrated, and "dreary" characters if they are set in the costumed past and sing in 3/4 time. A few commentators quibbled that *A Little Night Music* lacked the edge and bite of the previous Sondheim shows, that it was more charming than one expected. Yet Wheeler's script is full of nervous tension, sometimes sexual but other times questioning the decisions one has made. "Dearest Armfeldt," Charlotte says to her rival, "do regale us with more fascinating reminiscences from your remote youth." More than any other Sondheim collaborator, Wheeler writes with elegance and wit. Some librettists can match Sondheim's brash and acerbic lyrics, but none picks up on the songwriter's lyricism as Wheeler does. Old Madame Armfeldt observes, "To lose a lover or even a husband or two during the course of one's life can be vexing. But to lose one's teeth is a catastrophe." This kind of flowing rhetoric punctuated by a punch line is unique in Broadway musicals.

The same season as *A Little Night Music*, Wheeler worked with Joseph Stein on the libretto revision of the 1919 favorite *Irene* for its Broadway revival in 1973. They tightened up the plot, dropped half the score, added period songs, and ended up with a musical just as contrived and formulaic as the original. Critics carped, but audiences came in droves to see Debbie Reynolds as the title heroine. Wheeler's revision of *Candide*, on the other hand, was a major overhauling. Lillian Hellman's libretto for the original 1956 production was roundly blamed for the show's failure. Reading it today, one has trouble arguing against that opinion. It was true to Voltaire's novella in spirit and wickedness, but Hellman's writing was too heavy handed for the musical stage, and the more satiric and outlandish she tried to be, the less interesting she was. Broadway had pretty much chalked *Candide* up as an impossible situation. But Harold Prince thought otherwise, and with a new libretto by Wheeler and some Sondheim lyrics added to Leonard Bernstein's music, *Candide* finally became a hit in 1973. Its success can, quite simply, be attributed to Wheeler. Prince's inventive direction (the musical was staged as a slapstick environmental piece with the cast dashing about the theatre as the characters traveled the continents), and the new Sondheim lyrics were commendable, but it was the libretto that saved the day. Wheeler pretty much disposed of Hellman's script and started from scratch, turning the Voltaire work into a naughty fairy tale. The tone is sly yet playful, the story unfolding like a merry frolic filled with improbabilities and sublime foolishness. Voltaire (Lewis J. Stadlen) narrates the events so that the libretto retains some of the French author's wry commentary. But the dialogue that Wheeler created on his own is equally adept, taking on a mock verbosity:

> CANDIDE: Alas! An entire population wiped out by an erupting mountain. What benign law of the universe, I wonder, could have made such a cataclysm essential in this best of all possible worlds? Can it be that some slight error has taken place somewhere?

Candide, the most beloved of Broadway flops because of its famous score, entered the canon of revivable musicals thanks to Wheeler. It remains one of the most impressive rescues in Broadway history.

Prince, Sondheim, and Wheeler would collaborate one more time, and in many ways it was the crowning achievement for each of their careers. *Sweeney Todd, the Demon Barber of Fleet Street* (1979) is one of the few Sondheim musicals that was instigated by the songwriter himself. He saw a new version of the Victorian tale written by Christopher Bond in London in 1973 and was intrigued with the idea of musicalizing it, creating a "musical thriller" that could also comment on the social orders. The legend of Sweeney Todd (Len Cariou), a deranged barber who slit the throats of his customers and then turned the bodies over to the pragmatic Mrs. Lovett (Angela Lansbury), who made meat pies out of them, was a familiar tale in England but pretty much unknown in America. Turning the macabre story into a Broadway musical was quite a tall order, even for a Sondheim project, but Wheeler's adaptation met the inherent problems head on and succeeded. Although there are a lot of songs in *Sweeney Todd,* there is a lot of plotting as well. The score intermingles with the libretto more carefully than in any other Sondheim work; in fact, it may be *the* integrated musical of the era. Wouldn't Oscar Hammerstein be proud? Well, not really. Many audience members felt that *Sweeney Todd* was going too far. Sure, you can make a musical out of anything, but can you really make a musical about *anything?* Despite all its awards and accolades, the show lost money. A one-sentence description of the plot was enough to keep a good portion of the Broadway audience away. Happily, the musical claimed its rightful place after a few years. Perhaps the idea has settled in people's minds or enough have seen it and liked it for the show to be accepted today. One thing is for certain: time has not diminished its potency. Wheeler's script carefully balances the Grand Guignol elements with the musical comedy format as dialogue moves effortlessly in and out of the songs, and the characters' prose explodes into lyric verse. Wheeler even managed to retain Bond's ideas about the dog-eat-dog world of the industrial revolution that so interested Sondheim in the first place. Wheeler's libretto career, which also included the aborted musicals *Truckload* (1975) and *The Little Prince and the Aviator* (1982), some play doctoring on *Pacific Overtures* (1976), and the posthumous *Meet Me in St. Louis* (1989), concentrated on adaptations, but never was he in finer form than in *Sweeney Todd.*

While Wheeler was Sondheim's senior by a whole generation, the rest of the songwriter's collaborators would come from a younger generation. James Lapine was born in Mansfield, Ohio, in 1949 and educated at Franklin and Marshall and the California Institute of the Arts. He moved to New York in 1974 to pursue writing and directing in the theatre, but ended up working as a graphics designer for Yale University. His first play, an adaptation of Gertrude Stein's *Photograph,* was presented at Yale and then moved to Off Broadway in 1977. Lapine received recognition for his plays *Twelve Dreams* (1978) and *Table Settings* (1980) and for directing his own works and classics for the New York Shakespeare Festival. His first encounter with the musical form was directing (and guiding) William Finn's *March of the Falsettos* (1981) Off Broadway. Lapine's input was so important for the musical's sequel, *Falsettoland* (1990), that he was listed as co-librettist with Finn (see chapter 19). Because he had little background in musical theatre, Lapine brought a fresh outlook to the genre when he collaborated with Sondheim on *Sunday in the Park with George* (1984), his first libretto. Lapine broke many of the rules of libretto writing, sometimes out of experimentation, other times out of innocent ignorance. For Sondheim, who had learned the art form and all its unwritten precepts from Hammerstein himself, it was exciting to work with Lapine, whose ideas and suggestions did not seem to come out of the usual musical comedy mentality. The inspiration for *Sunday in the Park* is a Georges Seurat painting completed in 1886. Musicals have been based on a lot of things over the years, but a piece of art was a new one to Sondheim (and everybody else). The major figures in the painting became the characters in the musical, with Seurat himself (called George and played by Mandy Patinkin) as the hero (or antihero) of the piece. Act 1 concerns George's work on the pointillist painting, his bumpy relationship with his mistress Dot (Bernadette Peters), and the general neglect George gets from the Paris art community. Act 2 jumps ahead to 1984 with another artist named George (supposedly the great-grandson of Seurat) facing modern equivalents in the Chicago art world. While the French pointillist died in poverty, unable to interest anyone in his work, the new George must play the funding-and-patronage game, spending more of his energy on selling himself than on creating his multimedia works. The two stories come together at the end of the musical when twentieth-century George goes to the island setting of the Seurat painting and the ghost of Dot encourages him to pursue his artistic vision without worrying about acceptance or acclaim.

Lapine's whole conceit for the show was new and exciting: two different but related playlets, both real and painted characters, lots of insights into artists and art, and, even better, a glimpse into the process of *how* something is created. Here was the concept musical in full bloom. But something was missing. *Sunday in the Park* is filled with potent ideas, but a libretto is much more than ideas. Whenever Sondheim's strangely beautiful music stopped, the show seemed to come to a dead halt. Most of the characters were flatter than any canvas, and the dialogue sounded as stiff as dried paint. Lapine the writer wasn't quite up to Lapine the conceptual artist. The vibrant performances by Patinkin and Peters helped disguise the fact that even the central characters were lacking flesh and blood. When they sang, the imagery and emotions flowed; when they spoke, they sounded (dare I say it?) dreary. While most critics recognized that there were marvelous things in *Sunday in the Park*, audiences too often were bored. Not that this was a musical that was ever going to appeal to the tired businessman, but the show could have been as exciting as the ideas it offered. *Sunday in the Park* deservedly won the Pulitzer Prize, and it remains one of the most unique and thrilling of the concept musicals. But one has to wade through a lot of unconnected dots to get through it.

Lapine and Sondheim's next collaboration, *Into the Woods* (1987), also had an intriguing and refreshing premise. Act 1 musicalized a group of fairy tales all taking place in the same forest; Act 2 went beyond the traditional endings and explored the consequences of the characters' actions, raising questions about responsibility and community. Lapine went back to the original, darker versions of Cinderella, Rapunzel, Little Red Riding Hood, and other tales for his libretto. Then, to help tie these stories together, he created an original plot about a baker and his wife who are cursed with infertility by a vengeful witch. The familiar characters were played light and airy with all the happy endings converging at the end of the first act. But Lapine was on his own in act 2, and soon characters were being killed, guilt was being placed, and philosophical messages were being tossed about like magic beans. The cardboard figures of the playful first act started carrying on like Ibsen characters in the second, and when a handful of them were periodically bumped off to keep the plot moving, it was difficult to even pretend to care. Of course, the Sondheim score interrupts often enough that some blood starts flowing in these cartoon characters, but it only points out the incongruity of it all. Jack (of beanstalk fame) is written as ignorant, naive, and bumbling. Yet when he sings "Giants in the Sky," it is the voice of budding maturity and inspired observation. Then he returns to his usual stupidity. The baker's wife seems to have the insight of a fishwife, yet she manages to sing "Moments in the Woods," a delectable character song about her mixed emotions after a brief sexual indiscretion. Is this woman finally going somewhere? No, because she is crushed by a giant after she finishes the song. In no other Sondheim show is the gap between the heavenly score and the lead-footed dialogue more noticeable. Yet audiences were not bored with *Into the Woods*. Not only did it run two years on Broadway, but it has become the most often produced Sondheim show after the perennial favorite *Forum*.

For their third collaboration, Sondheim and Lapine considered another evening of two different but related playlets: a musical about bodybuilding and a dramatization of the Italian film *Passione d'Amore* (1981), which was based on a novel titled *Fosca*. How these two acts were going to relate to each other boggles the mind. But soon the second story grew too long, the bodybuilders were discarded, and they ended up with the musical *Passion* (1994). When the Italian Army officer Giorgio (Jere Shea) leaves his married mistress, Clara (Marin Mazzie), in Milan to go to his assignment at a military outpost, they plan to keep their passionate and perfect love alive through letters. At the outpost, Giorgio is fascinated by his captain's sickly and unappealing cousin Fosca (Donna Murphy). Her love for the handsome officer is off-putting at first, then slowly it penetrates Giorgio's gentlemanly demeanor. When Clara has to choose between her lover and losing her son, she breaks off with Giorgio, and he finally submits to Fosca's all-powerful love, the two of them ending tragically but enlightened. This handsome-boy-meets-ugly-girl story seemed a bit too traditional for either Sondheim or Lapine, and there was little in the telling (and singing) of it that was highly conceptual or unconventional (unless one considers a nude duet in bed conceptual). Yet *Passion* ended up being one of the most numbing of all Broadway musicals.

The libretto is straightforward and clear, if mostly stiff in dialogue and lifeless in character. Sondheim purposely wrote a score so low key and subtle that even the songwriter's strongest devotees were whispering "dull" to each other. On the other hand, one had to admit that this time the score and the libretto seemed to be cut from the same cloth. But just because Lapine threw out all the jokes, did Sondheim have to get rid of all the rhymes? *Passion* met with negative reviews, managed to win some major awards in a lean season, and held on for a few unprofitable months. At this writing, it is the last new Sondheim musical to be seen in New York. Everyone hopes it will not be his last; despite what T. S. Eliot says, better to go out with a bang than a whimper. As for Lapine, his directing career continues on. It is worth pointing out that he directed all three of his Sondheim collaborations, and one wonders if the collaborative team had gotten a bit thin in this trio of shows. Harold Prince, who did not produce the Lapine–Sondheim works, always brought his own vision as producer and/or director to the team of librettist and songwriter. It seems that a creative force of only two may not have been the most advantageous in these circumstances.

Sondheim's other "young" collaborator is John Weidman. Born in New York City in 1946, Weidman is the son of novelist, playwright, and sometime-librettist Jerome Weidman (see chapter 8). He was educated at Harvard, where he started writing humor pieces for the *Lampoon,* and in 1970 he founded the *National Lampoon* and served as its co-editor for a while. After teaching elementary school for three years, Weidman entered Yale Law School to pursue a legal degree. But after graduation in 1974, he found himself writing his first play, a nonmusical about Commodore Perry's arrival in Japan in 1853 to open up the "floating kingdom" for trade. Before Weidman knew it, Prince brought the play to Sondheim, and the result was *Pacific Overtures* (1976), perhaps the most neglected and underrated of the songwriter's works.

The libretto takes the point of view of the Japanese, cut off from the world for over a century and seeing the American ships as "black dragons" come to destroy their way of life. It is a history tale told in episodes involving everyone from the Shogun to common laborers, with two male friends used as reference points throughout: the samurai Kayama (Isao Sato), who is eventually seduced by Western ways and forsakes his Nippon heritage, and the fisherman Manjiro (Sab Shimono), who has seen the Western world and its enlightened ways but instead becomes a radical nationalist. It is a lively history lesson with such potent scenes as the Shogun's mother systematically poisoning her own son because she deems him too weak to rule, a brothel owner preparing her girls for the anticipated Americans, government officials coming up with a plan to meet with Perry and his staff without letting them touch sacred Japanese soil, three British sailors mistaking a noblewoman for a geisha girl and getting slaughtered by her father, and an American businessman introducing the rickshaw to the country. The libretto climaxes with Kayama and Manjiro, now on opposite sides of a bloody civil war over the question of the westerners, meeting again; Manjiro kills Kayama, but it is in vain because the Emperor decides to accept the Americans, and Japan will never be the same again. As if this plot were not foreign enough, Prince staged the musical in a pseudo-Kabuki style, and Sondheim came up with music that used Asian forms and lyrics that sometimes drew on Haiku poetry, all the time providing a palatable Broadway score. Boris Aronson designed what was arguably the finest scenery of his illustrious career, and with all the other elements in place, *Pacific Overtures* was one of the most beautiful productions ever to grace the Winter Garden Theatre.

Weidman's libretto is a marvel of pageantry, anecdote, character scenes, grandeur, and simplicity. A traditional Reciter (Mako) acts as a narrator at times, but then he also joins in the proceedings, playing a variety of characters. His commentary, from unsung Haiku poems ("The bird from the sea, / Not knowing pine from bamboo, / Roosts on *anything*.") to sly storytelling ("Giants with wild, coarse hair and faces gray as the dead. Americans! Look how they glare!"), kept the libretto from ever getting stuffy or solemn, and there was plenty of humor in the script as well. But like most Sondheim projects, there was a deep sense of tragedy underneath it all. Some Japanese American theatregoers were not endeared to a show that, on the one hand, praised Japan's ingenuity and rapid rise in the world and then, on the other hand, lamented how it sold its heritage for Western prestige and world power. The reviews were just about evenly divided into raves or pans, and the curious came to see the show for five months. Because of the difficulty in casting the all-Asian musical, revivals have been infrequent, though a scaled-down Off-Broadway production in 1984 met with success.

Enough time has gone by that *Pacific Overtures* can be fairly evaluated, and should a major revival bring it back to the attention of the public, it might gain the respect it deserves. When *Pacific Overtures* was in trouble out of town, Hugh Wheeler was brought in to help the beginner Weidman with the script. (Wheeler was credited with "additional material" in the program.) One might suspect that the most accomplished aspects of the libretto were Wheeler's, but Weidman would provide similar and even superior writing with *Assassins* (1991), which he wrote by himself. In the interim he worked on the revised script for the 1987 Broadway revival of *Anything Goes* and wrote for the popular television series *Sesame Street*. But these conventional writing experiences must have been little preparation for the dynamic, fearless libretto he wrote for *Assassins*. Again, the musical is a history piece, but history without chronological order or a traditional point of view. If *Pacific Overtures* looked at the opening of Japan from the Asian perspective, *Assassins* looks at the U.S. presidency (and America itself) from the killer's rifle scope. This very conceit struck some critics as anti-American, as if *Oedipus Rex* condones patricide or *West Side Story* advocate gang violence. These actual assassins (or would-be assassins) are a pathetic, funny, disturbing, even awe-inspiring group of individuals who cross over the borders of time to boast or complain to each other about the role they played in American history. John Wilkes Booth (Victor Garber) is the ringleader and the most intriguing of the lot, but each assassin is vibrantly written. Charles Guiteau (Jonathan Hadary) is a shameless self-promoter who considers death a small sacrifice to pay for fame. Leon Czolgosz (Terrence Mann) is a desperate idealist who has seen all his New World principles stepped on by his adopted country. Sara Jane Moore (Debra Monk) is a dysfunctional mother trying to find herself, while John Hinckley (Greg Germann) is a slave to his infatuation for movie star Jodie Foster. Perhaps Weidman's eeriest characterization is Lee Harvey Oswald (Jace Alexander), a self-deprecating loner who is enticed into killing JFK by the ghosts of the assassins who came before him. The climax of the musical is not a song but the scene in which Booth argues that the role of assassin is the refuge for the victims of this world:

BOOTH: Lee, when you kill a President, it isn't murder. Murder is a tawdry little crime; it's born of greed, or lust, or liquor. Adulterers and shopkeepers get murdered. But when a President gets killed, when Julius Caesar got killed . . . he was assassinated. And the man who did it . . . [he lets the sentence hang, unfinished]
OSWALD: Brutus.

> BOOTH: Ah! You know his name. Brutus assassinated Caesar, what?, two thousand years ago, and here's a high school drop-out with a dollar twenty-five an hour job in Dallas, Texas, who knows who he is. And they say fame is fleeting . . .

All the writing in *Assassins* is pointed and powerful. Weidman retains the adventurous spirit of an eager, young writer while he demonstrates the polish of an old pro. Sondheim also sounds like a young explorer as his score experiments with sounds and styles he'd not tackled before. Mixed notices and the nation's preoccupation with the Persian Gulf War kept the limited Off-Broadway run of *Assassins* from transferring to Broadway. But over the years the musical has made a name for itself across the country where dozens of theatre groups looking for demanding and rewarding musical theatre have success with it. Weidman's career after *Assassins* has been variable. He wrote the competent but uninspired adaptation for the musical *Big* (1996) and penned the nonbook for the "dance play" *Contact* (2000). There was much to recommend in *Big*, even though it seems much too traditional for Weidman's sensibility. *Contact* is an experiment in dance as storytelling and consists of three choreographed tales with recorded music and little dialogue. Each piece ends with a plot twist trying to be like O. Henry, but instead strikes me as the payoff for a beer commercial. *Big* failed to run, and *Contact* was a surprise hit. At this writing there is still a great deal of anticipation about *Gold*, a Weidman-scripted musical with a Sondheim score, originally titled *Wise Guys*, that has been in the workshop stage for some time.

With every Sondheim show, the perimeters of the musical form were challenged and pushed. The librettists for the Sondheim musicals are among the most courageous in the business. Consider the fact that about ninety percent of all musicals are based on a previous source, yet seven of the twelve Sondheim-scored shows have original librettos. The profit margins for the Sondheim musicals are slight, and the success ratio is debatable. But the integrity of writers like Larry Gelbart, Arthur Laurents, George Furth, Hugh Wheeler, James Lapine, and John Weidman cannot be questioned when they have refused to take the safe path and dared to provide librettos for Broadway's most demanding songwriter.

CHAPTER SIXTEEN
CARNIVAL ON THE ROOF: MICHAEL STEWART, JOSEPH STEIN, AND PETER STONE

By the 1960s, when the number of Broadway musicals each season continued to shrink, it became more difficult for songwriters and librettists to enjoy busy stage careers with frequently produced shows to their credit. Yet the librettists Michael Stewart, Joseph Stein, and Peter Stone managed to do just that. While all three careers extended beyond the 1960s, each did his finest work during that decade. All three proved to be fine craftsman with plenty of hits and flops to their credit, but in the 1960s each came up with at least one inspired and masterful show.

Michael Stewart was born in New York City in 1929 and educated at Queens College and Yale University. Like many other show business writers before him, Stewart honed his craft writing sketches for original revues at adult summer camps. He contributed sketches to such Broadway revues as *Alive and Kicking* (1950), *Razzle Dazzle* (1951), and *Shoestring Revue* (1955), and by 1956 was one of the television writers for Sid Caesar. Then Stewart struck gold with *Bye Bye Birdie* (1960), his first book musical to reach Broadway. The show had started as a high school musical called *Let's Go Steady* with a libretto by Warren Miller and Raphael Millian, but novice producer Edward Padula picked up the floundering production, brought on songwriters Charles Strouse (music) and Lee Adams (lyrics), and recruited Stewart to provide a better book. Stewart kept part of the high school romantic plot and added an adult story about show biz manager Albert Peterson (Dick Van Dyke); his client, the Elvis Presley–like Conrad Birdie (Dick Gautier); and Albert's long-suffering girlfriend Rose (Chita Rivera), who is still waiting for him to marry her, give up the pop music scene, and settle down as an English teacher. When Birdie is drafted (just as Elvis was), Albert hopes to cash in on a farewell performance in Sweet Apple, Ohio, where the all-American teenager Kim McAfee (Susan Watson) gets to kiss the rock-and-roll star goodbye on live television. In a secondary plot going back to the Andy Hardy movies, Kim's boyfriend, Hugo (Michael J. Pollard), is threatened by Kim's infatuation with the celebrity Birdie and actually slugs the not-so-wholesome singer on the air. Albert's hope for a commercial triumph collapses, Kim returns to Hugo, Birdie goes off to serve his country, and Albert and Rose reconcile and leave show business.

As familiar as it all may have seemed, *Bye Bye Birdie* was an original libretto in more ways than one. It was the first Broadway show to acknowledge (and lampoon) the rock sound that had already infiltrated records, movies, and television. It also dealt with the generation gap and foreshadowed the antiestablishment sentiment of shows later in the 1960s. In addition to the fretting McAfee parents (Paul Lynde and Marijane Maricle) who lamented the behavior of their "Kids," Stewart added Albert's mom (Kay Medford), a stock Broadway mother who hassles Albert and Rose, waylays their marriage plans, and illustrates that each generation should ignore the preceding one. Most of the characters throughout are stock types but are written with bold and cartoonish glee. Director Gower Champion's inventive staging and the bright and tuneful score helped make *Bye Bye Birdie* feel like a breath of fresh air, and the show was the sleeper of the season, if not one of the most celebrated of all Broadway sleepers. It remains popular today, especially with young audiences who view that bygone era with the same kind of manufactured nostalgia that makes *Grease* a favorite.

Stewart's writing took on a very different tone with *Carnival* (1961). His first of several adaptations, the show had a bittersweet, European temperament to it that was nothing like the all-American *Bye Bye Birdie*. The French waif Lili (Anna Maria Alberghetti) joins the traveling "Grand Imperial Cirque de Paris," where she is captivated by Marco the Magician (David Mitchell) but loved with true affection by the bitter and partially crippled puppeteer Paul Berthalet (Jerry Orbach), who communicates his feeling through his puppets. After nearly running away with Marco, Lili realizes that it is Paul whom she loves, and the show ends with minor key happiness. The tale had started out as a short story by Paul Gallico called "The Man Who Hated People" and was fashioned by screenwriter Helen Deutsch into the popular film *Lili* (1953). Stewart opened it up for the musical, yet managed to keep everything simple and delicate. Gower Champion was again the director, and he provided a few dazzling showstoppers, but the whole show still had a tenderness to it that also felt very foreign in a quaint way. Pierre Olaf as a wry commentator and Kaye Ballard as Marco's suspicious mistress Rosalie were also useful in tying the musical together, the former with his French authenticity and the latter with her Broadway chutzpah. *Carnival* was about as far from *Bye Bye Birdie* as one could get, yet Stewart penned both with professional ease.

Stewart's biggest success was *Hello, Dolly!* (1964), though it was probably one of the less challenging projects of his career. The story can be traced all the way back to the wily matchmaker Frosine in Moliere's *The Miser* (1668). (Some bits of Moliere's dialogue survive right up to the musical libretto.) British playwright John Oxenford made the same conniving matchmaker an important part of his 1835 comedy, *A Day Well Spent,* which was expanded by Austrian playwright Johann Nestroy into the 1842 farce *Einen Jux Will Er Sich Machen (He Wants to Play a Joke).* Thornton Wilder Americanized the tale in his comedy *The Merchant of Yonkers* (1938), which failed to run, but when he rewrote it as *The Matchmaker* (1954) with Dolly Levi now center stage, the show was a hit. Other aspects of the plot, such as the group of young folks out on the town looking for adventure, and an elderly merchant losing his wallet at a ritzy restaurant, can be traced back to *A Trip to Chinatown* (1891) (see chapter 6). I mention all these sources not to detract from Stewart's libretto but to point out that the story had been staged many times before. Opening up the plot for the musical form was not terribly difficult because Wilder's farce already has the expansive feel of a musical. More than any other show I can think of, the song cues (and even Jerry Herman's song titles) are right there in the original. All the same, Stewart's adaptation of the material into *Hello, Dolly!* is very proficient. Intended as a star vehicle for Ethel Merman, the libretto pads the part of Dolly unashamedly. When Merman declined and Carol Channing took on the role, she was able to fill out the oversized character with no problem. Subsequent Dollys found that, star or not, they had to perform the lady like a comic diva. It is not quite Wilder's matchmaker but a Broadway version of her—less wily and sly, more bombast and mother earth figure. Stewart eliminated the character of Aunt Flora and the scene in her New York townhouse, and rewrote the climax as a frantic courtroom scene with all the major characters gathered for some merry chaos and a sweet denouement. It may not measure up to the skillful plotting of the original, but it is bigger and more in the musical mode. Making things bigger seems to have been Stewart's main task in writing the libretto, and he certainly succeeded. Not many can take what was mostly a drawing room comedy and end up with a train scene, a city park full of dancers, and even a parade.

After three hits in a row, Stewart's career faced two decades of rollercoaster fluctuation. His script for a musical about computer dating called *How Do You Do, I Love You,* with a score by David Shire (music) and Richard Maltby Jr. (lyric), closed on the road in 1967. The next year he collaborated with his sister and brother-in-law, Fran and John Pascal, on the biomusical *George M!* (1968) about showman Cohan (Joel Grey).

Because Cohan's life had already been wonderfully (and inaccurately) portrayed in the film classic *Yankee Doodle Dandy* (1942), the stage version was up against a lot of fond memories. The librettists aimed for a more truthful telling of the man's career and marriages, yet the feeling was still that of a great big patriotic, happy-go-lucky Cohan musical. The result was not real enough to be illuminating, but was artificial enough to be entertaining. Cohan's songs and Joe Layton's vigorous direction and choreography made the show seem special. Probably a tough, revealing, and fascinating musical could be made from the Yankee Doodle's life, but *George M!* was not that musical.

Stewart's run of unprofitable adaptations continued in England, where his musicalization of Arthur Wing Pinero's comic romance, *The Amazons* (1893), closed in 1971 on its way to the West End. Back in the States, his libretto for *Sugar* (1972), based on the film favorite *Some Like It Hot* (1959), was discarded, and he was replaced by George Axelrod (who was later replaced by Peter Stone). Stewart's work on the problematic *Seesaw* (1973) was also dropped when he was replaced by Neil Simon (who himself was replaced by director Michael Bennett). Even more problematic was *Mack and Mabel* (1974), which *did* open with Stewart's name as librettist. Billed as "the musical romance of Mack Sennett's funny and fabulous Hollywood," the show reunited Stewart with songwriter Herman and director Champion. It was an original libretto, though filmmaker Mack Sennett (Robert Preston) and his favorite star, Mabel Normand (Bernadette Peters), were far from fictional and, it turned out, not exactly musical comedy fodder. He was a ruthless, unfeeling egomaniac, and she became a drug addict, got mixed up in some juicy scandals, and died of an overdose. The *Hello, Dolly!* team found themselves in Stephen Sondheim territory. Stewart tried to steer a path between the mindless fun of Keystone Kops and bathing beauties and the brutal reality of a doomed romance and wasted lives. It was probably a hopeless cause, especially when Champion just kept piling on the spectacle to hide the show's many flaws. Herman did provide what many consider the finest score of his career, and Preston and Peters were so charming that you could almost forget about Mack and Mabel. Perhaps an ingenious writer could have pulled it all together and made it work, but Stewart was unable to. *Mack and Mabel* is always being tinkered with, sometimes cutting out the parts of the tale that are a downer, but ultimately it ends up being a showcase for performers and Herman's glorious score.

After the profits from *Hello, Dolly!* started pouring in, Stewart lived much of the time in France, where in 1975 he ran across the Parisian hit comedy *Viens Chez Moi, J'Habite Chez une Copine (Come to My House, I Live at My Girl Friend's)* by Luis Rego and Didier Kaminka. The sex farce about wife swapping even had a few songs in it, and the show struck Stewart as ideal for a small-cast musical. He interested composer Cy Coleman, whom he had worked with during his tenure on *Seesaw,* in the project, and since Coleman's lyricist on that show, Dorothy Fields, had died in 1974, Stewart himself provided the lyrics and called the show *I Love My Wife* (1977). Word of mouth during the out-of-town run and previews were not encouraging, but surprisingly the critics mostly praised the little musical, and it ran 872 performances. Stewart reset the story in Trenton, New Jersey, where two married couples, feeling that they have somehow missed out on the sexual revolution, decide to drop their inhibitions and "turn on" with drugs and sex. They are disastrously inept in both areas of experimentation and, before any actual wife swapping can occur, they learn to be content with their spouses. Whether it was Stewart's idea or the original director Joe Layton's brainstorm is not clear, but the four were joined by four bearded musicians who performed on stage and kept appearing in various guises throughout the show. It was an unpretentious piece of entertainment that was professionally done. Stewart's lyrics ranged from clever to embarrassing, but the libretto is perky and playful. *I Love My Wife* may seem rather dated today, yet it has such an unabashed 1970s mentality that the musical seems nostalgic when revived, which is not often.

The Grand Tour (1979) was Stewart's last musical with Jerry Herman and his first of three shows with co-librettist Mark Bramble. Born in 1950 and raised near Baltimore, Bramble was educated at Emerson College in Boston and at New York University. Before he graduated from the latter in 1975, he interned as an assistant in the offices of producer David Merrick. Some of Bramble's librettos were produced Off-Off Broadway, and his reworking of the script of *Pal Joey* with Jerome Chodorov was presented with success in Los Angeles. Stewart and Bramble were approached by the producers of *The Grand Tour* when an earlier version fell through. The show was based on the 1944 comedy *Jacobowsky and the Colonel* by S. N. Behrman, which was an adaptation of the Austrian play *Jacobowsky und der Oberst* by Franz Werfel. Although the Behrman play was a success, most Americans knew the story from a 1958 film version called *Me and the Colonel* with Danny Kaye as a Jewish refugee who enlists the help of a Polish Colonel to keep one step ahead of the Nazis. Although the Colonel is initially anti-Semitic and resistant to the plan, he and the little Jew set off together and befriend each other in a subtle and amusing manner. The libretto remains true to the earlier versions, but sometimes the songs seem more like intrusions than embellishments to the story. (A wedding song-and-dance sequence that seemed to take place for no other reason than to please *Fiddler on the Roof* fans was roundly attacked by the critics.) Some of the writing is very accomplished, and Herman's score has as many touching moments as it has garish ones. But the original production suffered from weak direction and indecision about how the fragile story should be played. Ron Holgate was a robust and enjoyable Colonel, but Joel Grey's Jacobowsky was considered too artificial and overblown for the gentle character. *The Grand Tour* struggled for sixty-one performances and lost a lot of money, yet it seems to be a show that should be revised and revived; with the right elements in place, it might become what Broadway never saw.

Bramble and Stewart had much more success with *Barnum* (1980), though they provided journeyman's work at best. Suggested by the life of the greatest of all con men/showmen, Phineas Taylor Barnum, the musical used the format of a circus to tell a fascinating story—poorly. Most of the main attractions were worked in, from little General Tom Thumb (Leonard John Crofoot) to scenic designer David Mitchell's clever representation of Jumbo the elephant, but for plot the libretto belabored the marital problems of Barnum (Jim Dale) and his straight-laced New England wife Charity (Glenn Close). It seems she wants him to settle down, but he loves looking for the adventurous side of life, and they talked about it endlessly while the audience patiently waited for the next circus act. Once again Stewart provided the lyrics to Cy Coleman's music, and this time he came up with an admirable score, much more playful than any of the book scenes. Dale's winning and energetic performance and Joe Layton's tireless direction and choreography made *Barnum* seem like gold, and it ran a very profitable 854 performances. But like *George M!* it was a lost opportunity, a musical that could not begin to approach the genius of its subject.

Stewart's last hit show was *42nd Street* (1980), co-written with Bramble and with Gower Champion on board once again as director-choreographer. The preparations and previews were more ghastly than usual (even for a David Merrick production) as the ailing Champion saw the producer bring in other directors for "advice" while the scenery was rebuilt and the opening delayed. Yet when *42nd Street* finally opened, it looked like putting it together must have been a breeze. The announcement of Champion's death on opening night gave the show a sentimental boost, something lacking in the script, and it ran an astounding 3,486 performances. Since the musical was based on a movie *musical* (one of the first such transitions on Broadway but far from the last), it would seem that a stage adaptation would not be difficult. But the landmark 1933 movie was so famous and influential because it did not resemble a stage show. Even the production numbers in the movie's show-within-a-show did not conform to the rules of the stage. In a way, Stewart and Bramble had to take a piece of entertainment that defied the conventions of the theatre and turn it into a theatre piece. The solution seemed to lie in the musical numbers, nearly three times the number in the film. Songs from other Harry Warren (music) and Al Dubin (lyrics) scores were added, and the plot was downplayed until libretto credit was reduced to "Lead-Ins and Crossovers by. . . ." Merrick later restored the "Book by . . ." billing, but in this case there was some truth in advertising. There is precious little book in *42nd Street*, and what is there is either abrupt or downright confusing. Here is a musical where boy doesn't seem to get girl (Wanda Richert); it's not even clear which boy wants girl: producer Julian Marsh (Jerry Orbach), Billy Lawlor (Lee Roy Reams), or both. The comedy, provided mostly by wisecracking Maggie Jones (Carole Cook) and diva Dorothy Brock (Tammy Grimes), is cracklingly fun but in short supply. This is true of the score as well as the libretto. Of the dozen songs, only one ("Shuffle Off to Buffalo") comes close to being a comic number. Ironically, the dying Champion provided the only heart in *42nd Street*, a show touted as "The Song and Dance Extravaganza." That's even more truth in advertising; it is barely a book musical at all.

The rest of Stewart's career consisted of quick flops. *Elizabeth and Essex*, a musical based on Maxwell Anderson's historical drama *Elizabeth the Queen* (1930) that had been co-written with Bramble back in 1975, finally appeared Off Broadway and disappeared after a short run. *Bring Back Birdie* (1981), one of Broadway's most infamous sequels, reunited Stewart with songwriters Strouse and Adams and star Chita Rivera from the 1960 hit. Intended for amateur markets (particularly high schools who might want more Conrad Birdie), the musical ended up on Broadway, where it received one of the worst set of pans on record. The script caught up with the characters twenty years later, and they were a sorry lot. Birdie (Marcel Forestieri) is old and fat and the mayor of a hick burg in Arizona. Albert's mother (Maria Karnilova) returns as a vulgar bigamist. Even the marriage of Albert (Donald O'Connor) and Rosie (Rivera) is a little shaky, as their teenage offspring are into a Hare Krishna cult, a punk rock band, and extramarital sex. (They intended this for high schools?) The songs were sometimes bearable, but Stewart's book was a shambles with more subplots than a Dickens novel. The six-performance dud became a Broadway legend.

Unlike *Bring Back Birdie*, the idea behind *Harrigan 'n Hart* (1985) was a good one. Another biomusical, the show was about the two men who had helped create musical farce in America, comics Edward Harrigan (Harry Groener) and Tony Hart (Mark Hamill); but like Stewart's previous biomusicals, it failed to capture what made the originals special. Some songs by David Braham (music) and Harrigan (lyrics) from the actual shows were mixed in with some new numbers by Max Showalter (music) and Peter Walker (lyrics), but Stewart's script never fully explained what a Harrigan and Hart musical was like. Evidently, they were quite raucous, though you would never guess it from this watered-down version that even soft-pedaled Hart's notorious homosexuality. The musical ran one less performance than *Bring Back Birdie*.

Stewart's last project never made it to Broadway. *Pieces of Eight* (1985), a musicalization of *Treasure Island* with a score by Jule Styne (music) and Susan Birkenhead (lyrics), tried out in Edmonton, Canada, then faded away. A musical farce called *Nothing but the Truth*, co-written with Bramble, was unfinished when Stewart died of pneumonia in 1987 at the age of fifty-eight. His was a career of no fewer than six major hits, most of them continually revived.

Joseph Stein's writing career begins about the same time as Stewart's, but he is providing Broadway librettos by the mid-1950s, reaching the peak of his success at about the same time that *Hello, Dolly!* triumphs. Stein was born in New York City in 1912 and educated at the College of the City of New York and Columbia University's College of Social Research, with an eye on a career as a social worker. His first writing was for the radio, then by 1950 for television, writing for *All Star Revue*, Sid Caesar, and other video stars. By this time, Stein had also contributed sketch material for such Broadway revues as *Lend an Ear* (1948) and *Alive and Kicking* (1950). His first musical libretto, co-written with Will Glickman, was *Plain and Fancy* (1955), a genial show about an Amish community in Pennsylvania and a modest success. While Broadway musicals had enjoyed making fun of country rubes and rural sects since the days of the Cohan musicals, *Plain and Fancy* took a quaint and warm approach to the subject. New Yorkers Dan (Richard Derr) and Ruth (Shirl Conway) come to Bird-in-Hand, Pennsylvania, to look over a farm Dan has inherited before they sell it to Papa Yoder (Stefan Schnabel). The farm will be the dowry for Papa's daughter Katie (Gloria Marlowe), who is engaged to the upright Ezra Reber (Douglas Fletcher Rogers), even though she really loves Ezra's "shunned" brother Peter (David Daniels). Tradition is challenged, city ways confront country ways, and a happy ending is reached by everyone bending a little. As a folktale, it can be considered something of an ancestor to Stein's later *Fiddler on the Roof* (1964). The community nurtures the rustic characters but also threatens those who want to break away from the old ways. Here is a musical that actually has something to say about society. Yet with the sarcastic humor provided by the wisecracking Ruth and the overromantic local, Hilda (Barbara Cook), *Plain and Fancy* never gets unbearably folksy. And the songs by Albert Hague (music) and Arnold B. Horwitt (lyrics) are bright and knowing rather than solemn, even the Amish hymns filled with life-affirming optimism. It is a well-constructed libretto, an original one at that, and a musical that ought to be revived more often.

Stein and Glickman teamed up again on the book for *Mr. Wonderful* (1956), a showcase for the up-and-coming vocalist Sammy Davis Jr., but it was a book musical in name only. The first act told about the struggles of young Charlie Welch (Davis) as he tries to break out of small-time show business and into the big time; the second act was mostly his nightclub act. Jerry Bock, Larry Holofcener, and George Weiss collaborated on the score, which provided Davis with the hit song "Too Close for Comfort," but Stein and Glickman could not provide any characters or situations that were believable or entertaining. The show ran 383 performances on Davis's appeal, but lost money and did nothing for the authors' reputation. They hardly redeemed themselves with *The Body Beautiful* (1958), a gritty, realistic, but dull musical about the world of boxing. Young tyro Bob (Steve Forrest) tries to make it into the big ring, but underworld figures stand in his way until good (and love) triumphs. The show is memorable only because it marked the first collaboration of tunesmiths Jerry Bock (music) and Sheldon Harnick (lyrics). Even their score was forgettable, but *The Body Beautiful* did bring together the talents for Stein's later hit, *Fiddler on the Roof.*

Working solo for the first time, Stein wrote the libretto for the ambitious musical drama *Juno* (1959) based on the Sean O'Casey Irish classic *Juno and the Paycock* (1924). It was his first adaptation for Broadway, and he remained faithful to O'Casey, while opening up the one-set drama into a full-scale musical about, once again, community. The drama takes place in 1922 Dublin during the IRA "troubles" that overshadow the domestic problems of the Boyle family: the crusty drunkard Captain Jack Boyle (Melvyn Douglas), his long-suffering wife Juno (Shirley Booth), their love-hungry daughter Mary (Monte Amundsen), and their troubled son Johnny (Tommy Rall). Stein masterfully transposes the family's episodes into community ones. For example, in the O'Casey play, a gramophone is delivered to the Boyle household, and they celebrate with music; Stein has the Boyles show off their new toy to the neighborhood, the scene turning into a vibrant street song and dance that is suddenly stopped by the appearance of a mourning mother going to the funeral of her son who was killed by the British. The libretto is skillful throughout, and Marc Blitzstein's songs are probably the most moving and overwhelming of his quirky career. But *Juno*, with its many tragic elements (Mary gets pregnant, Johnny is shot dead,

Juno deserts the Captain, who escapes into another drunken stupor), was far too grim for Broadway, and it closed in two weeks. Perhaps no other failed musical of the decade deserves to be rediscovered more than *Juno*.

Stein's next adaptation, *Take Me Along* (1959), based on Eugene O'Neill's only comedy, *Ah, Wilderness!* (1933), was written with Robert Russell. (Bob Merrill provided the music and lyrics.) The librettists remained faithful to O'Neill's period piece about the coming of age of the lovesick youth Richard Miller (Robert Morse), but the focus of the story was thrown off when celebrity Jackie Gleason was cast in the secondary role of Sid, Richard's merry, alcoholic uncle. Despite this imbalance, much of *Take Me Along* is top-notch musical theatre (and not bad O'Neill, either). The show was a hit at 448 performances, but Stein's contribution seems unexceptional. He then turned to writing nonmusicals for a while, his most notable effort being the comedy *Enter Laughing* (1963), until he was invited to come on board for a Jewish musical based on the stories of Sholom Aleichem. Stein and the other creators believed that *Tevye and His Daughters*, as they first called it, would have limited appeal, but it was a project dear to them; they reasoned that the largely Jewish theatre audience would allow them to run long enough to at least break even. So they made no attempt to Broadway-ize the material. The Russian folktales would be told without glitz or glamour (although the producers did court big stars to play Tevye), and the Hebrew customs and terminology would not be secularized or translated. It would be a nice Jewish show.

In many ways, Stein's libretto for *Fiddler on the Roof* (1964) is a culmination of his earlier efforts at writing about a community. Here were the simple Amish, but without the city slickers to provide the jokes. One of the central scenes in *Plain and Fancy* was a traditional barn raising with all the locals taking part; in *Fiddler* it is a village wedding with all the traditional rituals intact. In Bird-in-Hand, two childhood sweethearts go against a father's wishes in order to marry; in the Russian town of Anatevka, three of Tevye's daughters go against parents, family, religion, and even community to wed. The dark shadow of oppression that was evident throughout *Juno* becomes more subtle but just as effective in *Fiddler*. A street dance is interrupted by a funeral in Dublin; a wedding is dispersed by a pogrom in *Fiddler*. Although filled with several colorful folk types, Anatevka is the main character of the show. I can think of no other successful musical in which community is the star. And, not to take away from Jerome Robbins's brilliant direction and the sterling score by Bock and Harnick, much of this must be credited to Stein. One has only to look at the musical's sources (the original Aleichem stories, Arnold Perl's stage adaptation *Tevye and His Daughters*, a Yiddish-language film version) to realize that the Stein libretto is by far the best of the lot. The musical is filled with stage traditions, but like the questioning characters it is about, it also flies against the Broadway musical formula. What can be more traditional and familiar than the scene in which Tevye (Zero Mostel) and the butcher, Lazar Wolf (Michael Granger), bargain? The father thinks they are talking about buying a milk cow, the butcher about marrying Tevye's daughter:

> TEVYE: Reb Lazar, there is no use talking about it.
> LAZAR: [upset] Why not?
> TEVYE: Why yes? Why should I get rid of her?
> LAZAR: Well, you have a few more without her.
> TEVYE: I see! Today you want one. Tomorrow you may want two.
> LAZAR: [startled] Two? What would I do with two?
> TEVYE: The same as you do with one!

Yet what could be more disturbingly untraditional than an exchange such as this?

> CONSTABLE: I am giving you this news because I like you. You are a decent, honest person, even though you are a Jewish dog.
> TEVYE: How often does a man get a compliment like that? . . . Thank you, Your Honor. You're a good man. If I may say so, it's too bad you're not a Jew.
> CONSTABLE: [amused] That's what I like about you, Tevye, always joking.

The Aleichem folk humor turns painfully unfunny at many points throughout *Fiddler on the Roof.* Occasionally, such moments occur in the score, but mostly it is Stein's libretto that gives the show its bite. (Notice that each act ends without a song.) He also manages to incorporate the script's many episodes into a beautifully balanced libretto. High craftsmanship meets inspired creativity. We are so familiar with the show now that we forget how exceptional *Fiddler* is. Much of it has become cliché because of that familiarity. But time and repetition cannot diminish Stein's (and one of Broadway's) finest accomplishments.

Community was also central to *Zorba* (1968), but the suspicious, narrow-minded little village in Crete was a nightmarish community. Nikos Kazantzakis's 1946 novel *Zorba the Greek* had been made into a memorable film in 1965. Stein, working solo again, incorporated the townsfolk into the tale of the aging but robust Zorba (Herschel Bernardi), the faded courtesan

Hortense (Maria Karnilova), whom he romances, and the young English-man, Nikos (John Cunningham), whom he befriends when the Brit comes to Crete to reactivate an old mine he has inherited. Stein's libretto begins with a gathering of locals who argue in song and prose about the meaning of life, then they reenact the story, becoming the principal characters as well as the townspeople. But this is no Anatevka. The villagers distrust the new-comers, envy the wealthy Hortense, and scorn a widow (Carmen Alvarez) because she won't remarry. When Hortense dies, they ransack her house before the state can claim the goods, and when a local youth commits sui-cide over his unrequited love for the widow, the locals stone her to death. The mine fails, Zorba and Nikos part ways, and life continues in the vicious little town. Aside from the play-within-a-play device, Stein sticks closely to the source material, and the John Kander (music) and Fred Ebb (lyrics) songs often add richness to this rather dire tale. Harold Prince's direction was also admirable. But too much of *Zorba* fails to take off. Some blamed Bernardi, who was proficient as the life-fulfilling Zorba, but he was not the wild-eyed Anthony Quinn, who played the role in the film. Fifteen years later, when *Zorba* was revived on Broadway with Quinn, it made money, running 354 performances (fifty-one times more than the original). There is not much to fault in Stein's libretto, but it remains a curiously cold musical.

Stein's final hit show, *Irene* (1973), was a dubious success. He was among the many who helped revise the 1919 libretto (Stein and Hugh Wheeler were the only authors credited), and what they came up with seemed painfully old fashioned without being nostalgic. The troubled re-vival was roundly panned, but audiences flocked to see Debbie Reynolds as the Irish lass Irene, and the show managed a small profit. Stein was brought in to doctor the musicals *Raisin* (1973) and *Doctor Jazz* (1975), the first a modest success, the second an unprofitable vehicle for Lola Falana. Then Stein adapted his own play *Enter Laughing* (based on Carl Reiner's autobiography) into the musical *So Long, 174th Street* (1976). The tale of the eager but inept actor David Kolowitz (Robert Morse) trying to break into the theatre seemed like probable musical comedy material, but the result was surprisingly leaden. Many blamed the dull score by Stan Daniels, but Stein's libretto was also lacking. To fill out the slight plot, he added fantasy sequences in which David saw himself as a ladies' man, a star, and so on. But David ends up being a pharmacist, and the show ended up closing in two weeks.

Also promising was *The Baker's Wife* (1976), a musicalization of the 1938 French comedy of the same title, but this notoriously troubled show never made it to Broadway, closing in Washington after a torturous tryout tour across the country. Over the years it has become a cult favorite (thanks largely to the superb score by Stephen Schwartz), and revised revivals are plentiful (including short stints Off Broadway in 1985 and in London in 1989). But *The Baker's Wife* is still one of the most problematic of all cult musicals. The plot is basically a triangle consisting of the middle-aged baker Aimable (Topol, later replaced by Paul Sorvino); his much younger and restless wife, Genevieve (Carole Demas, later replaced by Patti Lupone); and the womanizer Dominique (Kurt Peterson), who seduces her. When she runs off with Dominique, the grief-stricken Aimable stops baking, and the whole town finagles to get her back because they miss their fresh bread. Stein fills out the cast of characters with locals (an oversexed mayor, a pair of arguing innkeepers, battling neighbors), but instead of being quaint (as in Bird-in-Hand and Anatevka) or villainous (as in Crete), these French villagers were insipid and annoying. Most of the later revisions involved filling out these characters, but it only made the show longer and the townsfolk more obnoxious. There will always be someone trying to make *The Baker's Wife* work (Stein himself has revised it a few times), but the problem continues to be in the basic story, which seems to resist musicalization.

After serving as play doctor for the ailing *Hellzapoppin'*, a revue starring Jerry Lewis that closed out of town in 1977, Stein adapted another French film for the musical stage: *King of Hearts* (1978). The 1968 movie had become an antiestablishment favorite, as it argued that the only sane people in a war-torn world were the escaped lunatics from the local asylum. Offbeat Off-Broadway playwright Steve Tesich wrote the libretto when the show was tried out in summer stock, but Stein was brought on when the production was enlarged (most say bloated) for Broadway. As the British soldiers head toward a French village in 1918, the Germans occupying the town plant hidden bombs and take off, as do most of the inhabitants. When the naive British soldier Johnny Perkins (Don Scardino) arrives to scout out the town, it is peopled by the merry lunatics who pretend to be the mayor, a bishop, and other establishment figures. By the end of the story, Johnny is so disenchanted by the real world that he joins the folks in the insane asylum. It was a sweet, leftist tale that required a delicate kind of whimsy in order to be palatable. Stein's humorless libretto and the production's elaborate sets, circus acts, and even a coronation scene all help sink the expensive, overblown musical, which closed in a month. Like the movie, the show has a cult following of its own. Much of the score by Peter Link (music) and Jacob Brackman (lyrics) is laudable, and *King of Hearts* has been revived on occasion, often with the original Tesich libretto.

When Alan Jay Lerner was having trouble plotting *Carmelina* (1979), he enlisted the help of Stein, who got co-author credit. But neither man had had anything but box office failures for years, and this show did not prove to be an exception (see chapter 11). Stein worked solo again on *Rags* (1986), another unsuccessful musical that has developed a cult following, but this time there was much to admire in the ambitious project. In many ways *Rags* was a sequel to *Fiddler,* showing what happens to a group of Jewish immigrants when they arrive at Ellis Island in 1910. The central characters are Rebecca Herschkowitz (Teresa Stratas), who arrives in America with her young son David (Josh Blake) to look for her husband Nathan (Larry Kert); Bella Cohen (Judy Kuhn), another newcomer to New York who befriends Rebecca; and Saul (Terrence Mann), a radical union organizer. While there was some humor in the complicated plotting, much of it was dark and tragic: David is beaten up for his laborers' rights activities, Nathan turns out to be a stooge for Tammany Hall politicians, and Bella dies in a sweatshop fire. But there was also much that was warm and involving in the overlong libretto, and the score, by Charles Strouse (music) and Stephen Schwartz (lyrics), was exceptional throughout. After going through a series of directors, the production limped onto Broadway, where it lasted only four performances. But *Rags* refuses to disappear. Revivals Off Broadway and regionally continue to surface, and some of the many book problems have been solved over the years. Stein's work cannot be totally blamed, for there are some beautifully written scenes, and many of the characters come to life vividly; but there is no question that the libretto is the show's weakest link.

Joseph Stein has not been represented again on Broadway. After years of no activity, he provided the adaptation of Thornton Wilder's *The Skin of Our Teeth* (1942) into the Kander and Ebb musical *Over & Over;* but an out-of-town tryout in 1999 was so disastrous that it did not make any attempt to reach Broadway. Stein's career had not seen a profitable show in decades, but to many he still represented the reliable craftsmanship of libretto writing. The man who wrote about so many communities was beloved in the theatrical community. His hit-miss record was embarrassing, but his integrity record was champion material.

Peter Stone, on the other hand, has had a very impressive track record. Not only has he scripted a half dozen hit shows, but he has proved to be one of the most sought after play doctors on Broadway. He was born in Los Angeles in 1930, the son of a film producer and writer. Stone was educated on the East Coast, getting degrees from Bard College and Yale University before beginning a writing career in television. He would win awards for his work on such acclaimed programs as *Studio One, The Asphalt Jungle, The Defenders,* and *Androcles and the Lion* (a television musical with Richard Rodgers). Stone would also have a distinguished film career, writing original screenplays for a dozen movies, most memorably *Charade* (1963), and doing the film versions of *Sweet Charity* (1968) and *1776* (1972). His theatre career began with a script for a musical called *Friend of the Family* (1958), which was produced in St. Louis. Three years later he had his first Broadway credit, as librettist for *Kean* (1961). Most of Stone's musicals would be adaptations, but no assignment was more bizarre than turning a Jean-Paul Sartre philosophic biodrama about eighteenth-century British actor Edmund Kean into libretto form. Sartre's 1953 play, *Kean, ou Désordre et génie (Kean, or Disorder and Genius),* was based on an 1836 melodrama by Alexandre Dumas *père,* but the French philosopher-playwright was more interested in Kean's inner battle between reality and illusion than his many mistresses and scandalous behavior. Stone cut back on the philosophy and emphasized Kean's adventures in the boudoir over those of the theatre. In may ways the libretto resembles a costume operetta, and the score by George Forrest and Robert Wright was often in the operatic mode. Broadway favorite Alfred Drake was quite mesmerizing as Kean (for many, his Shakespeare scenes were the most rewarding aspect of the show), but the musical was neither fish nor fowl; the Sartre sensibility was gone, but so was most of the entertaining melodrama. *Kean* held on for a few months, and Stone's theatre career was launched.

Turning Elmer Rice's expressionistic *Dream Girl* (1945) into the musical comedy *Skyscraper* (1965) was a less daunting assignment. The original was a light comedy about Georgina Allerton, a bored bookseller who fantasizes about life all day long until she meets Mr. Right and she no longer needs her dreams. Much of Rice's script had dated poorly, so Stone wisely made Georgina (Julie Harris) more interesting by turning her into an antique shop owner who refuses to sell her building to speculators who want to demolish it to make room for a skyscraper. Georgina's fantasies were still romanticized views of her wishes, but they were more farcical in Stone's version, most of the scenes playing well. Particularly fun was her shop assistant Roger (Charles Nelson Reilly) who was transformed into an FBI agent, a British officer, a Southern gent, and even a toreador in Georgina's dreams. The score by James Van Heusen (music) and Sammy Cahn (lyrics) was merely serviceable, and what Harris lacked in singing talents she more than made up for in her considerable comic ability. *Skyscraper* was Stone's first musical *comedy,* and it managed to get moderately favorable reviews and run 241 performances.

CHAPTER SIXTEEN

Stone's finest hour would be his libretto for *1776* (1969), an assignment that forebode nothing but disaster. Sherman Edwards, a former high school history teacher whose career as a songwriter was slowly taking off, had spent years writing the book, music, and lyrics for a musical about the signing of the Declaration of Independence. Understandably, no producer would touch such an unlikely project. But Stuart Ostrow liked the songs and found the dramatic situation promising. What he didn't like was the libretto. So Stone was brought in, and after getting caught up in the history and characters more than in Edwards's book, he agreed to pen a new script. There was plenty of archival material available (letters by John and Abigail Adams, George Washington, and Benjamin Franklin were quoted profusely), but making the characters come alive was the real challenge. Stone's version of the Founding Fathers uses Gilbertian satire, patriotic speechifying, and even vaudeville. Since the real Franklin had written plenty of one-liners, many of the scenes involving him turned into comic sketches:

ADAMS: Dammit it, Franklin, you make us sound treasonous!
FRANKLIN: Do I? [thinks] Treason—"Treason is a charge invented by the winners as an excuse to hang the losers."
ADAMS: I have more to do than stand here listening to you quote yourself.
FRANKLIN: No, that was a new one!

But Stone placed just as much emphasis on the serious aspects of the situation, keeping the debates in the Continental Congress lively and even fiery rather than solemn or sanctimonious. The slavery issue, for example, is brought into the story powerfully. What could have been a comfortable sermon on human rights becomes a disturbing complication facing the Congress and, clearly implied, the country that is to be:

HOPKINS: It's a stinking business, Mr. Rutledge—a stinking business!
RUTLEDGE: Is it really, Mr. Hopkins? Then what's that I smell floatin' down from the North—could it be the aroma of hypocrisy? For who holds the other end of that filthy pursestring, Mr. Adams? [to everyone] Our northern brethren are feelin' a bit tender toward our slaves. They don't keep slaves, no-o, but they're willin' to be considerable carriers of slaves— to others! They are willin', for the shillin'— [rubbing his thumb and forefinger together] or haven't y'heard, Mr. Adams? Clink! Clink!

Some commentators felt that *1776* trivialized history, but it would be more accurate to say that Stone and Edwards Broadwayized it. They did not need to invent episodes to make the show interesting, but they did rearrange some events and consolidated details as any good stage adapter does. If ever a libretto was lacking the boy-meets-girl possibilities, this was it. So Stone brought in Adams's and Jefferson's wives, one as a confidante and the other for a bit of romance. The first spouse works well in the text; the second was a clumsy mistake. Newlywed Martha Jefferson (Betty Buckley) and her visit to Philadelphia to release her husband's sexual tension and free him up to write the Declaration is the libretto's weakest spot. Perhaps it was insurance that this talky, all-male story would have at least a bit of petticoat in it, but some found it more a distraction than a pleasant diversion. The question of how John Adams (William Daniels) and his colleagues were going to get everyone to agree to sign the Declaration was much more interesting than the testosterone needed to write it. *1776* is talky, with perhaps more book scenes than any other Broadway musical, but the talk is never dull. In fact, Stone's wit is much more polished than Edwards's lyrics, and the silliness sometimes attributed to the musical can be found mostly in the songs. When the show opened during the height of the Vietnam War, it was denounced as both blindly patriotic by some and leftist with an antiwar agenda by others. Over the years *1776* has been revived frequently (a 1997 Broadway revival was highly praised) and successfully stands on its own as a fascinating and entertaining musical. It is also a one-of-a-kind musical, unique in its handling of history as musical theatre. One has only to look at the many failed imitations that followed, such as *1600 Pennsylvania Avenue* (1976), *Rex* (1976), and *Teddy and Alice* (1977), to realize what a miraculous thing *1776* is.

While none of Stone's subsequent musicals matched the success of *1776,* many of them were profitable, sometimes for reasons having nothing to do with the quality of the show. *Two By Two* (1970), for example, was able to run in the black because of Danny Kaye's presence. Stone adapted Clifford Odets's *The Flowering Peach* (1954) into a musical vehicle for the star's return to Broadway after three decades of popular movies. The Odets comedy took a light but philosophical approach to biblical Noah and his family, making the spry old man into a Sholom Aleichem–kind of character. Stone's Noah was much broader (or was that Kaye?), and what were mildly amusing Yiddish jokes in the original became leaden geriatric jokes in the musical. Richard Rodgers provided some lovely music, but Martin Charin's lyrics were so feeble that Kaye's frequent ad-libs started to sound good. Like *Two By Two,* Stone's next project, *Sugar* (1972), had a harrowing preparation. The composer, lyricist, librettist, director, the scenery, and a handful of the actors were all replaced during the efforts to make the film favorite *Some Like It Hot* (1959) into a musical. Jule Styne (music) and Bob Merrill (lyric) were the final songwriters, and Stone was the surviving librettist, though Neil Simon was brought in to punch up the comedy in some of the scenes. Despite the title, the plot still centered on Chicago musicians Jerry (Robert Morse) and Joe (Tony Roberts), who witness a mobster killing, so they disguise themselves as women and join Sweet Sue and Her Society Syncopators, an all-girl band traveling to a gig in Miami. One of the girls, Sugar (Elaine Joyce), falls for Joe (when he's not in drag), and elderly millionaire Osgood Fielding Jr. (Cyril Ritchard) is smitten with Jerry (when he *is* in drag). It was a classic comedy plot, and the possibilities for musical numbers were built into the original. But what looked like a sure thing turned out to be rather routine and even dull at times, saved by some expert clowning (especially by Morse). Stone's libretto is not inferior, but neither is it anything special. Producer David Merrick's shrewd publicity machine allowed *Sugar* to run 505 performances, but its only major revivals have been ones in which celebrities carry the show.

In 1981, Stone adapted another film comedy, the Tracy–Hepburn vehicle *Woman of the Year* (1942), for the musical stage, retaining the title but little else. The movie's heroine, a diplomat's daughter and current affairs journalist, became Tess Harding (Lauren Bacall), a television talk show host. Spencer Tracy's crusty sports reporter became Sam Craig (Harry Guardino), a newspaper cartoonist. When he does a series of satirical panels making fun of "Tessie Cat," the two celebrities lock horns, make amends, marry, separate, and then reconcile. The plot was different enough that few compared the libretto to the original film, and both audiences and critics found something to enjoy in the harmless diversion. (The songs, by Kander and Ebb, were far from their best, but were similarly pleasant.) Because of expensive costs and poor budgeting, the musical managed to run 770 performances and still lose money.

By this time Stone was looked on as one of the most astute play doctors in the business, called in to help troubled shows, or, as in the case of *My One and Only* (1983), to totally rewrite the libretto. A deconstructivist revival of the Gershwins' *Funny Face* (1927), helmed by avant-gardist Peter Sellers, was in such a panic on the road that practically the whole creative staff was replaced. Timothy Myers's libretto was pretty much discarded, and Stone wrote a new script that kept nothing from the original except an aviator character and a few of the Gershwin songs. Barnstormer Billy Buck Chandler (Tommy Tune) and championship swimmer Edith Herbert (Twiggy) meet, fall in love, but get mixed up with a bootlegging minister (Roscoe Lee Browne) and a Russian spy (Bruce McGill) before the happy ending. It was a thinner plot than even the most frivolous 1920s musical, but Tune's staging and choreography was magical, and the score, copped from various Gershwin shows, was still better than anything else heard on Broadway of late. As far as Stone's contribution goes, it was a professional patch-up job and little else. But it worked, and *My One and Only* ran two years. Although he was not officially credited, Stone also did patch-up work on the book for *Grand Hotel* (1989), another Tune show that became a hit. Even though Stone was in on *The Will Rogers Follies* (1991) from the beginning, his libretto seems like a last-minute attempt to save a floundering show. The idea of making a musical about the life of the beloved comic seemed like an exciting idea, until one realized that Rogers's life was devoid of conflict, romance, or drama. (Rogers's death in an airplane crash was often foreshadowed but never included in the libretto.) So Stone turned his musical bio into a *Follies* show and made fun of the fact that, like any Ziegfeld extravaganza, nothing much was going to happen. Keith Carradine made no attempt to impersonate Rogers, and the score by Cy Coleman (music), Betty Comden, and Adolph Green (lyrics) made little effort to sound like *Follies* songs; both star and tunesmiths got by on charm, aided yet again by director-choreographer Tune's theatrics. This show was so thin, libretto-wise, that it made *My One and Only* look like *War and Peace*. But once again, Stone knew what worked, and the show "worked" for 983 performances.

He was faced with a more formidable task when asked to turn the sinking of the *Titanic* into a musical. Here was a show that was going to take all the ingenuity of a *1776* to pull it off. Composer-lyricist Maury Yeston had worked with Stone during his rescue duties on *Grand Hotel*, and they collaborated again on *Titanic* (1997), a show that became a hit against great odds. It was Stone's first libretto since *1776* that was not a comedy, and like that earlier show, it had to make a situation gripping even though everyone in the audience knew the outcome of the plot. The tone of *Titanic* is rather grim throughout, and there is a solemnity in some of the writing that turns much of the musical into a church service. (Yeston's songs are similarly hymn-like at times.) With all the jokes about a sinking-ship musical running through the theatre community, perhaps the creators wanted to nip the giggles in the bud. The result was an ambitious and sometimes impressive musical, but one that thrived on large-scale awe rather than empathy with the characters. The ship itself is the main character, and the rolling, titling, and descending scenery supported its star faithfully. But the moments that worked best in *Titanic* were the little human touches that outweighed the oceanliner itself: the hopeful girls from

Ireland dreaming about a new life, the ship's architect basking in the joy of creating the greatest moving object on earth, a stoker sending a love letter back to his sweetheart via the newfangled telegraph, and so on. The libretto contains some of Stone's best writing in decades. It is a shame that one must sit through such hokum as the blissfully happy Straus couple (Larry Keith and Alma Cuervo) or the melodramatics of the villainous steamship chairman, J. Bruce Ismay (David Garrison); they are historical figures but needn't be portrayed so simplemindedly.

Stone's most recent Broadway credit is the book revisions for the 1999 revival of *Annie Get Your Gun* (1946). It is another patch-up job, but unfortunately here was a libretto that needed to be rethought and touched up rather than sanitized and watered down. Removing or rewriting the Indian sections of the original script could possibly be justified, but adding an irritatingly dull subplot and reordering the position of some of the songs struck even the most unenlightened theatregoers as a bad idea. Stone presents the plot as part of the Wild West Show, implying that modern audiences could not sit through such tripe unless it was all pretend. But the revival was a hit *despite* the new libretto, the songs, and the various stars carrying a show that was far less effective than the original. Perhaps this time Stone's instincts about what works were not so reliable.

Stewart, Stein, and Stone are perhaps the last of a certain breed of Broadway librettist. All three worked in the postwar style of scriptwriting, learning their skills in television and Broadway revues and pursuing the book musical as a practical but ethereal craft. Each was adept at both adaptation and original writing, each made significant contributions (particularly in the 1960s), and each suffered from the changing tastes and temperaments on Broadway. Yet even taking their least accomplished shows into consideration, there are few librettists working today who understood the musical theatre like this trio did. Even when they were not inspired artists, they were always top professionals.

CHAPTER SEVENTEEN
GETTING AN ACT TOGETHER: GRETCHEN CRYER AND OTHERS IN THE 1960s AND 1970s

B y the 1960s, a Broadway (or an Off-Broadway) libretto could take many different forms. There were still plenty of book musicals that told a story in a sequential manner, going through the plot in a causal and usually logical way. But now there were also musicals whose librettos were loose and aimless, as in *Hair* (1968); slapdash and improvised, such as *Godspell* (1971); or even taking the shape of a pseudodocumentary, as with *A Chorus Line* (1975). It was also during this period that powerful director-choreographers, from Bob Fosse to Michael Bennett to Tommy Tune, sometimes outshone the material they presented, and the libretto, along with the score, just became fodder for an auteur to dazzle his audience. Just as often, a major star kept a show running because the musical was constructed around the conceit that the central character is not a person but a larger-than-life celebrity. It almost seemed like we were back in the pre-Harbach days, when everything in a musical was more important than the book.

But there are a handful of libretto writers in the 1960s and 1970s not already discussed who made notable contributions to the Broadway musical. The actress-lyricist-playwright Gretchen Cryer, with her composer-partner Nancy Ford, was the first significant female team to write and score American musicals. Cryer was born Gretchen Kiger in Dunreith, Indiana, in 1935 and educated at DePauw University, where she met Ford, and the two started to collaborate on contemporary musicals. They ended up in New York, where Ford got jobs as a rehearsal and pit pianist while Cryer pursued her acting career, appearing in such musicals as *Little Me, 110 in the Shade,* and *1776.* Married for a time to actor David Cryer, she became Gretchen Cryer and kept the name after the two divorced. The first Cryer–Ford collaboration to appear Off Broadway was *Now Is the Time for All Good Men* (1967), an inventive piece about an English teacher who becomes a conscientious objector during the escalating Vietnam War. The score was typical of much of the team's work, a congenial blending of pop, light rock, folk, and some Broadway brass. The libretto was also typical of Cryer, exploring uncomfortable issues and centering on a character in crisis. As melodramatic as the show was, it got preachy only on occasion, and there was plenty of humor, even if it was sometimes the acid kind.

The Last Sweet Days of Isaac (1970) was billed as a rock musical when that new genre was beginning to flower, but the score is again an eclectic mix of different musical styles, and the rock numbers tend to be satiric. Cryer's libretto consists of two playlets about the lack of communication in the modern age. The first is a lighthearted two-hander that mocks the issues of the day and illustrates the foils of being too much in touch with the world. The neurotic and overromanticized Isaac Bernstein (Austin Pendleton) is only thirty-three years old but always sees death around the corner, so he tries to live each day to the fullest, recording all his thoughts on a portable tape recorder he carries around with his menagerie of musical instruments. When Isaac gets stuck for an hour in a stalled elevator with uptight secretary Ingrid (Fredricka Weber), he teaches her to open up, express her feelings, and consider making love to him. It takes Ingrid much of the hour to totally give in to her feelings, only for her to realize that she truly loves someone else. Isaac's sexual frustration is very funny because, in his mind, it's philosophical: he thinks he wants to touch her mind. The two part when the elevator is fixed, she discovering her own feelings and Isaac still in search of a "transparent crystal moment." The playlet is perhaps the most literate of all the rock musicals of the era, and though hopelessly dated, it still has its wit. (Isaac: "I must confess at one time I considered self-immolation about the time it was so big in Thailand.") Unfortunately, the second playlet is more ponderous and, though often moving, too pat. Seventeen-year-old Isaac is in a prison cell where he tries to communicate by way of a television screen with the girl in the next cell and with the world at large. There are some powerful moments, as when Isaac watches on the news his own death during an antiwar demonstration, or when he and the girl try to make love to each other's image on the screen. But *The Last Sweet Days of Isaac* was a show only for its time, and that time is gone. One song argues that rather than taking a jet plane to San Francisco, it is better to walk there so that one can savor each step along the way. This is a very spiritual thought if you start, say, in Oakland. But for the rest of the world it's a pretty foolish concept. Yet in 1970 such an idea could fly. The show ran 485 performances Off Broadway and still has a cult following of sorts.

Cryer and Ford's only Broadway musical was *Shelter* (1973), a short-lived piece of allegory about television commercial writer Michael (Terry Kiser), who, instead of living with his wife and seven internationally adopted children, inhabits a television studio set complete with a multitude of multimedia devices and a computer named Arthur. One of Michael's few human contacts is a cleaning woman named Wednesday November (Susan Browning), to whom he makes love, his only experience that is not enjoyed through technology. It is a pretentious libretto, and the score (recorded but never released) is thought to be unworthy of the team. *Isaac* managed to spoof all of Marshall MacLuhan's then-popular theories. *Shelter* wallowed in them, Tony Walton's set pulsating with slides and lighting effects. When Cryer and Ford presented their next show five years later, they returned to Off Broadway where they belonged, and traded high tech and mass media for interpersonal communication. The result, *I'm Getting My Act Together and Taking It on the Road* (1978), was one of the longest runs of the decade and (still) the only satisfying "feminist" musical ever written. Perhaps "feminist" is not the right word. *I'm Getting My Act Together . . .* takes one woman's point of view: that of soap opera star Heather Jones (Cryer), who was once a pop singer of trite and chart-climbing ballads like "In a Simple Way I Love You." Divorced, confused, and facing her thirty-ninth birthday, Heather is not a feminist, but she has learned something about the roles men and women play, and she's written a series of songs that she wants to perform on her upcoming tour. As she and her two backup singers audition the new numbers for her manager, Joe (Joel Fabiani), lively and revealing discussions spring up, ranging from troubled marriages to self-image. Heather has always performed in the manner that men, from her father to her husband to her manager, have outlined for her. Now that she is gradually discovering herself, she questions the roles that the two sexes have played so long. It may all sound rather turgid and preachy, but both the score and the libretto are lively, thought provoking, and sometimes disturbing:

> JOE: Look, honey, nobody has to know [that you're thirty-nine]. On the soap opera you don't play thirty-nine . . .
> HEATHER: I'm thirty-nine! Look at these lines in my face. And this morning I found a gray hair.
> JOE: We'll fix it with the lights. Nobody will see those lines. Don't worry.
> HEATHER: I'm not worried! Who said I was worried? You're worried! You're the one.
> JOE: I know sometimes you look like you've been through the wringer, but—

HEATHER: I look like I've been through the wringer because I have been through the wringer! That's who I am! A person who's been through the wringer . . .
JOE: Well, I don't know how I'm going to sell that.

Much of the musical is a reaction to the women's movement that was very prominent in the late 1970s and seemed to infiltrate all the arts (except the Broadway musical). Joe complains to Heather: "Women are getting very hostile these days. Do you know why there are so many faggots out on the streets? It's because women are getting so hostile. . . . The only place he's safe is with another man." Cryer's libretto does not offer any solutions to the male–female dilemma, which makes it all the more upsetting. Some dismissed the musical as a feminist diatribe, but more saw it as a show that struck a nerve. Like *Isaac* and all the other Cryer–Ford collaborations, *I'm Getting My Act . . .* was a product of its time and is not easily revived. Are we more sophisticated today and have the answers that the script poses? Probably not. But too few are asking those same questions today. When they do ask once again, this musical will be back on the boards.

Another team that met in college and stuck together for years was that of Tom Jones and Harvey Schmidt. Jones was born in Littlefield, Texas, in 1928 and attended the University of Texas, where he met art student Schmidt, and the two started writing musicals together. Once established in New York, they provided songs to various Off-Broadway revues and wrote a one-act musical of Edmond Rostand's play *Les Romanesques* for a summer theatre workshop. Encouraged to expand the playlet into a full-length but simple production, the team came up with *The Fantasticks* (1960). As with all their later shows, Jones wrote libretto and lyrics and Schmidt composed the music. Parts of the book are written in rhymed verse with musical accompaniment, so the show sometimes has a narrative ballad quality that might be found in an old folktale. Much has been written about the simplicity and universal appeal of *The Fantasticks*. It is the first truly international American musical, playing in countries that still hadn't seen *Oklahoma!* I believe it is Jones's libretto that accounts for the musical's widespread appeal. The songs are delightful pastiches of everything from folk to tango to jazz, but it is in the writing that the show reaches out to so many cultures. Considering the fact that *The Fantasticks* started as a domestic French comedy and was reworked into a Latin-flavored *Romeo and Juliet* musical (this idea was dropped once *West Side Story* opened), the show exists in its own time and place. The Spanish touches show up in some of the songs, but the libretto takes the form of a modern fairy tale divorced from any one culture. There are few references to the rest of the world in *The Fantasticks*, and the makeshift scenery and costumes keep the musical from settling in any one point in time or place. No wonder it was a hit around the world; it was about every boy, girl, father, and illusion that ever existed. *The Fantasticks* remains the quintessential Off-Broadway musical: small, intimate, inventive, literate, and slightly unconventional. It ran there for forty-one years and never needed to transfer to Broadway. The gem didn't require a fancy setting; it shone brightly in a black box, and, being timeless, it will continue to light up stages everywhere.

Jones's librettos for subsequent musicals with Schmidt are far less accomplished but always have a touch of whimsy in them to remind you that this team wrote *The Fantasticks*. Small in scale but pure Broadway razzle-dazzle was *I Do! I Do!* (1966), which Jones adapted from the two-character comedy *The Fourposter* (1951) by Jan de Hartog. This musical chronicle of a marriage over the decades is also vague in its time setting, but there is no question about its locale: a Broadway musical. Jones lost the quaint innocence of the original play and instead wrote a surefire vehicle for stars (Mary Martin and Robert Preston in the original production). The score is very competent and had its requisite star turns, but the dialogue is a series of one-line jokes or compact sentiments that fill in the gaps between songs and decades. Perhaps Jones and Schmidt were not so happy with the success of *I Do! I Do!* because for their next show, *Celebration* (1969), they returned to primitive theatre, going back to its tribal roots and exploring such basic conflicts as the battle of the seasons, good versus evil, youth against old age, and (once again) disillusioned love. Jones's libretto is a true original, an all-out allegory that echoed the simplicity of *The Fantasticks* but was much darker, more brutal, and sexier. An Orphan (Michael Glenn-Smith) hopes to bring his garden back to life but is sidetracked by the con man Potemkin (Keith Charles), who brings him into the clutches of Mr. Rich (Ted Thurston) and into the arms of the waif Angel (Susan Watson). But nothing is what it seems in the cold, dark world, and there is much disappointment and painful realization before youth, spring, and love conquer all. As pretentious as it sounds, Jones's libretto is self-mocking, straightforward, and even entertaining—a sort of musical *King Lear* with a hopeful ending. The original production used masks and other tribal touches to give the illusion that this was ancient storytelling told around a fire. A lot of it worked, and some of the writing had that cockeyed kind of simplicity that made *The Fantasticks* special:

> ANGEL: We're too different. Take our backgrounds, for example. You grew up green. But my life wasn't like that. I grew up gray.

ORPHAN: Gray?
ANGEL: I lived in a gray house, and I had a gray mother and a gray father, and I went to a gray high school and studied Grey's Shorthand so I
could be a gray little secretary all my dull, gray life. But I'm not going to
do it!

Although it sought to be timeless, *Celebration* was really a product of the re-
bellious 1960s and is seldom produced today. Yet the way the show echoes
its time is what made it so appealing. Jones and Schmidt wrote many other
shows, most of them never getting beyond the workshop or tryout stage.
Philemon (1975) is perhaps the best of the lot. It is a fable set in ancient Roman times, about a clown who masquerades as a Christian and soon finds
himself questioning his own values. As late as 2001, the team was represented Off Broadway with *Road Show*, a piece about a traveling carnival
that recalled *The Fantasticks* only in its bare-bones production.

One of the best Jones–Schmidt scores (but not a Jones libretto) can be
found in *110 in the Shade* (1963), a musical version of *The Rainmaker* (1954)
that its author, N. Richard Nash, adapted himself. Born Nathaniel Richard
Nusbaum in Philadelphia in 1913, Nash had several plays produced during
his career but few hits. His first libretto was for the Lucille Ball vehicle
Wildcat (1960), an awkward musical set during the early days of oil booms.
Nash's libretto for *110 in the Shade* opened up the play nicely, and without
adding a lot of chorus numbers and extra characters, it managed to feel like
a Broadway show even as it retained its intimacy. Spinster Lizzie Curry
(Inga Swenson) is a beautifully realized character in both the play and the
musical, yearning for love but at the same time fearing it. Like Marian Paroo in *The Music Man* (1957), Lizzie sees right through a con man who
comes to town, the mesmerizing rainmaker Starbuck (Robert Horton), but
he awakens something inside of her, so that when he moves on she is able
to wed the local sheriff who has long courted her. It is a well-constructed,
conventional libretto that works. Had Jones written the book, it might have
taken a more interesting turn but might not have been as satisfying. *110 in
the Shade* had a profitable run of 331 performances, yet is not revived nearly
as often as it should be.

Nash's other notable Broadway musical was *The Happy Time* (1968),
another intimate musical about a small town and a visitor who arrives to
upset everyone, yet ignites a spark in one maturing person. Nash's libretto was a radical departure from the 1950 comedy of the same name
by Samuel Taylor. In fact, the main character in the musical, the wan-
derlust photographer Jacques Bonnard, is not even in the play. The ado-

lescent Bibi (Michael Rupert) is growing up in the French Canadian town of St. Pierre under the watchful eyes of his strict parents. In Taylor's comedy, two hedonistic uncles provide the temptations for the young Bibi (one even gives the boy his collection of ladies' garters) until he is old enough to fall for the girl next door. It was a slight but pleasing domestic comedy that could be a hit only in the 1950s. Nash (and director Gower Champion) tried to transform the little play into a glittering Broadway hit with plenty of slides and other multimedia inappropriate to the story. Nash turned the two uncles into a black sheep uncle, Jacques (Robert Goulet), and a dirty old man of a *grandpere* (David Wayne). John Kander (music) and Fred Ebb (lyrics) provided a delicate and tender score, but the libretto lost the warmth of the original, and Champion's overproduced theatrics killed any intimacy. Oddly enough, the musical's plot is still too slight to sustain itself, and *The Happy Time* has joined the ranks of very rarely produced musicals.

Taylor had nothing to do with *The Happy Time* but did write a skillful libretto of his own for *No Strings* (1962), the only musical with both music and lyrics by Richard Rodgers. Samuel Taylor was born in Chicago in 1912 and wrote for radio before finding success on Broadway in 1950 with his French Canadian comedy. His subsequent hits included *Sabrina Fair* (1953) and *The Pleasure of His Company* (1958). Taylor's libretto for *No Strings* is an original tale about an American writer, David Jordan (Richard Kiley), who suffers from writer's block, so he bums about Europe and falls in love with an international model, Barbara Woodruff (Diahann Carroll). Although there was no mention of race until the last scene, the romance was an interracial one, Barbara hailing from Harlem but now living well in the less-race-conscious world of European fashion. David and Barbara traipse across the continent avoiding commitment; like the orchestra, they have no strings (of attachment). But when they do decide to marry and return to his home in Maine, the issue of race and different lifestyles looms large:

BARBARA: But I would like to take all my beautiful Paris dresses! May I?
DAVID: [smiling] You won't have much use for 'em there.
BARBARA: Oh, I can wear them to the Saturday-night dances. [a moment] They do have Saturday-night dances?
DAVID: [quietly] Yes, quite often.
BARBARA: [with a small smile of irony] But we won't go.
DAVID: Of course we'll go!
BARBARA: Once. To show we're not cowards.

But it is not to be. The two part on friendly but bittersweet terms, each reprising separately Rodgers's lovely "The Sweetest Sounds." It is *The Student Prince* all over again, but the issue is not Ruritanian social order but contemporary conditions. Taylor's libretto is highly underrated, and while the subject at hand is less relevant these days, it is a musical that still holds together well.

Neil Simon, America's most successful playwright, is not thought of as a librettist, but he scripted a half dozen musicals and was a reliable play doctor on others in the 1960s and 1970s. He was born Marvin Neil Simon in 1927 and, as everyone knows from his autobiographical plays, grew up in New York City and started writing comedy sketches in his teens for radio and early television. His first play, *Come Blow Your Horn*, appeared on Broadway in 1961; there was barely a season after that in which a Simon work was not running. His first libretto was *Little Me* (1962), a vehicle for his old television boss, Sid Caesar. Although it has a continuous plot (the rise and fall and rise of a gal from the wrong side of the tracks), the libretto breaks down into a series of comic sketches. Here is a typical exchange:

> NOBLE: My name is Noble Eggleston, and I live up on the Bluff. In the biggest and best house.
> BELLE: Oh! And I'm Belle Schlumpfert.
> NOBLE: Gosh, that's a pretty name.

In many ways, *Little Me* is like those slapdash musicals put together in the 1930s to highlight a beloved clown, yet Simon's script is still funny on paper and can be revived by other gifted comics. The musical is filled with the zesty one-liners that Simon is famous for, and while there is little character development even in the central character, the plot progression is solid. Cy Coleman's music is appropriately merry and filled with pastiche, while Carolyn Leigh's lyrics capture the Simon style and blend with the text, something that rarely happens in later Simon musicals.

Sweet Charity (1966), for example, has better lyrics. Dorothy Fields teamed with Coleman this time, and the score is one of the era's brightest. But the dialogue and the songs do not blend together, and Fields's wit, which is considerable, is in a different vein than Simon's. The musical is a new version of Federico Fellini's 1957 film *Nights of Cabiria* about an Italian streetwalker whose heart is as innocent as a schoolgirl's. Simon reset the tale in Manhattan and called the heroine Charity Hope Valentine (Gwen Verdon), a dance hall hostess at the Fandango Ballroom who always falls for the wrong guy. Like *Little Me*, the libretto is a series of misadventures, but there is character development this time around, and sometimes the humor is warm and honest rather than just jokes:

> CHARITY: [to movie star Vittorio Vidal] There was this scene. I couldn't see it too good 'cause it was very foggy. Anyway, you had just finished making wild love to her—which is why I think it was foggy—and she started to cry, like this . . . [cries] "Mario. Mario." And then . . . you bent down and kissed every one of her fingers. From pinkie to thumb. And then you said—and I remember every word exactly—you said, "Without love, life has no purpose." Wow! Did that ever hit home. You got me right where I live. I went through the whole picture and six Milky Ways just to hear that line again. "Without love, life has no purpose."
> VIDAL: Is that what you believe?
> CHARITY: Oh sure. Don't you? Doesn't everybody?

Although it too is a star vehicle, *Sweet Charity* is solid enough to be revived with other comic-dancing talents. The musical has as much heart as Charity herself and continues to win audiences over.

Perhaps Simon's finest libretto is *Promises, Promises* (1969), though that might be because the source material is so strong. He adapted Billy Wilder and I. A. L. Diamond's screenplay for *The Apartment* (1960) into an urban musical with few plot or character changes. Simon opens up the story somewhat but never loses sight of what made the film so pleasing. Chuck Baxter (Jerry Orbach), the eager young executive who loans his apartment out as a trysting place for senior colleagues and their mistresses, is the most interesting character in the Simon musical canon. He thinks he is a shrewd and manipulating businessman, but at heart he's a scared young man looking for love, equally scared when he finds it. Chuck's eventual casting off of "promises" and compromises to become his own man is an emotional triumph for himself and the audience. *Sweet Charity* has heart, but *Promises, Promises* has guts. The pop score by Burt Bacharach (music) and Hal David (lyrics) is very satisfying, but it seems to run parallel to the libretto, the two overlapping in only a few spots. And Simon's quirky, on-the-edge dialogue sometimes turns pretty banal when the characters switch over to David's lyrics. All the same, it is a commendable show. Simon's knack for sharp, concise libretto writing put him in demand as a doctor when others' musicals were in trouble. *Seesaw* (1973) and *A Chorus Line* (1975) are two shows he contributed to during this time, the former for structure problems and the latter for much-needed jokes.

Simon surely kept the jokers in steady supply in *They're Playing Our Song* (1979), a very popular musical comedy that had one of the thinnest books of the decade. Songwriters Vernon Gersch (Robert Klein) and Sonia Walsk (Lucie Arnaz) begin by collaborating on pop songs but soon fall into a roller-coaster romance, the ups being nothing but molehills and the dips even more boring. There were only the two characters, backed by a chorus of six who acted as their alter egos; yet with all these levels of expression, neither character had anything worth exploring. So Simon filled the script with forced one-liners and threw in some bargain-basement pathos when the song cues were slow in coming. Marvin Hamlisch (music) and Carole Bayer Sager (lyrics) provided the songs, which wavered between pop and Broadway, capturing the sound of neither. As for the lyrics, they sounded like Sager had never even *seen* a Neil Simon play, let alone being able to match his style.

In the case of *The Goodbye Girl* (1993), David Zippel was given the task of providing Simon-like lyrics, and he got pretty close. The trouble was that Simon's humor fell flat most of the time, so it was not too difficult to match. Adapting his own 1977 screenplay for Broadway, Simon lost sight of what was charming about the original tale: a romance between a would-be actor (Martin Short) and a would-be dancer (Bernadette Peters), forced to share the same Manhattan apartment. Hamlisch again provided the music, much of which was pleasantly tuneful. But the dreary characters and the laborious plotting turned the show into the only musical flop of Simon's career. He has not returned to the musical stage since, which is a shame because Broadway can surely use a Simon musical once in a while.

Another major talent represented on Broadway too seldom was Joe Masteroff, who wrote two of the best librettos of the 1960s. Masteroff was born in Philadelphia in 1919 and educated at Temple University. He received his theatre training as an assistant to playwright Howard Lindsay, then turned to writing himself, his first Broadway play, *The Warm Peninsula* (1959), enjoying a modest run. Masteroff's first libretto was *She Loves Me* (1963), which he adapted from a 1937 Hungarian play that had already been filmed as *The Shop around the Corner* in 1940 and *In the Good Old Summertime* in 1949 (and later to be remade again as *You've Got Mail* in 1998). The tale of two bickering employees at a Budapest parfumerie who are also, unbeknownst to each other, sweethearts by mail became a romantic valentine of a musical with Masteroff's delicate adaptation. The comedy is gentle, the romance is subdued, and the score (by composer Jerry Bock and lyricist Sheldon Harnick) is an entrancing series of songs that flow in and out of the libretto like, well, the smell of perfume. All the characters are drawn with humor and fondness, even the cad (Jack Cassidy as the two-timing Mr. Kodaly) being more fun than he is disturbing. The old-world charm is in Bock's waltzing music but can also be enjoyed in Harnick's beautifully subdued lyrics and Masteroff's script:

> MISS RITTER: Tell me—what's he like? Tell me all about him. I love to suffer.
> AMALIA: Well—
> RITTER: Is he tall?
> AMALIA: [evasively] Oh—so-so.
> RITTER: So-so six feet? So-so five feet?
> AMALIA: I never measured.
> RITTER: Color of hair? Color of eyes?
> AMALIA: Eh—sandy hair. Not really light. Not really dark.
> RITTER: And the eyes—?
> AMALIA: Blueish—greenish—
> RITTER: [beginning to smell something fishy] Brownish?
> AMALIA: A little.
> RITTER: Is he handsome?
> AMALIA: It's difficult to say. I mean—at times he is—and then again at times he's not . . .
> RITTER: Would you like a piece of good advice? [Amalia nods] Just this: don't ever lose him in a crowd.

She Loves Me was applauded by the press but was a hard sell in the early 1960s, when a Broadway musical had to be bigger than life. After its run of 302 performances, the show faded from mainstream memory but became one of the most beloved of all cult musicals. A well-received Broadway revival in 1993 brought new recognition to *She Loves Me,* and it finally entered the repertory of revived musicals.

Nothing could have been more different from this tender musical soufflé than the hard-hitting *Cabaret* (1966), which Masteroff wrote using Christopher Isherwood's *Berlin Stories* and a dramatization by John Van Druten called *I Am a Camera* (1951). So much has been written about this landmark musical that ushered in a new era of musical theatre that an entire chapter would be needed to do it justice. But let us try to determine what Masteroff's role was in the creation of this modern classic. No one can say exactly where the idea of doing two musicals—the story of Sally and Cliff and the cabaret scenes—came from. Kander and Ebb wrote a handful of cabaret numbers in German and English for director-producer Harold Prince. One of them, sung by a creepy, leering emcee, prompted the team to create the role of the Master of Ceremonies (Joel Grey), a character not in any of the source material. From there the show went in parallel directions, one score for the plot and another for the cabaret. *I Am a Camera* is a one-set drama, so Masteroff used two Isherwood stories ("Goodbye to Berlin" and "The Last of Mrs. Norris") to fill out the locales and characters. Soon the cabaret numbers were commenting on and enhancing the book scenes, and *Cabaret* as we know it was born.

But how do we know it? Because of the popular 1972 film version and the long-running 1998 Broadway revival (both of which made substantial changes in script and score), *Cabaret* is one of those musicals, like *Show Boat* and *Follies,* that has several identities. The concept of telling a powerful story with musical interruptions is so strong that the show survives all the fine tuning (or is it tinkering?) that others have imposed on it. Whether Cliff is bi-, homo-, or heterosexual; whether Sally is British or American; whether the songs are relegated only to the cabaret or to the story as well; whether the point of the show should be sly and sarcastic rather than delivered with sledgehammer theatrics—these are merely details in a musical that will always be exceptional. Again, I insist that Masteroff's libretto (no matter how many ideas the rest of the team contributed) is key to the success of *Cabaret.* Ideas are wonderful, but it takes a writer to put them on stage. And Masteroff writes superbly. Consider one exchange from the original script:

> CLIFF: Where's your coat? Did you leave it at the club or was it stolen?
> SALLY: I left it at the doctor's office.
> CLIFF: Were you sick last night? Is that why you didn't come home?
> SALLY: [toasting] Hals and beinbruch. It means neck and leg break. It's supposed to stop it from happening—though I doubt it does. I doubt you can stop anything from happening. Any more than you can change people. I mean. . . . Oh, darling—you're such an innocent, really! My one regret is I honestly believe you'd have made a wonderful father. And I'm sure someday you will be. Oh yes, and I've another regret: That greedy doctor! I'm going to miss my fur coat. [Cliff slaps her]

Masteroff wrote another very different kind of libretto for Kander and Ebb's *70, Girls, 70* (1971), a geriatric musical comedy based on the British farce by Peter Coke, *Breath of Spring* (1958), which had been filmed as *Make Mine Mink* (1960). At least we suspect he wrote a different kind of libretto; Masteroff walked during tryouts (as did other members of the production team), and no one is quite sure who wrote the agreeable mess that finally opened on Broadway. Masteroff's last two musical projects never made it to Broadway, so his musical career pretty much consists of *She Loves Me* and *Cabaret*. But what a legacy to be remembered by!

The 1960s was the beginning of the era of one-play wonders: artists who wrote or composed a smash musical and then were hardly ever heard of again. Sometimes on Broadway it was easier to have a hit than a career. Consider *Man of La Mancha* (1965), one of the decade's most prestigious offerings and a staple in the musical theatre repertory. Creating a musical-ization of Cervantes' Spanish epic *Don Quixote* must have been its own "Impossible Dream," but Dale Wasserman's libretto is expert in every way. It is practical, using the play-within-a-play format to solve the logistics of the many scenes and characters. The libretto is also inspired, letting us see Quixote's adventures through the eyes of his author and bringing a second level of understanding to this fanciful and ultimately tragic tale. The audi-ence empathizes with both Quixote and Cervantes (both originally played by Richard Kiley, the role of his career), and a story that might have been a melodramatic curiosity at best becomes a masterful piece of musical theatre:

> CAPTAIN (of the Inquisition): . . . the following is summoned to give answer and submit his person for purification if it be so ordered: Don Miguel de Cervantes.
> CERVANTES: How popular a defendant I am. Summoned by one court before I've quite finished with another. Well? How says the Judge?
> GOVERNOR (of the Prisoners): [weighing the package in his hands] I think I know what this contains. The history of your mad knight? [Cer-vantes nods assent. Handing him the package] Plead as well there as you did here and you may not burn.
> CERVANTES: I've no intention of burning . . .
> GOVERNOR: I think Don Quixote is brother to Don Miguel.
> CERVANTES: [smiling] God help us—we are both men of La Mancha.

Wasserman had written a nonmusical version of Cervantes' book earlier for television and called it *I, Don Quixote,* but as well constructed as his libretto is, *Man of La Mancha* cries out for music, and the songs by Mitch Leigh (music) and Joe Darion (lyric) have the soaring kind of panache that the story and characters require. Score and libretto seemed to be breathing in unison in this show, and it looked like Wasserman–Leigh–Darion would become one of the great Broadway collaborations. But it never happened. None of the threesome ever worked again with any of the others, and Wasserman never saw another libretto of his on a New York stage.

A similar fate befell William F. Brown and Charlie Smalls, the creators of *The Wiz* (1975). Brown's adaptation of L. Frank Baum's *The Wizard of Oz* was sassy, clever, and very efficient. Comparisons to the beloved 1939 film version were not possible because *The Wiz* was its own animal. Not only was it told as a contemporary (very 1970s) story and used an African American idiom, it was wonderfully self-mocking and satirized the show business aspects of its own presentation. (When Dee Dee Bridgewater, as the good witch Glinda, made her big entrance, one character prefaced it by noting that she must be approaching because you can hear her theme song.) Smalls's score was a burst of musical energy rarely seen on a Broadway stage, and the show, so troubled in tryouts and previews that the producers planned on closing it on opening night, went on to run 1,672 rousing performances. Quite an impressive debut. But, alas, quite a swan song as well. Brown and Smalls never returned.

Almost as joyous as *The Wiz* but more richly textured was *Purlie* (1970), which Ossie Davis, Peter Rose, and Peter Udell scripted from Davis's play *Purlie Victorious* (1961), a sly comedy about an eager preacher trying to collect a legacy from a bigoted Southern landowner. The material cried out to be musicalized, and the songs by Gary Geld (music) and Udell (lyrics) were splendid all around. The score (and the dazzling original cast) made *Purlie* a hit, but it was the razor-sharp libretto that made it work. The characters were types, but they breathed fire, and the story was slight but bounced along merrily. Black musicals and revues proliferated during this time, but none was as much fun as *Purlie*. It stayed on Broadway for two years and remained popular on tour and in revival for some time. Davis never returned to the musical form, but Rose, Udell, and Geld scored another hit with *Shenandoah* (1975) and wrote a handful of admirable shows that never caught on: *Angel* (1978), *Comin' Uptown* (1979), and *The Amen Corner* (1983).

The Robber Bridegroom (1976), with a backwoods setting reminiscent of *Purlie,* was also a celebratory musical that told a tall tale. Robert Waldman and Alfred Uhry adapted Eudora Welty's 1942 novella of the same name and turned it into a folk legend enacted by a group of square-dancing Mississippi townspeople—a kind of hillbilly *Man of La Mancha* with its play-within-a-play format. The story, about a dashing bandit who steals "with style" and captures the heart of a plantation owner's daughter, was silly and improbable, complete with a villain who conversed and sang with the detached head of his brother. Waldman composed the folk tunes, Uhry wrote the farcical lyrics, and the songs were a highly pleasing mixture of bluegrass and Broadway. The show was not a runaway success in New York but was a hit on tour and has enjoyed many happy revivals since. But the team of Waldman and Uhry did not continue. Uhry turned (very successfully) to playwriting and years later did write a laudable libretto for *Parade* (1998) (see chapter 19).

Two more musicals by one-play wonders must be mentioned: *Your Own Thing* (1968) and *The Grass Harp* (1971). Donald Driver scripted the libretto for the former, a wacky, contemporary (very late 1960s) version of Shakespeare's *Twelfth Night*. Illyria becomes Manhattan and the world of the music business, Viola is a singer who disguises herself as a member of the all-male rock group The Four Apocalypse, Olivia and Orsino become record producers, and Sebastian looks a lot like his sister Viola because the boys are all wearing their hair long these days. It is a rollicking takeoff on the familiar mistaken identity tale (the Orsino character wonders if he is gay since he is drawn to the disguised Viola) and even has its touching moments, particularly during some of the quieter songs by Hal Hester and Danny Apolinar. Like its title expression, *Your Own Thing* was so "with it" that it was quickly dated. But what a promising debut and what a disappointment that nothing much came of it. (Driver did write the book and lyrics for the unappreciated *Oh, Brother!* thirteen years later.) As for *The Grass Harp*, one of the cultists' most fervent favorites, its libretto, based on a 1951 Truman Capote novella, was so offbeat that audiences were either immediately enthralled or turned off. Kenward Elmsie did the adaptation, retaining the quirky flavor of Capote's story of an eccentric spinster who escapes from the real world by moving into a treehouse. Her repressed sister, a lusty cousin, an outspoken housekeeper, and a traveling lady evangelist were among the unconventional characters who popped in and sang the memorable songs by Claibe Richardson (music) and Elmsie (lyrics). The two authors continued to write together, but we are still waiting for something special to come of it.

I don't suppose you can call Jerome Lawrence and Robert E. Lee one-play wonders since they wrote a handful of plays, *Inherit the Wind* (1955) among them. But they had only one successful musical, *Mame* (1966), and it was a giant hit. The twosome had adapted Patrick Dennis's 1955 book *Auntie Mame* into a popular play and movie, so it was not such a giant leap to script the libretto. In fact, those familiar with the sources found few surprises in *Mame* because Lawrence and Lee changed hardly a thing. It is more of an editing job than a true adaptation. But Mame Dennis is a character who was bigger than life, and she is an ideal musical comedy heroine. Jerry Herman gave her the songs to sing, and he was able to match the source material in both his music and his lyrics. While both score and libretto strike me as a bit too manufactured to be truly joyous (the characters are so busy celebrating Auntie Mame that we rarely see much in her that gets them so excited), it is a show that works like gangbusters and always will. When Lawrence and Lee attempted a much more challenging project, turning Jean Giraudoux's quixotic 1948 play *The Madwoman of Chaillot* into a Broadway musical, the result was the very unsatisfying *Dear World* (1969) starring Angela Lansbury, the original Mame. Jerry Herman again provided the score, and in some songs he attempted to capture the French whimsy of the original. But Lawrence and Lee's book was earthbound, and the delicate fantasy turned vulgar and embarrassing. So maybe the team was a one-play wonder after all.

All the musicals mentioned in the last several pages were adaptations. Yet the two longest-running shows of the 1970s boasted original librettos. Jim Jacobs and Warren Casey (two more one-play wonders) wrote the libretto, music, and lyrics for *Grease* (1972), the campy, nostalgic favorite on stages everywhere. Not only were the songs all pastiche, but the script was filled with the sort of clichés that filter the 1950s into something to be enjoyed by those who never really knew the decade. Each character is a simplistic type, from perennial virgin to perennial slut, from cool greaser to uncool nerd. The plotting is awkward (particularly in the second act), but it never runs out of stereotypic episodes. The ending, in which Cinderella gets her prince by becoming cheap and brazen, is a cheat but is probably the only conclusion such a hackneyed kind of story could have. It is difficult to defend *Grease* (and I certainly have no ambition to do so), but one must admit that it works. Yes, it is extremely popular—on Broadway, on film, in revival, in every high school in the nation—and, no, it is not just a fluke. *Grease* delivers, and whether you like the product or not, it delivers regularly and in a package that continues to sell.

A Chorus Line (1975) is the other long run of the decade. Its libretto is by James Kirkwood, Nicholas Dante, an invisible Neil Simon, a very visible Michael Bennett, and dozens of dancers who spilled their guts out for a microphone and saw it all become a Broadway musical. I started this chapter by calling *A Chorus Line* a pseudodocumentary, but that is not accurate. A documentary views its subject objectively and from a proper distance. *A Chorus Line* is written *by the subject* and is far from objective. Kirkwood and Dante shaped the material (hours of taped interviews with dancers), and Simon spiced up the confessions with some jokes, but the chorus members are the true authors, and what they may lack in structure or theatricality they make up for in sincerity and vulnerability. It is this show, not *Grease,* that's the fluke. Intended as a workshop that might develop into a performance piece that gypsies could appreciate, *A Chorus Line* found itself appealing to outsiders. Sure, theatre folk love it, but that's not enough to keep a show on the boards for years. The musical's wide appeal is the fluke. Who thought that even infrequent theatregoers would embrace it and return to love it again? One could point out the libretto's many flaws—too much exposition, little character growth, no satisfying climax, awkward repetition, and so on—but this is not a show about words or plot or even, ultimately, characters. Concept musicals can get around all that. Neither is it a show about the songs, though Marvin Hamlisch's music and Edward Kleban's lyrics have their strong points. No, *A Chorus Line* is about dance and dancers, and its true exposition, development, and climax come in the form of movement. It doesn't need a libretto, just a concept. What would Oscar Hammerstein have thought?

THE KISS OF RAGTIME: TERRENCE MCNALLY

Few American playwrights in the last decades of the twentieth century enjoyed a more prodigious career than Terrence McNally, his work consistently being produced from 1969 on, and rarely a season going by without a new play of his seen in New York or regionally. Although a handful of his works eventually transferred to Broadway, McNally is considered an Off-Broadway playwright. In fact, he might be considered the quintessential Off-Broadway writer because his plays often echoed the major themes of that alternative venue. In some ways the history of Off Broadway can be charted by looking at McNally's works, from his early satires on the establishment, such as *Adaptation* (1969) and *Where Has Tommy Flowers Gone?* (1971), to groundbreaking works about homosexuality, as in *The Lisbon Traviata* (1989) and *Love! Compassion! Valor!* (1994), to mature works dealing with midlife crises, as seen in *Lips Together, Teeth Apart* (1991) and *A Perfect Ganesh* (1994). If Off Broadway thrived on controversy, McNally was always in the thick of it. His provocative one-act *Sweet Eros* (1968), in which a naked woman was tied to a chair, raised eyebrows in its day, and three decades later his *Corpus Christi* (1998), about a homosexual Jesus and his gay followers, caused its own scandal that got nationwide media attention. McNally could also write a heterosexual love story, as in *Frankie and Johnny in the Clair de Lune* (1987), and provide a first-class star vehicle, as with *Master Class* (1995) with Zoe Caldwell. He even excelled at the tricky genre of farce, his *The Ritz* (1975) remaining one of the best American examples of its type. But what McNally did not attempt until late in his career was libretto writing. When he finally did, he usually found himself handling difficult projects for producers looking to present demanding musical theatre fare. The results varied in success and quality, but there was no question that a superb craftsman was at work.

McNally was born in St. Petersburg, Florida, in 1939 but grew up in Corpus Christi, Texas. He was educated at Columbia University, where his writing was first produced. Soon after graduation, his stage adaptation of Dumas's *The Lady of the Camellias* (1963) was briefly seen on Broadway. It would be one of his very few works based on previous material until his musical adaptations in the 1990s. McNally's first original script on Broadway was *Things That Go Bump in the Night* (1965), another short run, but it was Off Broadway where his one-acts were gaining him notice, particularly the long-running *Adaptation*. Never a household name, McNally became an established figure Off Broadway with dozens of plays to his credit. They all might be classified as comedies, though bittersweet and even tragic endings were not unheard of. Critical reaction was usually mixed. Commentators praised McNally's vivid and often outlandish characters and fertile dialogue but sometimes found fault with his plotting. A recurring complaint concerned the resolution of the story line. Often the playwright came up with an intriguing situation, filled it with sparkling characters and dialogue, and then had fun with all the complications. But rarely was he able to bring the story to any kind of satisfying conclusion. Some critics (and theatregoers) declared that McNally's endings were weak; others considered them Chekhovian.

Since most of McNally's musicals are adaptations, this problem did not arise so much in his librettos. But it was definitely an issue in his first effort, *The Rink* (1984). Songwriters John Kander (music) and Fred Ebb (lyrics) began working on a small Off-Broadway musical scripted by the promising young playwright Albert Innaurato. It dealt, as all of Innaurato's plays did, with Italian Americans, in this case a mother and her estranged daughter. When the project was fumbling, its director, Arthur Laurents, suggested that McNally be asked to write the script. What began as basically a two-character, intimate musical ended up on Broadway with a huge and intricate set, a small chorus of males who played various roles, and two major stars: Chita Rivera and Liza Minnelli. Laurents dropped out, and A. J. Antoon directed what was still a two-hander but now on a expensive scale. Anna Antonelli (Rivera) has been running a roller skating rink on a crumbling boardwalk for decades. Her husband Dino abandoned her long ago, and she hasn't heard from her daughter Angel in seven years. But Anna has saved up enough money that, with her sale of the rink, she can now live for herself and not for others. Angel (Minnelli), returning from another failed love affair, shows up and wants to settle in her former home; when she finds out that the rink is to be sold, she is furious. Anna is just as furious as they open old wounds and dredge up the past, complete with flashbacks of Dino's charismatic but unreliable behavior, Anna's promiscuity, and Angel's drug-filled travels.

There are plenty of dramatics in *The Rink*, as well as one of Kander and Ebb's most underrated scores, but the libretto doesn't seem to go anywhere. A series of bitter revelations alternating with some brilliant star turns barely manage to sustain the piece, and the ending, a sort of reconciliation between mother and daughter when Angel's daughter (whom Anna didn't even know existed) shows up, was forced. Audiences, most coming to see Rivera and Minnelli dance and sing while dressed in spangles, were disappointed in the unglamorous characters, even if they had to admit that both gave masterful performances. Critics blamed the book, which surely had its drawbacks, yet often McNally's writing is funny and touching. Neither Anna nor Angel is the Italian cliché one might expect, and their dialogue is sometimes knowingly terse:

> ANGEL: I was never good enough for you. You never once told me I was pretty.
> ANNA: You were pretty.
> ANGEL: You were prettier.
> ANNA: It wasn't a contest.
> ANGEL: You make it feel like one.

McNally learned about libretto writing the hard way (he has not written an original musical since), and when he teamed up with Kander and Ebb nearly a decade later, the result was a much happier experience. *Kiss of the Spider Woman* (1993) was as unlikely a candidate for a Broadway musical as *The Rink,* although this time Chita Rivera did wear spangles. Manuel Puig had adapted his 1976 novel into a nonmusical play, and this was then turned into a successful art-house film in 1985. McNally's task of musicalizing the tale of two prisoners in a Latin American jail was far from enviable. When the show was first presented as an experimental workshop in 1990 in Purchase, New York, the critical and audience reaction was very negative. But with recasting and major rewriting by McNally, the show, which played first in Canada and London, arrived on Broadway in a tighter and more potent form. The action of the story is set mostly in a small jail cell with dream sequences or flashbacks used to bring on other locations and characters. Luis Albert Molina (Brent Carver), a flagrant homosexual window dresser serving an eight-year sentence as a sexual offender, escapes from his nightmarish situation by fantasizing about Aurora (Rivera), a movie screen beauty who is also, it turns out, a symbol of death as the Spider Woman. His new cell mate is Valentin Arrequi Paz (Anthony Crivello), a political prisoner who refuses to give the police information about his fellow revolutionaries on the outside. The two men are opposites in many ways, but over time the desolate circumstances they share bring them together, the two even becoming lovers. When Albert is freed with the hopes that he will lead the authorities to Valentin's comrades, the window dresser contacts the revolutionaries. Arrested again, Albert refuses to reveal their names and is murdered by the warden right in front of Valentin. McNally concludes the libretto not with this grisly scene but with one more fantasy sequence with Albert now singing and dancing on the silver screen and comforting Valentin with "I find I walk in Technicolor now!"

There is certainly no problem with plot resolution in *Kiss of the Spider Woman*. It has two endings, both of them highly satisfactory. The Kander and Ebb score takes care of many of the flashbacks and dream sections, so McNally's book concentrates on the cell scenes and the relationship between Albert the effeminate escapist and Valentin the brutal realist. The writing also fluctuates back and forth between these extremes, from warm and sentimental moments to a prison scene in which a poisoned Valentin suffers bowel spasms and Albert helps clean up his filthy cell mate. Harold Prince directed the demanding musical with such precision that both aspects of the script, the tender and the harsh, were involving. McNally's dialogue is less slangy and conversational than in *The Rink;* instead, it has a simple and direct flavor to it as in a fable, though a nightmarish fable. Albert has his expansive moments ("The nicest thing about being happy is that you never think you'll be unhappy again."), but most of the writing is down to earth. Despite its unlikely subject, *Kiss of the Spider Woman* was a hit, and McNally pulled off a difficult task with success. Perhaps that is why he was approached by the same producers for an even more gargantuan libretto challenge: turning E. L. Doctorow's epic novel *Ragtime* into a Broadway musical. Doctorow had written one play, the short-lived, talky *Drinks before Dinner* (1978), and was not interested in dramatizing *Ragtime,* especially after the 1981 film version penned by Michael Weller failed. The Canadian producers hired the team of Lynn Ahrens (lyric) and Stephen Flaherty (music) to write the score, but even though Ahrens had written the librettos for her previous shows with Flaherty, they wanted McNally for the difficult book chore. Aside from the complex, overlapping stories, dozens of characters, and passage of time, *Ragtime* posed an added problem in that it was written in a detached, formal style that distanced the reader from the tale even as it fascinated one. Many of the major characters are given generic names (Mother, Father, Younger Brother, and so on) and seem to be viewed through dusty old photographs or primitive silent films.

This cool and remote method of telling the story was one of the highlights of the best-selling novel, and McNally knew he could not ignore it. So he opens the stage version with a child viewing his family through a stereopticon, the double image combining into a clear one. Characters are not introduced dramatically or by a narrator but by the characters themselves speaking *about* themselves in the third person. The effect was a bit off-putting to some theatregoers, but most realized that this was not going to be traditional storytelling and accepted the premise easily. McNally continues the idea throughout, sometimes having a character from one story act as commentator for another story. The plot crisscrossing that was so engrossing on the page turned into a ballet of sorts on stage, one set of characters passing by another set and visually tying the stories together. Again the director (Frank Galati) and the production staff must also be credited with the powerful visual storytelling. But ultimately, McNally was the force that made this huge show work.

Both the novel and the musical center on three major plots: the coming apart of an upper-class white family in suburban New Rochelle, the arrival and indoctrination of an immigrant peddler who eventually makes his American dream come true, and the courtship between a black musician and a servant girl and the bloody rampage he goes on when he is insulted and she is accidentally killed by the police. The three tales continually overlap each other: the servant girl works for the white family, the WASP brother joins the musician's gang, the frustrated New Rochelle mother ends up in the arms of the immigrant, and so on. Factual characters, such as Harry Houdini, Evelyn Nesbit, Henry Ford, Emma Goldman, and Booker T. Washington, are drawn into the fiction logically and effectively. Time passes, people change, ideas are explored, and characters grow. It is ambitious in the way that *Show Boat* was seven decades earlier. And while the Ahrens–Flaherty score did not produce the popular kind of standards that the Kern–Hammerstein show did, *Ragtime* boasts a superior set of songs that ranks high by any yardstick.

When a musical has as much plot and as many principal characters as *Ragtime,* there is little room for anything else. But McNally's libretto is much more than a well-organized retelling of events. *Ragtime* is also about social change and a world that is moving from the innocence of the nineteenth century to the reality of a world war. The libretto for *Ragtime* manages to illustrate this without taking time out for speeches or explanations. The same Little Boy (Alex Strange) who opened the show with his stereopticon is used throughout the script to plant ideas and foreshadow future disasters. His nightmare about Houdini at the beginning of the second act frightens him into warning his mother that there will be explosions; soon Coalhouse Walker (Brian Stokes Mitchell) and his men are blowing up buildings. While flying his toy airplane, the Little Boy also issues warnings to the unseen Archduke Ferdinand about his impending assassination and the outbreak of the Great War. By the end of the musical, the boy is viewing life not through a stereopticon but with an early manual movie projector. While much of this is in Doctorow's novel, it is McNally who selects the most potent items and plants them so carefully in the narrative.

But *Ragtime* is not without its faults. As the show was previewing in Toronto, it was polished into an appealing consumer product that struck some as too fabricated. There is probably some truth to the complaints that *Ragtime* is the result of astute marketing rather than inspired creativity. This has nothing to do with the advertising and selling of the show but rather with the way that the musical sometimes panders to a congenial public's desires. The African American characters, for example, are blameless and faultless. Coalhouse has impregnated and deserted his sweetheart Sarah (Audra McDonald), but he is played and accepted as a dashing and righteous hero. The immigrants are usually as flawless as the WASP Americans are narrow and wrongheaded. Some of this goes back to the novel, but there is no justification for the score's three or four similar anthems for the oppressed, other than the fact that audiences in Toronto (and elsewhere) ate them up like candy. *Ragtime* is bold, inventive, and stirring, but it seems to have one eye on the box office at all times. Yet I don't think this much diminishes McNally's libretto and the way it manages to do the near impossible. The show was a major hit, though a run of 861 performances was not enough to pay for the expensive production. Subsequent touring versions and future productions will turn *Ragtime* into a profitable and revivable favorite.

McNally moved on to a more questionable hit with *The Full Monty* (2000). If *Ragtime* hoped to say something worthwhile as it wanted to be liked, *The Full Monty* only wanted to be liked and dare not say anything much at all. Based on a 1997 low-budget British film that was suspect in every aspect except its wide popularity, *The Full Monty* was workshopped in New York, tested out in San Diego, and quickly moved to Broadway before its timeliness could fade. David Yazbek provided the Las Vegas lounge–like score, and McNally concocted a libretto that teased and pleased audiences and a surprising number of critics. The film was about a group of out-of-work laborers in Sheffield, England, who decide that there is money to be made as male strippers, even though they are far from the Adonis type. They see the key to their success as doing "the full monty," the British expression for stripping down to nothing. For Broadway the show was set in Buffalo, New York, a place where no one would know the title expression unless they had seen the film. Buffalo, the butt of many jokes over the decades, as the new locale was the first of the script's many easy laughs. (The city of Buffalo was far from amused to hear the news.) Now turned into unemployed steelworkers, the gang becomes blue-collar Polacks (another easy joke) and other ethnic types, and McNally adds a crusty old rehearsal pianist, Jeanette Burmeister (Kathleen Freeman), for homespun wisdom: "You know what Kate Smith used to say about a bad rehearsal? Usually meant a bad performance." Since much of the film was one long tease until the final strip scene, McNally went one better by adding a male stripper called Keno (Denis Jones) near the top of the show so that audiences wouldn't get restless. Both the score and the libretto have lots of jokes that center on different terms for male genitalia, something the ladies in the script lovingly refer to as "The Goods." Every effort McNally makes to humanize these self-admitted losers (love for a dying mother, concern over losing custody of a son, even a gentle romance between two of the guys) seems to fall flat and points out that this musical is only about "The Goods."

A much more enticing challenge awaited McNally when he turned to *The Visit* (2001), a musicalization of the 1956 problem play by German dramatist Freidrich Duerrenmatt. Kander and Ebb wrote the score, Chita Rivera starred, and critical reaction was guarded when it tried out in Chicago. Its appearance on Broadway, at this writing, is questionable. McNally's next project, a musicalization of another low-budget British film, *A Man of No Importance* (1994), is also a challenging idea and may prove to be very intriguing. (Ahrens and Flaherty are providing the score.) But most McNally musicals are intriguing, to say the least. He often takes on exciting projects, works with talented collaborators and distinctive directors, and comes up with a show that pushes the boundaries of musical theatre, even as he provides satisfactory entertainment. As more musicals these days seem to be either sung through, conceptual, or even fragmentary, a fine craftsman like McNally is a writer to be appreciated. He knows how a musical works and is not afraid to construct a solid libretto with an artistic vision.

CHAPTER NINETEEN
THE PRODUCERS:
THE 1980s, 1990s, AND BEYOND

How ironic, and somewhat disconcerting, to realize that *The Producers* (2001), the first megahit of the new century, was written by two men who are two generations older than one would expect with a hot new musical. And how alarming to think that the musical they wrote might well have been, with the deletion of a few choice words, the best musical of, say, 1960. Constant revivals on Broadway have convinced audiences that the most entertaining shows are the old shows. Is *The Producers* now telling them that old-style musicals are the only kind of new musical enjoyment left? The book musical in the 1980s and 1990s had gotten very serious indeed, and a number of them were excellent. But a musical comedy? A show with no pretensions other than laughter and no agenda except to avoid agenda? There weren't many. One had to see revivals or thinly disguised revivals like the "new" Gershwin musicals *My One and Only* (1982) and *Crazy for You* (1992). In the eyes of many, there was plenty of art but not much fun. Of course, the art musical could be entertaining. Not everything was as grim as *Floyd Collins* (1996) or *Marie Christine* (1999). Yet those two musicals were written by some of the newest and most exciting artists on the theatre scene. So the future looked promising. But for escapist shows like *The Producers*, you had to turn to old-timers.

Both Mel Brooks and Thomas Meehan were show business veterans when they put together *The Producers*. Brooks was born Melvin Kaminsky in Brooklyn in 1926 and was writing for television by the time he was in his early twenties. The movie of *The Producers* (1968) was his feature film writing-directing debut, and it was followed by many other popular movies. Yet Brooks was no stranger to Broadway before his triumph in 2001. He had co-written the libretto for *Shinbone Alley* (1957), a musical fantasy based on Don Marquis's animal characters *archy and mehitabel*, and penned the book for *All American* (1962), a vehicle for Ray Bolger with a collegiate setting. Neither ran very long, and the comic lunacy of Brooks's later writing is absent from both. Thomas Meehan was born in New York City in 1929 and also worked in television for many years. A frequent contributor to the *New Yorker* magazine, he also co-wrote some of Brooks's screenplays. Meehan had much better luck on Broadway than Brooks, writing the libretto for *Annie* (1977) his first time out. Using the famous comic strip characters, he fashioned a well-built libretto that was both efficient and amusing. Even with its substandard score and uninspired production values, *Annie* was a giant hit, but Meehan rarely got credit for it. The show worked masterfully and still works because of its strong libretto.

When Meehan's knack for structure and plotting combined with Brooks's zany premise and off-the-wall characters, the result was *The Producers*, with the most hilarious musical comedy libretto in decades. The musical's script is an improvement over the film's screenplay, and one cannot help but credit Meehan. The characters were wildly funny but mere grotesques in the movie, and the plot, as farcical as it was, had some dull spots and did not resolve itself. The musical libretto fleshes out some of the characters without losing their amusing insanity, and the story is better plotted and comes to a highly satisfactory conclusion. Much of the film's famous lines remain intact, and Brooks and Meehan were able to go even further in the libretto, moving from isolated one-liners to extended comic scenes. Just as Brooks's score is ripe with parody throughout, the dialogue also has lots of fun echoing clichés from the past:

> CARMEN GHIA: [to Roger De Bris on opening night] You can do it, you know you can do it, and I know you can do it. You've been waiting all your life for this chance. And I'm not going to let you pass it up. You're going out there a silly hysterical screaming queen and you're coming back a great big passing-for-straight Broadway star!

Yet the script has plenty of moments that delight for their own sake, not depending on parody or camp. The scenes between shyster producer Max Bialystock (Nathan Lane) and mousy accountant Leo Bloom (Matthew Broderick) have the flavor of vaudeville yet are enjoyable in an irreverently modern way. Much has been made of the way *The Producers* flaunts political correctness, and several believe its popularity is due in some part to audiences' weariness with the elements of political correctness in the arts during the last decades of the twentieth century. But one must remember that the musical comedy of the past was never politically correct (had such a term existed in those days), and the scripts by George S. Kaufman, E. Y. Harburg, and others traded on bursting bubbles and targeting sensitive issues. Brooks and Meehan are not so much being daring as they are being old fashioned. But sometimes it takes a lot of daring to write what you think is funny and not worry about ruffling feathers. This is where *The Producers* triumphs. Old hat can be pretty impressive when worn with style and devil-may-care abandon.

Leaving the veterans behind, let us look at some of the new talent, the Broadway (and Off-Broadway) musical's future. In his own way, William Finn is as zany and farcical as Brooks. His musicals have a frantic edge to them as they plunge into the neurotic side of life recklessly and, often, hysterically. Finn was born in Boston in 1952 and educated at Williams College, where he wrote offbeat minimusicals while he majored in English. After graduation he wrote history textbooks for the junior high school level to support himself, while his quirky little musicals were being workshopped Off-Off Broadway. *In Trousers* (1979), the first of the Marvin Plays, saw three different productions in out-of-the-way venues but was not appreciated until after Finn's later success. It is a chaotic, exciting, and messy concoction of ideas that sometimes seems more like a bizarre session with a psychiatrist than a musical. Finn writes libretto, music, and lyrics, and since all his shows are sung through, the three elements are inseparable. His hero Marvin is married with an eight-year-old son, but he has trouble sleeping, haunted as he is by visions of past and present lust. As a fourteen-year-old, he played the role of Columbus in the school play and made amorous advances to his teacher-director, Mrs. Goldberg. But Melvin has also recently begun an affair with a man, the unseen stud Whizzer, and he cannot get the image of their lovemaking out of his head. Marvin decides to leave his wife for Whizzer, but because of his neuroses, it is not a happy ending for anyone. As he wryly notes, "The thing about explorers is: they discover things that are already there."

When Finn continued Marvin's story in the popular *March of the Falsettos* (1981), director James Lapine helped him structure his wild and erratic ideas, and the result was much more cohesive. When Marvin (Michael Rupert) leaves his wife Trina (Alison Fraser) for Whizzer (Stephen Bogardus), she goes to see Marvin's psychiatrist Mendel (Chip Zien) for help, and the two fall in love. Marvin's son Jason (James Kushner), starting to show the same signs of confusion as his father, is upset with the developments in his family ("My Father's a Homo," he sings), yet Jason likes Marvin's lover and consents to getting psychiatric help only when Whizzer encourages him. Father and son come to a wistful but truthful understanding by the end of the musical. The writing in all the Marvin Plays is often staccato, like an opera going out of control. All five characters remain on stage for most of the action, providing narration or shouting comments. From its ribald opening number, "Four Jews in a Room Bitching," to the delicate conclusion, "Father to Son," *March of the Falsettos* is a seamless musical ride that travels to many places in a very small space.

Finn's career then went through a series of disappointments. His *America Kicks Up Its Heels* (1983) never got beyond workshop stage, and when *Dangerous Games* (1989) and *Romance in Hard Times* (1989) were presented in first-class houses, they quickly closed. So much had happened in gay lifestyle in the 1980s, the AIDS epidemic in particular, that Finn returned to his alter-ego Marvin, and continued the story with *Falsettoland* (1990), the most mature work of the trilogy. Lapine played such a vital part in the development of the new installment that Finn listed him as co-librettist (though again the musical was sung through, so Lapine's contribution was probably structural). Two neighboring lesbians were added to the dramatis personae, one of them a doctor who sees the first signs of a new and terrible disease (she sings, "Something Bad is Happening"). Jason (Danny Gerard) is giving both his parents grief about his upcoming bar mitzvah, and again he relies on Whizzer for advice. But Whizzer is dying of AIDS, so Jason insists that the ceremony be held in his hospital room. The eruptive relationship between Melvin and Whizzer comes to a quiet resolution before the latter dies, and Melvin is finally, perhaps, coming to understand himself. While it may not have the uncontrolled glee of the first two musicals, *Falsettoland* is not a ponderous or angry diatribe like so many of the AIDS plays that proliferated at the time. It retains its wacky sense of humor, as in a risible scene in which the characters watch Jason play baseball or in the stepfatherly advice that Mendel gives Jason, saying it is all right to hate your folks because God hated his parents too. The musical is rich with understanding even as it offers no easy solutions.

The last two parts of the trilogy were altered, then combined under the title *Falsettos* (1992) and were presented with success on Broadway; Finn finally got widespread recognition. Still, many believed that his talent was limited to one narrow range of characters and ideas. It was *A New Brain* (1998) that proved otherwise. The musical was autobiographical, exploring Finn's experience when a brain tumor was detected and he thought his life was over. Such a morbid premise became his most life-fulfilling show. Gordon Schwinn (Malcolm Gets) writes songs for the children's television show character Mr. Bungee (Chip Zien) but dreams of creating a body of songs that say something worthwhile. When he collapses in a restaurant one day and is hospitalized, his friends gather around him, including his ex-lover Roger (Christopher Innvar) and Gordon's mother Mimi (Penny Fuller). Treatments in the hospital bring on hallucinations of the present, such as a tormenting Mr. Bungee, and the past, with memories of a gambling father and his past happiness with Roger. The tumor is operated on successfully, and by the time Gordon comes back to life his perspective has changed, deciding he will now live for "Time and Music." *A New Brain* recalls *In Trousers* with its collage-like approach to the material, but the new work is in total control, and Finn's voice is still humorously inventive even as it sounds more sane. Its limited run Off Broadway was not widely noticed, but since then *A New Brain* has gained a strong following and has received many productions.

We can look forward to future works by William Finn (his musicalization of *The Royal Family* has already been workshopped) but must content ourselves with only a handful of musicals by librettist-lyricist Howard Ashman (1950–1991). He was born Howard Elliott Gershman in Baltimore and educated at Goddard College and Indiana University. Ashman contributed lyrics to several Off-Off-Broadway musicals and revues, teaming up with composer Alan Menken on one of them. Their first book musical together was *God Bless You, Mr. Rosewater* (1979), a musicalization of Kurt Vonnegut's novel about an eccentric millionaire in middle America. It only enjoyed a short run, but their next project, *Little Shop of Horrors* (1982), turned into a long-running Off-Broadway hit and saw hundreds of productions across the country and around the world. Like *The Producers,* the stage version is superior to its movie source. The 1960 low-budget film, about a plant that needs human blood to survive, was a cult favorite, but it was a slapdash affair often enjoyed because of its outrageous premise, cheap production values, and corny acting. Ashman turned the little flick into a campy spoof of both the sci-fi movie genre and the early 1960s lifestyle, fleshing out the plot and developing the cartoon-like characters. He added a Greek chorus of sassy street urchins, and he and Menken provided a superb score that often went beyond pastiche to its own kind of comic book reality. *Little Shop of Horrors* remains very popular because its satire of the sci-fi B movies of the 1960s can be enjoyed even by audiences unfamiliar with its targets.

Ashman teamed up with composer Marvin Hamlisch for *Smile* (1986), a Broadway version of a 1975 film of the same name about a small-time beauty pageant. It also was a satire but a low-key one, and as much as Ashman tried to make the characters sympathetic, the contestants were generally an unlikable lot. Despite a laudable score, *Smile* quickly folded and has pretty much disappeared. The experience was so disheartening that Ashman (and Menken) took up the Disney Studio's lucrative offer to score animated films. They had three hits in a row, *The Little Mermaid* (1989), *Beauty and the Beast* (1991), and *Aladdin* (1992), but Ashman had died from AIDS before the last went into production. He did not write the screenplays for Disney films but contributed much to the plot structure and character development. When *Beauty and the Beast* was turned into a stage musical in 1994, Ashman finally had a Broadway hit, but only as a lyricist.

It also took a while for Lynn Ahrens to have a Broadway hit, even though she had been writing expert librettos for a decade. Ahrens was born in New York City in 1948 and studied to become a journalist at Syracuse University. But soon she was writing commercials and children's shows for television. Her collaboration with composer Stephen Flaherty began with their Off-Broadway musical farce *Lucky Stiff* (1988), a daffy tale about a weak-willed shoe salesman who suddenly finds adventure in his life when he inherits a fortune from his uncle. But he can collect the money only if he takes the uncle's corpse to Monte Carlo for a posthumous vacation. There he meets mobsters trying to locate the uncle's money and an animal rights activist who is hoping to get the deceased's fortune for her home for stray dogs. Ahrens based her fast-moving, slaphappy libretto on a novella called *The Man Who Broke the Bank at Monte Carlo* by Michael Butterworth. The score is so tightly integrated into the plot that *Lucky Stiff* seems to be sung through, even though it does stop for some ridiculous dialogue scenes. The songs are as eccentric as the script, and the little musical is one of the funniest of its era. Because its initial production had a very limited run, it took a long time for *Lucky Stiff* to catch on, and it is still being discovered by theatres looking for a sly and farcical little musical comedy.

When Ahrens musicalized a Rosa Guy novel set in the Caribbean, the result was *Once On This Island* (1990), a richly textured musical in a very different vein. Told by a group of villagers as local folk legend, the plot follows the adventures of Ti Moune (La Chanze), an orphan girl who one day saves the life of the island aristocrat Daniel (Jerry Dixon), and they fall in love. But his wealthy family has another bride in mind for him, so Daniel forsakes Ti Moune, who dies and is transformed into a magical tree that overlooks Daniel's home. Years later, Daniel's young son meets a mysterious peasant girl sitting in the tree, and the legend comes full circle. It is a bewitching tale beautifully told, and the Flaherty–Ahrens score is a pleasing mixture of island music and Broadway ballad. *Once On This Island* transferred from Off Broadway to Broadway with success and finally brought the team some recognition. Ahrens would not write the libretto for her next two projects but provided lyrics for the problematic musical *My Favorite Year* (1992) and the highly acclaimed *Ragtime* (1998) (see chapter 18). She co-wrote the adept adaptation of Dickens's *A Christmas Carol* (1994), which played at Madison Square Garden seasonally, and provided nimble lyrics for Alan Menken's tuneful music. Her next venture with Flaherty was *Seussical* (2000), a musical based on a handful of stories by "Dr. Seuss" that had a forced but unprofitable run on Broadway. Both Ahrens and Flaherty wrote the libretto, which tried to hold the evening's various tales together by having characters from different stories overlap, and they used recurring songs to tie the piece together. But despite another superb score and some fine performances, *Seussical* did not have wide enough appeal to run. Hopefully, it will reappear someday with a more satisfying libretto. Until then, we look forward to future projects by this very talented team.

Michael John LaChiusa writes libretto, music, and lyrics for his shows, and like Ahrens he seems comfortable in various styles and periods. He was born in Chautauqua, New York, in 1962 and attended a junior college in Boston for a while before moving to New York to pursue a theatre career. LaChiusa first grabbed the attention of critics and audiences alike with his Off-Broadway musical *First Lady Suite* (1993), an odd but disarming piece that looked at bits of history with a fresh viewpoint. The musical consists of four playlets, mostly sung through, about a quartet of presidents' wives. Jacqueline Kennedy is seen through the eyes of two personal secretaries as they fly to Dallas on *Air Force One* on November 22, 1963. Mamie Eisenhower, alone in her White House bedroom on her birthday, slips into a nightmare of sorts that involves opera singer Marian Anderson and Ike's affair with another woman. Presidential daughter Margaret Truman is lampooned as she tries to perform for the Christian Democrat Mothers and Daughters but is upstaged by her mother Bess. The final playlet is a lyrical fantasy with Amelia Earhart flying in her plane over Washington with Eleanor Roosevelt and her rival Lorena Hickok. *First Lady Suite* is highly unusual, very intriguing, and pure LaChiusa.

Even finer was *Hello, Again* (1993), a loose adaptation of Arthur Schnitzler's 1903 comedy of amoral manners, *La Ronde*. The original is a series of sexual encounters that encompasses (and connects) all levels of Viennese society, from prostitute to duke. LaChiusa's version jumps through time, each coupling taking place in a different period and the characters continuing the "round" without regard for age or class. For example, a homosexual toy boy seduced by a businessman on board the *Titanic* survives the shipwreck and then shows up hustling a screenwriter in a 1970s discotheque. This ricocheting through the ages allows LaChiusa to imitate different kinds of popular music, from waltz to boogie-woogie. But it also allows his libretto to comment on sexual mores of each time period and to find a sometimes comic, sometimes bitter frame of reference. Much of the storytelling is told by the songs, but there are sections of dialogue that are craftily delightful. When the toy boy asks his seducer, Carl, if they will keep in touch once they arrive in New York, Carl blandly replies, "The ship has struck an iceberg. We are sinking. Lifeboats are being lowered. We will die soon." The youth admits, "Oh . . . that's good. I never heard that one before." As with Schnitzler's play, the cycle of lovers goes full circle, and we end up with a prostitute and a senator, two extremes of society that prove to be closer than you think. But LaChiusa is not so much interested in class as in attitudes, and *Hello Again* speaks about American mores as vividly as Schnitzler did about his world.

There was much less humor in LaChiusa's next two musicals, and both projects were too dark to find wide audiences on Broadway, where they premiered. Yet both are exceptional pieces of musical theatre. A Broadway musical based on *Medea* sounds like one of Mel Brooks's jokes from *The Producers,* but that is the premise for *Marie Christine* (1999), an opera-like musical that is as unrelenting as its source. LaChiusa sets his version in late nineteenth-century America with Medea as the New Orleans Creole aristocrat Marie (Audra McDonald), who has magical powers and falls into a passionate affair with the sea captain Dante Keyes (Anthony Crivello). She sacrifices her wealth and even her brother to help him. But when Keyes gets involved with Chicago politics and sees a Creole mistress as a dangerous liability, he tries to get custody of their sons and push Marie out of the picture. As in the Euripides tragedy, Marie poisons Dante's high-society fiancée and murders her own children. LaChiusa tells this still-disturbing tale *Man of La Mancha* style, with Marie in prison awaiting trial and relating the story to her fellow female prisoners. It is a well-plotted libretto that manages to tell the classic story in a new yet logical manner. The music and lyrics soar with emotion, and *Marie Christine* attempts to go where few musicals have considered going. But the result is perhaps too effective. The piece seems more appropriate for opera, and its future probably lies in opera houses.

Equally nightmarish but much more palatable is *The Wild Party* (2000), a gin-soaked orgy of sardonic humor and hot jazz that is based on Moncure Marsh's 1928 poem of the same title. George C. Wolfe co-authored the libretto with LaChiusa, and it also is unrelenting in its approach to the material. None of Marsh's characters is particularly lovable, and the musical made no efforts to disguise their raunchy and misguided behavior. In a savage spoof of vaudeville, we meet flapper Queenie (Toni Collette) and her violent-tempered lover, Burrs (Mandy Patinkin). Their relationship as shaky as always, they decide to throw a party to cover up their discontent. But the party brings old and new rivals, an orgy of sorts takes place, and Burrs ends up shot to death. There is plenty of humor in both the libretto and the wonderfully pastiche score, but it is an angry and uncomfortable humor. *The Wild Party* is a show perhaps easier to admire than to enjoy, but it is another impressive step forward for LaChiusa. What part he will play in the future of American musical theatre is impossible to say. But his future work will be looked at with great anticipation.

Mentioning George C. Wolfe brings us to the first of a list of musicals from the 1980s and 1990s that should not be excluded from this chapter. Wolfe's libretto for *Jelly's Last Jam* (1992) is a complex and an ambitious one. He views the early jazz pioneer Jelly Roll Morton (Gregory Hines) in a surreal presentation set in some life-after-death limbo with an ominous Chimney Man (Keith David) presiding. Morton was not presented sympathetically, his destructive ego and sense of bigotry overshadowing his musical accomplishments. Here was another dark musical and one that refused to slip into an old-style "Negro revue." Luther Henderson adapted Morton's music, and Susan Birkenhead contributed some unmemorable lyrics. But *Jelly's Last Jam* centered on character and dance and explored ideas about racial types. After its Broadway run, it pretty much faded from sight, but it is a unique and accomplished musical all the same.

A much more popular (and resilient) look at African Americans in show business is *Dreamgirls* (1981), a rather traditional backstager about a singing trio that was the Supremes in all but name. Tom Eyen, an author of avant-garde plays two decades earlier, wrote the libretto and the lyrics for Henry Krieger's Motown-like music. The story of the ups and downs of the all-girl group was interesting enough, but *Dreamgirls* was most effective when it paralleled the shifting roles that blacks played in America during the 1960s and 1970s. Although it was sometimes melodramatic, Eyen's script was neither angry nor simpleminded. The lavish staging Michael Bennett gave the musical often overshadowed the more subtle aspects of the libretto, but it remains a show that works on many different levels. *Dreamgirls* ran four years and was a hit on tour as well. *Baby* (1983), a small-scale Broadway musical, could hold on for only seven months, despite some good notices and a commendable score by David Shire (music) and Richard Maltby Jr. (lyrics). Sybille Pearson wrote the succinct libretto about three couples, two expecting a child and one trying to conceive. It is a surprisingly literate script that avoids cliché or simple stereotypes. Here is a musical in which the audience closely identifies with all six central characters. There is no villain; the conflict comes from within as each couple journeys to some kind of self-understanding. Dismissed as too clinical by some (it isn't; the premise just sounds that way), *Baby* was immensely pleasing, and it has found audiences regionally. Surely it belonged Off Broadway rather than on, for it plays best in small, intimate spaces.

Two British classics came to Broadway in very different guises during this period: the rollicking *The Mystery of Edwin Drood* (1985) and the delicate *The Secret Garden* (1991). Rupert Holmes wrote libretto, music, lyrics, and even orchestrations for his music hall treatment of Charles Dickens's final (and unfinished) novel. Audiences either loved the participatory nature of the evening or cringed in horror as they were asked to sing along and even decide on the ending of the story. Holmes creates the music hall milieu quickly and then uses it to tell a rather intricate tale in a fun and giddy manner. The dialogue may not be very Dickensian, but it sure is Victorian "variety," as heroes, villains, fallen women, and suspicious foreigners dash on and off and even drop character for the occasional sing-along or specialty number. Holmes's score goes far beyond parody as he re-creates parlor songs, Gilbert and Sullivan patter numbers, jolly "knees-up" ditties, and so on. Holmes is American (he previously had some pop songs on the charts), but *Drood,* as its title was later shortened to, is very British, and it is amazing that it appealed to Broadway at all. But subsequent productions across the country have proven the piece to be an audience pleaser. Holmes has written some nonmusical mystery plays since, but what we really need is another musical from this gifted artist. The same can certainly be said for Marsha Norman (book and lyrics) and Lucy Simon (music), who wrote *The Secret Garden.* Far from a simple, straightforward adaptation, Norman's libretto takes the Frances Hodgson Burnett classic and turns it into a dreamy, haunted tale about rebirth. Set against the realistic tale of an orphan girl discovering a hidden garden (and family secrets) in the grim Yorkshire moors, the stage is peopled with the ghosts of deceased characters and lingering memories. The libretto seems to comment on Burnett's Victorian story even as it retells it for the musical stage. Like *Drood,* the score is a marvelous pastiche of songs of the period along with some embracing Broadway ballads. *The Secret Garden* is also very British (the Yorkshire dialect of some of the characters is a challenge to American audiences) but has seen many productions across the country. How disheartening to think that over a decade has gone by and still Broadway hasn't seen another musical by Norman and Simon.

If British classics, why not a German favorite? Luther Davis, who had written the libretto for *Kismet* (1953) and had not been heard of much since, penned the script for *Grand Hotel* (1989), a brilliant director-choreographer showcase for Tommy Tune but a solid piece of writing as well. *Kismet* veterans Robert Wright and George Forrest (music and lyrics together) had been tinkering with this show for decades, but by the time it reached Broadway it had added songs by Maury Yeston. It is an impressive (and surprisingly cohesive) score, and Tune staged the numbers in unconventional ways. Yet Davis's libretto is rather conventional and told its many stories together with efficiency and style. Tune was exploring the different levels of Berlin society in his presentation, but the success of the show ultimately rested on a strong book. The story, based on a Vicki Baum novel (and later a play and a movie), looked at various patrons and employees at an expensive Berlin hotel in the 1920s. A popular star-studded film version in 1932 was engrossing melodrama, but the musical dug a bit deeper and managed to tie the different subplots together thematically. Whereas the movie ended with a melancholy observation about people passing through life, the musical celebrates new life: the front-desk worker Erik sings a welcome to his newborn son on the phone as the dying bookkeeper Kringelein leaves for Paris, where he will take care of the pregnant, unmarried stenographer Flaemmchen and her future child. *Grand Hotel* might have been a traditionally pleasing musical play in the 1950s, but in the 1980s it became an absorbing theatre piece.

Linda Woolverton adapted her own screenplay for the Broadway version of *Beauty and the Beast* (1994) and understood the difference between the two media, for she did a first-class job. Critics were expecting a theme park show (and several insisted that that was what they saw), but the libretto for the musical is in the traditional Broadway mode, with new scenes and songs (by Tim Rice doing lyrics for Menken's music) added to turn an animated feature into a full-fledged musical. The Beast, who hardly sang in the film, was further developed in the script and in the score, and the libretto concentrated more on the character change that the prince-turned-monster underwent. The spectacle and high-tech effects were, of course, Disney ingenuity at its best, but again it was a sturdy story that held the show together. Future productions unable to re-create the Broadway razzle-dazzle will probably prove to be very enjoyable as well. *Beauty and the Beast* is a timeless tale, and the stage version triumphs because it tells its story so well.

Woolverton was joined by director Robert Falls and playwright David Henry Hwang in writing the libretto for Disney's *Aida* (2000), and the result was much less effective (though still a hit). They did not so much adapt the

Ghislanzoni libretto from Verdi's 1871 opera as tweak it, and the show ended up being artificial in its characters and plotting. The great tragic story seems to resist a mod rock retelling, and glitzy Egyptians that are so campy in, say, *Joseph and the Amazing Technicolor Dreamcoat* (1972) are just plain embarrassing in an updating hell-bent on being serious. The character of Amneris (Sherie René Scott), for example, is first portrayed as a vapid Valley Girl and then awkwardly turns into a self-sacrificing woman of honor. The slave girl Aida (Heather Headley) is unflinchingly perfect, and the dashing warrior Radames (Adam Pascal) is right out of bad operetta: noble, stiff, and mindless. Perhaps the show could have been brought to life with an exceptional score, but the songs by Elton John (music) and Tim Rice (lyrics) are from each man's bottom drawer. *Aida* is a bad idea that just happened to make a lot of money.

Yet it *is* possible to take a new look at an old opera, as Jonathan Larson proved with *Rent* (1996). This was much more than tweaking, as he found parallels between the Parisian Bohemians of the 1890s and the Greenwich Village artists of a century later. *Rent* is a true adaptation that brings new light to an old tale (Puccini's *La Boheme*) rather than just marketing it. Larson's rock musical is sung through, so the lyrics become the libretto, and what a fascinating plot he makes of the old story! Love triangles, performance artists, hetero- and homosexual characters, street people, and rising "new money" Yuppies all crisscross in a complex yet enthralling libretto that uses the old opera when convenient and then goes off in its own direction when it chooses. Larson took a real rock (as opposed to a Broadway rock) approach to the show, but he understood how to introduce characters, relay expositions, illustrate the passage of the time, and indicate the change in relationships like a Broadway traditionalist. It is a well-constructed libretto that feels loose and unstructured. Larson's untimely death caused much speculation about what his future in musical theatre might have been. Some of this speculation was fueled when an earlier work of his, retitled *Tick Tick . . . Boom* (2001), was staged. It has many similarities to *Rent* and might even be viewed as an early draft of the later show. But *Tick Tick* also has vivid characterizations and tells its slight story in a thrilling way. Larson was not a one-play wonder; fate just made it seem that way.

As the century came to a close, two noteworthy musicals opened whose librettos, I believe, are of significant quality. *Floyd Collins* (1996) received only a limited Off-Broadway run but has slowly gained attention. The musical is based on a true story about a Kentucky man who, while exploring a cave on his property in 1925, got trapped one hundred feet below ground. The attempts to rescue him got national media attention, and the tragic episode (Floyd died before he could be saved) became a circus of sorts, bringing in the crowds that Floyd had hoped to attract when he opened his cave to the public for tours. Tina Landau's libretto is highly inventive, beginning with a long sequence with Floyd alone inside his discovery, singing duets with his echoing voice about how he will market his newfound fortune. Then the accident occurs, and Landau brings in the outside world, from devoted family members to the sensation-seeking press to entrepreneurs whose idea of marketing parallels Floyd's. Much of the show is sung, and Adam Guettel's score is perhaps the most unusual and challenging of the decade. From hillbilly folk songs to carnival-like Tin Pan Alley ditties to tricky minimalist concert pieces, it is a puzzling and estimable score that fits effectively with Landau's oddly involving libretto. *Floyd Collins* is a show that will never become widely popular because it purposely avoids many of the familiarities that an audience demands and expects. (And this from a songwriter who is Richard Rodgers's grandson!) But there is so much to savor in *Floyd Collins* that, mainstream or not, it adds richness to the American musical.

Parade (1998) also failed to find a mainstream public and probably never will, but it will be produced on occasion and will provide a gripping theatre experience. It also is based on a true event, the kangaroo court trial and subsequent lynching of a Jewish factory manager in Atlanta, Georgia, in 1913. Leo Frank (Brent Carver) is accused of murdering one of his employees, an adolescent girl whom he hardly knew. Like Floyd Collins's accident, the murder gets national attention, and Frank is railroaded by the media and a bigoted community that distrusts a Northern Jew. Alfred Uhry, a successful playwright who penned such prize-winning plays as *Driving Miss Daisy* (1987) and *The Last Night of Ballyhoo* (1997), wrote the libretto based on facts, hearsay, and his own vivid imagination. It is not a propaganda piece, though it might easily have gone that way in less talented hands. Uhry finds the humanity in many of the characters and, for the most part, avoids extreme stereotypes. Newcomer Jason Robert Brown wrote the penetrating music and lyrics, and there is nothing of the novice about them. Here is a first-class songwriter-storyteller, and working with Uhry's libretto, the two certainly told their grim story well. But no musical about the Leo Frank case could be widely popular on Broadway. It's the nature of the beast.

What is popular at the end of the century? *The Lion King* (1997), of course. It is the most successful show of the decade and is probably headed for a run that will leave those British long runs far behind. And who wrote this mammoth hit? One suspects that director Julie Taymor did, since it seems she did everything else; but the credited librettists are Roger Allers and Irene Mecchi. Who? Allers is an animator who helped shape the film version of *The Lion King*, and Mecchi is one of the co-authors of the screenplay. Their libretto adheres to the movie closely, yet allows opportunity for additional songs by Elton John (music), Tim Rice (lyrics), and others and added scenes to fill out the characters a bit more. Since the source is well plotted, the musical is also built sturdily, telling a *Hamlet*-like fable in clear and uncluttered terms. The dialogue is not exceptional, but neither is it dull or forced. It is a well-crafted, competent libretto with a likable if unexceptional score. So why is it the biggest hit since *My Fair Lady?* Because the American musical has changed, and it is now possible to make extraordinary magic out of ordinary songs and story. Taymor's manner of telling this capable tale is where the magic lies, and that is both an exciting and a sobering thought. The flashy director-choreographers of the 1960s and 1970s surely put their personal stamp on their shows, sometimes turning routine material into pure gold. But even *Pippin* (1972) or *Seesaw* (1973) started with a libretto that had a spark of something special. Julie Taymor's ingenious sense of visuals and staging (though she is not a choreographer) don't seem to rely on any material at all. This woman might present the proverbial phone book next, and it still might be magic! *The Lion King* may be the first American musical classic that achieves that distinction not because of its book or score but by its staging.

So is this the future of the Broadway musical? Probably not. Despite its runaway success, *The Lion King* is unlikely to produce many clones. (For one thing, there aren't enough Julie Taymors.) Book musicals will continue to depend on a story, even if that story comes from movies with plots that are as diverse as *The Full Monty* (2000) and *Sweet Smell of Success* (2002). Librettos will continue to lampoon or comment on other musicals, though it is hoped that the result will be better than *Bat Boy* (2001) or *Urinetown* (2001), two musicals that clumsily ape older styles and think they have said something new. There will even be the occasional "special" musical that isn't a musical at all, such as *Contact* (1999). Because anything and everything can be turned into a Broadway musical these days, the possibilities are endless. But regardless of how crazy things get, the librettist will remain the backbone of the book musical. There are so many stories, old and new, that need to be told on the musical stage. And it all starts with the librettist. How else can boy lose girl?

BIBLIOGRAPHY

General Works on the American Musical Theatre

Abbott, George. *Mister Abbott.* New York: Random House, 1963.

Alpert, Hollis. *Broadway: 125 Years of Musical Theatre.* New York: Arcade, 1991.

Atkinson, Brooks. *Broadway.* Rev. ed. New York: Macmillan, 1974.

Banham, Martin, ed. *The Cambridge Guide to Theatre.* New York: Cambridge University Press, 1992.

Baral, Robert. *Revue: The Great Broadway Period.* Rev. ed. New York: Fleet Press, 1970.

Bell, Marty. *Broadway Stories: A Backstage Journey through Musical Theatre.* New York: Limelight Editions, 1993.

The Best Plays. 81 eds. Edited by Garrison Sherwood and John Chapman (1894–1919), Burns Mantle (1919–1947), John Chapman (1947–1952), Louis Kronenberger (1952–1961), Henry Hewes (1961–1964), and Otis Guernsey Jr. (1964–2000). New York: Dodd, Mead, 1894–1988; New York: Applause Theatre Book Publishers, 1988–1993; New York: Limelight Editions, 1994–2000.

Block, Geoffrey. *Enchanted Evenings: The Broadway Musical from* Show Boat *to* Sondheim. New York: Oxford University Press, 1997.

Bloom, Ken. *American Song: The Complete Musical Theatre Companion, 1900–1984.* New York: Facts on File, 1985.

———. *Broadway: An Encyclopedic Guide to the History, People and Places of Times Square.* New York: Facts on File, 1991.

Blum, Daniel, and John Willis. *A Pictorial History of the American Theatre, 1860–1980.* 5th ed. New York: Crown, 1981.

Bordman, Gerald. *American Musical Comedy: From* Adonis *to* Dreamgirls. New York: Oxford University Press, 1982.

———. *American Musical Revue: From* The Passing Show *to* Sugar Babies. New York: Oxford University Press, 1985.

———. *American Musical Theatre: A Chronicle.* 3rd ed. New York: Oxford University Press, 2001.

———. *American Operetta: From* H.M.S. Pinafore *to* Sweeney Todd. New York: Oxford University Press, 1981.

———. *The Oxford Companion to American Theatre.* 2nd ed. New York: Oxford University Press, 1992.

Botto, Louis. *At This Theatre: An Informal History of New York's Legitimate Theatres.* New York: Dodd, Mead, 1984.

Bowers, Dwight Blocker. *American Musical Theater: Shows, Songs, and Stars.* Washington, D.C.: Smithsonian Institution Press, 1989.

Burton, Jack. *The Blue Book of Broadway Musicals.* Rev. ed. Watkins Glen, N.Y.: Century House, 1974.

Drone, Jeanette M. *Index to Opera, Operetta and Musical Comedy Synopses in Collections and Periodicals.* Metuchen, N.J.: Scarecrow Press, 1978.

———. *Musical Theatre Synopses: An Index.* Metuchen, N.J.: Scarecrow Press, 1998.

Engel, Lehman. *The American Musical Theater: A Consideration.* New York: CBS Legacy Collection Books, 1967.

Ewen, David. *New Complete Book of the American Musical Theatre.* New York: Henry Holt, 1976.

Fields, Armond, and L. Marc Fields. *From the Bowery to Broadway: Lew Fields and the Roots of American Popular Theatre.* New York: Oxford University Press, 1993.

Flinn, Denny Martin. *Musical: The Grand Tour.* New York: Schirmer, 1997.

Ganzl, Kurt, and Andrew Lamb. *Ganzl's Book of the Musical Theatre.* New York: Schirmer, 1989.

———. *Ganzl's Encyclopedia of the Musical Theatre.* New York: Schirmer, 1993.

Goldman, William. *The Season: A Candid Look at Broadway.* New York: Harcourt, Brace and World, 1969.

Gottfried, Martin. *Broadway Musicals.* New York: Abrams, 1980.

———. *More Broadway Musicals.* New York: Abrams, 1991.

Green, Stanley. *Broadway Musicals of the 1930s.* New York: Da Capo, 1982.

———. *Broadway Musicals Show by Show.* 5th ed. Milwaukee: Hal Leonard, 1999.

———. *Encyclopedia of the Musical Theatre.* New York: Dodd, Mead, 1976.

———. *The World of Musical Comedy.* New York: A. S. Barnes, 1980.

Guernsey, Otis L., ed. *Curtain Times: The New York Theatre, 1965–1987.* New York: Applause Theatre Book Publishers, 1987.

Henderson, Mary C. *Theater in America.* New York: Abrams, 1986.

Hischak, Thomas S. *The American Musical Theatre Song Encyclopedia.* Westport, Conn.: Greenwood, 1995.

———. *Stage It with Music: An Encyclopedic Guide to the American Musical Theatre.* Westport, Conn.: Greenwood, 1993.

———. *The Theatregoer's Almanac.* Westport, Conn.: Greenwood, 1997.

Jackson, Arthur. *The Best Musicals from* Show Boat *to* A Chorus Line. New York: Crown, 1977.

Kislan, Richard. *Hoofing on Broadway: A History of Show Dancing.* New York: Prentice Hall, 1987.

———. *The Musical: A Look at the American Musical Theater.* Englewood Cliffs, N.J.: Prentice Hall, 1980.

Laufe, Abe. *Anatomy of a Hit: Long-Run Plays on Broadway from 1900 to the Present Day.* New York: Hawthorn, 1966.

———. *Broadway's Greatest Musicals.* New York: Funk and Wagnalls, 1977.

Lerner, Alan Jay. *The Musical Theatre: A Celebration.* New York: McGraw-Hill, 1986.

Mandelbaum, Ken. *Not since Carrie: Forty Years of Broadway Musical Flops.* New York: St. Martin's, 1991.

Mates, Julian. *America's Musical Stage: Two Hundred Years of Musical Theatre.* Westport, Conn.: Greenwood, 1985.

McSpadden, J. Walker. *Operas and Musical Comedies.* New York: Crowell, 1958.

Miller, Scott. *Deconstructing Harold Hill: An Insider's Guide to Musical Theatre.* Portsmouth, N.H.: Heinemann, 2000.

———. *Rebels with Applause: Broadway's Groundbreaking Musicals.* Portsmouth, N.H.: Heinemann, 2001.

Mordden, Ethan. *Beautiful Mornin': The Broadway Musical in the 1940s.* New York: Oxford University Press, 1999.

———. *Better Foot Forward: The History of American Musical Theatre.* New York: Grossman, 1976.

———. *Broadway Babies: The People Who Made the American Musical.* New York: Oxford University Press, 1983.

———. *Coming up Roses: The Broadway Musical in the 1950s.* New York: Oxford University Press, 1998.

———. *Make Believe: The Broadway Musical in the 1920s.* New York: Oxford University Press, 1997.

———. *Open a New Window: The Broadway Musical in the 1960s.* New York: Palgrave-St. Martin's, 2001.

Peterson, Bernard L. *A Century of Musicals in Black and White.* Westport, Conn.: Greenwood, 1993.

Rosenberg, Bernard, and Ernest Harburg. *The Broadway Musical: Collaboration in Commerce and Art.* New York: New York University Press, 1993.

Salem, James M. *A Guide to Critical Reviews: The Musical, 1909–1989.* Metuchen, N.J.: Scarecrow Press, 1991.

Sennett, Ted. *Song and Dance: The Musicals of Broadway.* New York: Metro, 1998.

Sheward, David. *It's a Hit: The Back Stage Book of Longest-Running Broadway Shows, 1884 to the Present.* New York: Watson-Guptill Publications/BPI Communications, 1994.

Simas, Rick. *The Musicals No One Came to See.* New York: Garland, 1987.

Smith, Cecil, and Glenn Litton. *Musical Comedy in America.* 2nd ed. New York: Theatre Arts Books, 1981.

Suskin, Steven. *More Opening Nights on Broadway: A Critical Quotebook of the Musical Theatre, 1965–1981.* New York: Schirmer, 1997.

———. *Opening Night on Broadway: A Critical Quotebook of the Golden Era of the Musical Theatre.* New York: Schirmer, 1990.

Swain, Joseph P. *The Broadway Musical: A Critical and Musical Survey.* New York: Oxford University Press, 1990.

Thelen, Lawrence. *The Show Makers: Great Directors of the American Musical Theatre.* New York: Routledge, 2000.

Toll, Robert C. *On with the Show: The First Century of Show Business in America.* New York: Oxford University Press, 1976.

Traubner, Richard. *Operetta: A Theatrical History.* Garden City, N.Y.: Doubleday, 1983.

Wilmeth, Don B., and Tice Miller, eds. *Cambridge Guide to American Theatre.* New York: Cambridge University Press, 1993.

Woll, Allen. *Black Musical Theatre: From* Coontown *to* Dreamgirls. Baton Rouge: Louisiana State University Press, 1989.

Works on Theatre Librettists and Songwriters

Adler, Richard, with Lee Davis. *You Gotta Have Heart: An Autobiography.* New York: Donald I. Fine, 1990.

Arbold, Elliot. *Deep in My Heart: Sigmund Romberg.* New York: Duell, Sloane and Pearce, 1949.

Armitage, Merle. *George Gershwin: Man and Legend.* New York: Duell, Sloane and Pearce, 1958.

Bach, Bob, and Ginger Mercer, eds. *Our Huckleberry Friend: The Life, Times and Lyrics of Johnny Mercer.* Secaucus, N.J.: Lyle Stuart, 1982.

Bach, Steven. *Dazzler: The Life and Times of Moss Hart.* New York: Knopf, 2001.

Barrett, Mary Ellin. *Irving Berlin: A Daughter's Memoir.* New York: Simon & Schuster, 1994.

Bergreen, Laurence. *As Thousands Cheer: The Life of Irving Berlin.* New York: Viking, 1990.

Bernstein, Leonard. *Findings.* New York: Simon & Schuster, 1982.

Bordman, Gerald. *Days to Be Happy, Years to Be Sad: The Life and Music of Vincent Youmans.* New York: Oxford University Press, 1982.

———. *Jerome Kern: His Life and Music.* New York: Oxford University Press, 1980.

Burrows, Abe. *Honest Abe: Is There Really No Business Like Show Business?* Boston: Little, Brown, 1980.

Burton, Humphrey. *Leonard Bernstein.* Garden City, N.Y.: Doubleday, 1994.

Cahn, Sammy. *I Should Care: The Sammy Cahn Story.* New York: Arbor House, 1974.

Citron, Stephen. *Noel and Cole: The Sophisticates.* New York: Oxford University Press, 1993.

———. *The Wordsmiths: Oscar Hammerstein II and Alan Jay Lerner.* New York: Oxford University Press, 1995.

Cohan, George M. *Twenty Years on Broadway.* New York: Harper, 1924.

Comden, Betty. *Off Stage: My Non-Show Business Life.* New York: Limelight Editions, 1996.

David, Lee. *Bolton and Wodehouse and Kern.* New York: James H. Heineman, 1993.

Dietz, Howard. *Dancing in the Dark.* New York: Quadrangle Books/New York Times Book Co., 1974.

Donaldson, Frances. *P. G. Wodehouse: A Biography.* New York: Knopf, 1982.

Drew, David. *Kurt Weill: A Handbook.* Berkeley: University of California Press, 1987.

Duke, Vernon. *Passport to Paris.* Boston: Little, Brown, 1955.

Eells, George. *The Life That Late He Led: A Biography of Cole Porter.* New York: Putnam, 1967.

Engel, Lehman. *Their Words Are Music: The Great Theatre Lyricists and Their Lyrics.* New York: Crown, 1975.

Ewen, David. *American Songwriters.* New York: H. W. Wilson, 1987.

———. *George Gershwin: His Journey to Greatness.* Westport, Conn.: Greenwood, 1977.

———. *Richard Rodgers.* New York: Holt, 1957.

———. *The World of Jerome Kern.* New York: Holt, 1960.

Fordin, Hugh. *Getting to Know Him: A Biography of Oscar Hammerstein II.* New York: Random House, 1977.

Freedland, Michael. *Irving Berlin.* New York: Stein and Day, 1974.

———. *Jerome Kern.* New York: Stein and Day, 1981.

Furia, Philip. *Ira Gershwin: The Art of the Lyricist.* New York: Oxford University Press, 1996.

———. *The Poets of Tin Pan Alley: A History of America's Great Lyricists.* New York: Oxford University Press, 1990.

Gelbart, Larry. *Laughing Matters.* New York: Random House, 1998.

Gershwin, Ira. *Lyrics on Several Occasions.* New York: Viking, 1973.

Goldstein, Malcolm. *George S. Kaufman: His Life, His Theatre.* New York: Oxford University Press, 1979.

Gordon, Eric A. *Mark the Music: The Life and Work of Marc Blitzstein.* New York: St. Martin's, 1989.

Gordon, Joanne. *Art Isn't Easy: The Achievement of Stephen Sondheim.* Carbondale: Southern Illinois University Press, 1990.

Gottfried, Martin. *Sondheim.* New York: Abrams, 1993.

Grafton, David. *Red, Hot and Rich: An Oral History of Cole Porter.* New York: Stein and Day, 1987.

Grattan, Virginia L. *American Women Songwriters: A Biographical Dictionary.* Westport, Conn.: Greenwood, 1993.

Green, Benny. *P. G. Wodehouse: A Literary Biography.* New York: Routledge, 1981.

Green, Stanley. *Rodgers and Hammerstein Fact Book.* Milwaukee: Lynn Farnol Group/Hal Leonard, 1986.

———. *The Rodgers and Hammerstein Story.* New York: John Day, 1963.

Guernsey, Otis L., ed. *Broadway Song and Story: Playwrights, Lyricists, Composers Discuss Their Hits.* New York: Dodd, Mead, 1985.

———. *Playwrights, Lyricists, Composers on Theatre.* New York: Dodd, Mead, 1974.

Hamlisch, Marvin, with Gerald Gardner. *The Way I Was.* New York: Scribner, 1992.

Hamm, Charles. *Irving Berlin.* New York: Oxford University Press, 1997.

Hammerstein, Oscar, II. *Lyrics.* Rev. ed. Milwaukee: Hal Leonard, 1985.

Harris, Charles K. *After the Ball: Forty Years of Melody.* New York: Frank Maurice, 1926.

Hart, Dorothy. *Thou Swell, Thou Witty: The Life and Lyrics of Lorenz Hart.* New York: Harper & Row, 1976.

Herman, Jerry, with Marilyn Stasio. *Showtune.* New York: Donald I. Fine Books, 1996.

Hischak, Thomas S. *Word Crazy: Broadway Lyricists from Cohan to Sondheim.* New York: Praeger, 1991.

Hyland, William G. *Richard Rodgers.* New Haven, Conn.: Yale University Press, 1998.

———. *The Song Is Ended: Songwriters and American Music, 1900–1950.* New York: Oxford University Press, 1995.

Jablonski, Edward. *Gershwin.* Garden City, N.Y.: Doubleday, 1987.

———. *Harold Arlen: Happy with the Blues.* Garden City, N.Y.: Doubleday, 1961.

Jablonski, Edward, and Lawrence D. Stewart. *The Gershwin Years.* Garden City, N.Y.: Doubleday, 1958, 1973.

Kahn, E. J. *The Merry Partners: The Age and Stage of Harrigan and Hart.* New York: Random House, 1955.

Kasha, Al, and Joel Hirschhorn. *Notes on Broadway: Conversations with the Great Songwriters.* Chicago: Contemporary Books, 1985.

Kaye, Joseph. *Victor Herbert.* New York: Crown, 1931.

Kendall, Alan. *George Gershwin: A Biography.* New York: Universe Books, 1987.

Kimball, Robert, ed. *Cole.* New York: Holt, Rinehart and Winston, 1971.

Kimball, Robert, and William Bolcom. *Reminiscing with Sissle and Blake.* New York: Viking, 1973.

Kimball, Robert, and Alfred Simon. *The Gershwins.* New York: Atheneum, 1973.

Laurents, Arthur. *Original Story: A Memoir of Broadway and Hollywood.* New York: Hal Leonard, 2001.

Lees, Gene. *Inventing Champagne: The Worlds of Lerner and Loewe.* New York: St. Martin's, 1990.

Lerner, Alan Jay. *The Street Where I Live.* New York: Norton, 1978.

Loesser, Susan. *A Most Remarkable Fella: Frank Loesser and the Guys and Dolls in His Life.* New York: Donald I. Fine, 1993.

Marx, Samuel, and Jan Clayton. *Rodgers and Hart: Bewitched, Bothered and Bewildered.* New York: Putnam, 1976.

McCabe, John. *George M. Cohan: The Man Who Owned Broadway.* Garden City, N.Y.: Doubleday, 1973.

McLean, Lorraine Arnal. *Dorothy Donnelly: A Life in the Theatre.* Jefferson, N.C.: McFarland, 1999.

Meyerson, Harold, and Ernie Harburg. *Who Put the Rainbow in* The Wizard of Oz? *Yip Harburg, Lyricist.* Ann Arbor: University of Michigan Press, 1993.

Mordden, Ethan. *Rodgers and Hammerstein.* New York: Abrams, 1992.

Morehouse, Ward. *George M. Cohan: Prince of the American Theater.* Philadelphia: Lippincott, 1943.

Nolan, Frederick. *Lorenz Hart: A Poet on Broadway.* New York: Oxford University Press, 1994.

———. *The Sound of Their Music: The Story of Rodgers and Hammerstein.* New York: Walker, 1978.

Peyser, Joan. *Bernstein: A Biography.* New York: Ballantine, 1988.

———. *The Memory of All That: The Life of George Gershwin.* New York: Simon & Schuster, 1993.

Rodgers, Richard. *Musical Stages: An Autobiography.* New York: Random House, 1975.

Rose, Al. *Eubie Blake.* New York: Schirmer, 1979.

Rosenberg, Deena. *Fascinating Rhythm: The Collaboration of George and Ira Gershwin.* New York: Dutton, 1991.

Sanders, Ronald. *The Days Grow Short: The Life and Music of Kurt Weill.* New York: Holt, Rinehart and Winston, 1980.

Schwartz, Charles. *Cole Porter: A Biography.* New York: Dial, 1977.

———. *Gershwin, His Life and Music.* Indianapolis: Bobbs-Merrill, 1973.

Secrest, Meryle. *Leonard Bernstein.* New York: Knopf, 1994.

———. *Somewhere for Me: A Biography of Richard Rodgers.* New York: Knopf, 2001.

———. *Stephen Sondheim.* New York: Knopf, 1998.

Shatzky, Joel, and Michael Taub, eds. *Contemporary Jewish-American Dramatists and Poets.* Westport, Conn.: Greenwood, 1999.

Shivers, Alfred. *The Life of Maxwell Anderson.* New York: Stein and Day, 1983.

Simon, Neil. *The Play Goes On: A Memoir.* New York: Simon & Schuster, 1999.

———. *Rewrites: A Memoir.* New York: Simon & Schuster, 1996.

Taylor, Deems. *Some Enchanted Evenings: The Story of Rodgers and Hammerstein.* New York: Harper, 1953.

Taylor, Theodore. *Jule: The Story of Composer Jule Styne.* New York: Random House, 1979.

Waters, Edward. *Victor Herbert: A Life in Music.* New York: Macmillan, 1955.

Whitcomb, Ian. *Irving Berlin and Ragtime America.* New York: Limelight Editions, 1988.

Willson, Meredith. *But He Doesn't Know the Territory.* New York: Putnam, 1959.

Winer, Deborah Grace. *On the Sunny Side of the Street: The Life and Lyrics of Dorothy Fields.* New York: Schirmer, 1997.

Wodehouse, P. G., and Guy Bolton. *Bring on the Girls! The Improbable Story of Our Life in Musical Comedy.* New York: Simon & Schuster, 1953.

Zadan, Craig. *Sondheim and Co.* 2nd ed. New York: Harper & Row, 1986.

INDEX

Baum, Vicki, 239
Bavaar, Tony, 122
Bayes, Nora, 28
Be Yourself, 46
Bean, Orson, 114
Beaton, Cecil, 128
Beauty and the Beast, 234, 239
Beauty of Bath, The, 13
Beggar on Horseback, 46
Begum, The, 60
Behman, Louis, 2
Behrman, S. N., 187
Belafonte, Harry, 105
Bell, Marion, 121
Bells Are Ringing, 112–13
Benchley, Robert, 45
Bennett, Arnold, 106
Bennett, Michael, 172, 186, 203, 237
Bergman, Ingmar, 173
Berlin, Irving, 46, 50, 52, 60, 70, 71–72, 95, 153
Bernard, Sam, 86
Bernardi, Herschel, 193–94
Bernstein, Leonard, 98, 110, 112, 128, 145–47, 152–53, 175
Besoyan, Rick, 159–60
Between the Devil, 132
Big, 182
Big Fish, Little Fish, 173
Bigley, Isabel, 41, 154
Billie, 8–10
Billion Dollar Baby, 111–12
Birkenhead, Susan, 190, 237
Bissell, Richard, 76–77
Bizet, Georges, 38
Black Crook, The, 55, 77, 98

Blackbirds of 1928, 90
Blaine, Vivian, 154
Blake, Josh, 196
Blitzstein, Marc, 137–38, 191
Blood, Sweat and Stanley Poole, 171
Bloomer Girl, 102, 103
Blossom, Henry, 61
Blossom Time, 64
Blyden, Larry, 42
Bock, Jerry, 80, 153, 191–92, 212–13
Body Beautiful, The, 191
Bogardus, Stephen, 231
Bogart, Humphrey, 165
Boland, Mary, 50–51
Bolger, Ray, 74–76, 229
Bolin, Shannon, 78
Bolton, Guy, 7, 11–22, 68, 82
Bonanza Bound, 112
Bond, Christopher, 175–76
Bontemps, Arna, 142
Booth, Shirley, 53, 76, 99, 191
Bordman, Gerald, 57
Bordoni, Irene, 52
Bosler, Virginia, 121
Bosley, Tom, 79
Bostwick, Barry, 151
Bova, Joe, 158
Bow, Clara, 31
Boy Friend, The, 112
Boy Meets Girl, 135
Boys from Syracuse, The, 75, 82, 136
Brackman, Jacob, 195
Braham, David, 59, 190
Bramble, Mark, 187–90
Breakfast at Tiffany's, 155
Breath of Spring, 214

INDEX

ABOUT THE AUTHOR

Thomas S. Hischak is professor of theatre at the State University of New York College at Cortland and a member of the Dramatists Guild. He is the author of nine books on theatre, popular music, musical theatre, and film musicals, including *Word Crazy: Broadway Lyricists from Cohan to Sondheim* (Praeger, 1991), *American Theatre: A Chronicle of Comedy and Drama 1969–2000* (Oxford University Press, 2001), *The Theatregoers Almanac* (Greenwood, 1997), and *Stage It with Music: An Encyclopedic Guide to the American Musical Theatre* (Greenwood, 1993). He is also a playwright with over two dozen published plays. He lives in Cortland, New York, with his wife and two children.